The Princeton Review®

Cracking the

SAT
Subject Test™
in U.S. History

2nd Edition

The Staff of The Princeton Review

PrincetonReview.com

Penguin
Random
House

The Princeton Review
555 W. 18th Street
New York, NY 10011
E-mail: editorialsupport@review.com

Published in the United States by Penguin Random House LLC,
New York, and in Canada by Random House of Canada, a division
of Penguin Random House Ltd., Toronto.

Terms of Service: The Princeton Review Online Companion Tools
("Student Tools") for retail books are available for only the two
most recent editions of that book. Student Tools may be activated
only twice per eligible book purchased for two consecutive
12-month periods, for a total of 24 months of access. Activation
of Student Tools more than twice per book is in direct violation
of these Terms of Service and may result in discontinuation of
access to Student Tools Services.

ISBN: 978-1-5247-1083-5
eBook ISBN: 978-1-5247-5762-5
ISSN: 2373–8839

SAT Subject Tests is a trademark of the College Board, which is
not affiliated with The Princeton Review.

The Princeton Review is not affiliated with Princeton University.

Editor: Meave Shelton
Production Editors: Jim Melloan and Kathy G. Carter
Production Artist: Gabriel Berlin

Printed in the United States of America on partially recycled paper.

10 9 8 7 6 5 4 3 2 1

2nd Edition

Editorial
Rob Franek, Editor-in-Chief
Casey Cornelius, VP Content Development
Mary Beth Garrick, Director of Production
Selena Coppock, Managing Editor
Meave Shelton, Senior Editor
Colleen Day, Editor
Sarah Litt, Editor
Aaron Riccio, Editor
Orion McBean, Associate Editor

Penguin Random House Publishing Team
Tom Russell, VP, Publisher
Alison Stoltzfus, Publishing Director
Jake Eldred, Associate Managing Editor
Ellen Reed, Production Manager
Suzanne Lee, Designer

Acknowledgments

The Princeton Review would like to extend special thanks to Grace Roegner Freedman, Dan Komarek, Casey Paragin, Christine Parker, Jonathan Edwards, Candice Brenner, Claudia Landgrover, and Erik Kolb for their contributions to previous editions; to Gina Donegan for her contributions to this edition; and to Jonathan Chiu, National Content Director for High School Programs, for his expert oversight.

Special thanks to Adam Robinson, who conceived of and perfected the Joe Bloggs approach to standardized tests and many of the other successful techniques used by The Princeton Review.

We are also, as always, very appreciative of the time and attention given to each page by Jim Melloan, Kathy G. Carter, and Gabe Berlin.

Contents

Get More (Free) Content

1 Go to **PrincetonReview.com/cracking.**

2 Enter the following ISBN for your book: 9781524710835.

3 Answer a few simple questions to set up an exclusive Princeton Review account. (If you already have one, you can just log in.)

4 Click the "Student Tools" button, also found under "My Account" from the top toolbar. You're all set to access your bonus content!

Need to report a potential **content** issue?

Contact **EditorialSupport@review.com**.
Include:
- full title of the book
- ISBN number
- page number

Need to report a **technical** issue?

Contact **TPRStudentTech@review.com** and provide:
- your full name
- email address used to register the book
- full book title and ISBN
- computer OS (Mac/PC) and browser (Firefox, Safari, etc.)

The Princeton Review®

Once you've registered, you can...

- Take a full-length practice SAT and/or ACT

- Get valuable advice about the college application process, including tips for writing a great essay and where to apply for financial aid

- If you're still choosing between colleges, use our searchable rankings of *The Best 382 Colleges* to find out more information about your dream school.

- Access comprehensive study guides and a variety of printable resources, including additional bubble sheets, score conversion tables, and lists of key terms

- Check to see if there have been any corrections or updates to this edition

- Get our take on any recent or pending updates to the SAT Subject Test in U.S. History

Look For These Icons Throughout The Book

ONLINE ARTICLES

PROVEN TECHNIQUES

APPLIED STRATEGIES

MORE GREAT BOOKS

COLLEGE ADVISOR APP

Part I
Orientation

Chapter 1
Knowing the Basics

The SAT Subject Tests are a series of one-hour exams developed and administered by Educational Testing Service (ETS) and the College Board. Unlike the SAT, the SAT Subject Tests are designed to measure specific knowledge in specific areas, such as biology, history, French, and math. They are scored separately on a 200–800 scale.

How Are SAT Subject Tests Used by College Admissions?

Because the tests are given in specific areas, colleges use them as another piece of admissions information, and, in some cases, to decide whether applicants can be exempted from college requirements. For example, a certain score may excuse you from a basic English class or a foreign language requirement.

Should I Take the SAT Subject Tests?

About one-third of the colleges that require SAT scores also require that you take two or three SAT Subject Tests. Your first order of business is to start reading those college catalogs and websites. College guidebooks, admission offices, and guidance counselors should have the information you need to keep up with the changes.

As to which tests you should take, the answer is simple. Take the SAT Subject Tests

- on which you will do well
- that may be required by the colleges to which you are applying

The best possible situation, of course, is when you can achieve both goals with the same subject test.

Some colleges have specific requirements; others do not. **Again, start asking questions before you start taking tests**. Once you find out which tests, if any, are required, determine which will show your particular strengths. Colleges that require specific tests generally recommend that you take two subject tests from the following five groups: laboratory science, history, foreign language, math, and English.

As for timing, take the tests as close as possible to the corresponding coursework you may be doing. For example, if you plan to take the SAT Subject Test in U.S. History, and you are currently taking a U.S. history class, don't postpone the test until next year.

Check out The Princeton Review's entire series of review books for the SAT Subject Tests!

When Are the SAT Subject Tests Offered?

In general, you can take from one to three subject tests per test date in August, October, November, December, January, May, and June at test sites across the country. Not all subjects are offered at each administration, so check the dates carefully.

How Do I Register for the Tests?

To register by mail, pick up *The SAT and SAT Subject Tests Student Registration Booklet* at your guidance counselor's office. You can also register at the College Board website at collegereadiness.collegeboard.org/sat. This site contains other useful information such as the test dates and fees, as well as background information and sample questions for each subject test. If you have questions you can talk to a representative at the College Board by calling (866) 756-7346.

How and When Will I Get My Scores?

You may have your scores sent to you, to your school, and to four colleges of your choice. Additional reports will be sent to additional colleges for—you guessed it—additional money. Scores are made available to students via the College Board's website. To find out about the timeline of when scores are made available, please visit collegereadiness.collegeboard.org/sat.

What's a Good Score?

That's hard to say, exactly. A good score is one that fits within the range of scores the college of your choice usually looks for or accepts. However, if your score falls below the normal score range for Podunk University, that doesn't necessarily mean you won't get in. Schools are often fairly flexible in what they are willing to look at as a "good" score for a certain student.

Along with your score, you will also receive a percentile rank. That number tells how well you scored in relation to other test takers. In other words, a percentile rank of 60 means that 40 percent of the test takers scored higher than you and 60 percent scored lower than you.

A Couple of Words About Score Choice

You can choose which SAT Subject Test scores you want colleges to see, which is great! For one thing, if you take more than one SAT Subject Test on a given test date, you'll be able to choose which tests from that date you'd like to submit to colleges. So if, for example, you take the French test followed by the chemistry test, but you don't think the chemistry test went very well, you can simply opt out of having that chemistry score sent to your schools.

The score-reporting policy will be optional for students. This means that you aren't required to opt in and actively choose which specific scores you would like sent to colleges. If you decide not to use the score-reporting feature, then all of the scores on file will automatically be sent when you request score reports. For more information about the score-reporting policy, go to the College Board website at CollegeBoard.org.

Why Read This Book?

You could certainly take the SAT Subject Test in U.S. History today and get some of the questions right. But you'd probably miss a good portion of the questions you could have gotten right if you understood test taking a little better.

You could also review all of your old U.S. History assignments, hoping they'd be less boring this time around. You could even try one of those gargantuan study guides, crammed with ten thousand little snippets of information. But you'd still miss a good portion of the questions you could have gotten right if you just understood how to take the test. Face it: The only way to beat a standardized test is to develop a system or a strategy that allows you to answer the questions correctly and to get a higher score. Don't be haphazard in your approach to the test: The secret is to learn to work and study methodically. Knowledge of history will, of course, help you out. But to answer the questions, it isn't so much what you know as how you apply your knowledge.

The SAT Subject Test in U.S. History is not just about knowing history. In other words, getting a good score on this test depends upon more than just the depth of your history knowledge or your scholastic abilities. Scoring high on this test or, frankly, any other standardized test, comes right down to the sharpness of your test-taking abilities. But don't be intimidated—this is actually a cause to rejoice. Why? Because the simple skills of test taking, which you can master quickly, will put you—not the College Board—in the driver's seat!

> The best way to improve your score is to learn *how* to take the SAT Subject Test in U.S. History

This is where The Princeton Review comes in. Our mission is to understand, analyze, and simulate standardized tests so we can help students beat these tests and make their scores soar. Since 1981, we have been breathing down the necks of the College Board, studying its every move, and watching every alteration it makes to its tests. Then we devise and deliver test-beating techniques to our students. Our proven techniques here at The Princeton Review have taken us far from our base in New York City to locations across the country and around the world.

The Test Is Predictable

Unlike our knowledge of history itself, these tests don't change very much from year to year. That's because the writers of the tests, unlike the writers of history, do not change, probably because they are not asked to change. The people at the College Board do not regularly release previously administered tests; that is, they don't make many of their tests publicly available. Consequently, it is easy for them to write the same test, with the same types of questions, every year. And this makes it easy for us to know and understand the test and to find ways to beat it. This book is the result of serious research specifically on the most recent SAT Subject Tests in U.S. History.

The Test Balances Facts with Concepts

Mastering the SAT Subject Test in U.S. History requires a combination of both factual knowledge and a basic understanding of historical concepts and general themes. Some questions are very straightforward, asking you simply to identify people, places, documents, or events. For these questions, factual knowledge is key. Other questions require you to reason your way to the answer using a combination of factual and conceptual knowledge. Therefore, it isn't enough to know who Millard Fillmore was; for every factoid you know, you should also be sure to be able to identify why this person or thing is important. Context is key!

However, there is one more very important part to doing well on the SAT Subject Test in U.S. History: You need to understand how the test writers construct the test, the questions, and especially the answers so you can avoid ETS traps and use Process of Elimination (which we'll describe in Chapter 2) to find answers. Remember, no one is born a good test taker or a bad test taker. A good test taker realizes the importance of knowing both what to expect from a test and how to deal with the information. The fact is, it's not just about history: The better you know and understand the SAT Subject Test in U.S. History, the better you will score.

Factoid Heaven

In the content review section of this book, we've included lots of sidebars and special text boxes full of lists, definitions, timelines, and other useful information. To strengthen your factoid knowledge, make flashcards of the names, places, and events that are unfamiliar to you. Flash cards make for convenient review on the go, and even the act of making them helps you learn!

Take a Hike

Here's an analogy to explain The Princeton Review's strategy. Suppose you and a friend are hiking in the woods. You want to take it easy for a while, but your friend wants to keep hiking. So he says he will leave you a trail, and you can follow him and catch up whenever you are ready. Sounds good to you, so he leaves and you take a nap. Now suppose, after you wake up, you go looking for his trail. Several things could happen at this point.

Imagine that your friend left a marker every few inches, dropping small and insignificant items to mark the trail: first a penny, then a button, then a toothpick, later a small piece of string. It's as if he were just cleaning out his pockets, not really paying any attention to what he was doing. Following this trail would be painstakingly slow and difficult; every few seconds you'd have to stop, pick up the tiny little something, and hope that you're still moving in the right direction. Meanwhile, your friend would be at the campsite having dinner.

Now imagine that your friend is a very organized and together person. He knew that you'd wipe out after the first mile, so he came prepared. He brought along signs marked with large fluorescent arrows (made on 100 percent biodegradable recycled paper, of course) and pinned them on trees, spacing them about 20 yards. So when you wake up, you hit the trail running. It's easy to see the signs, and you can follow them quickly through the forest. With the arrows, you always know you're going in the right direction. At this pace, you meet up with your friend in no time, and you crack open some franks and beans together.

You see, if this book were to present to you an unorganized and detail-laden series of facts, as many other guides do, you would have a slim chance of remembering any of the information, important or insignificant, on the day of the test. So you would have a slim chance of scoring high. The content review section describes the most important eras for the test, what you need to know about each era, and how you should apply this knowledge with other test-taking techniques. Do not fear; we'll show you how to get the right answers. Other SAT U.S. History review books are like your disorganized friend, who either doesn't know or doesn't care how to be a good guide. But this book is like your organized friend. It helps you approach your history review like a well-marked trail. In the following chapters, we will present this history trail to you—the story of the last 400 (or 4,000) years clearly divided into important time periods.

We hope you find The Princeton Review approach to be an easy and fun way to think about history. It is most definitely the way to "score more" on the SAT Subject Test in U.S. History.

Is There Any Other Material Available for Practice?

The questions in the majority of books on the market bear little, if any, resemblance to actual SAT Subject Test questions. The College Board publishes a book called *The Official Study Guide for All SAT Subject Tests*, which contains full-length tests of all of the SAT Subject Tests offered. The College Board also has a stand-alone book for the SAT U.S. and World History Subject Tests, which has additional practice tests. You can also visit collegereadiness.collegeboard.org/sat/practice for more information and practice questions.

Chapter 2
Learning the
Techniques

Break the continuum of history into easily digestible chunks!

THINK "ERA" FOR ERROR-FREE THINKING

History is a long continuum of time that consists of many overlapping events and people, some of which had a greater impact than others. It is easy to be intimidated by all the stuff you have to know, or think you have to know, for the SAT Subject Test in U.S. History. But you don't have to remember all this information as one historically jumbled mass.

The easiest way to think about hundreds of years of history is to break the continuum into bite-sized chunks. This book refers to each time period, each chunk of history, as an era. You can organize all the history facts you know into eras, or historical time slots. Just keep all the tidbits of important information in a particular time period under one heading in your mind (and in your notes). The heading should be some name—a person, an event, a war—that reminds you of the era. When you have the vast and varied amount of information organized into only a few important eras, you will find it easier to recall the material on the test.

The history review chapters in this book are organized into eras and are designed to give you the information you need to know about each time period. From now on, whenever you learn anything about a certain time period, file it away in your brain under the title of its era. In fact, you probably do this already for some time periods.

Think About the 1960s

What comes to mind? Maybe it's the Beatles, dancing hippies, and Vietnam. Or perhaps the space race, the Cold War, Martin Luther King Jr., and John F. Kennedy. Whatever you remember is helpful; the specifics don't really matter. The point is that when you think about the era of the 1960s, you should automatically recall some key events and people connected to that time.

Now answer this question:

This question may seem specific, but you need to know only the important details to answer it.

1. The civil rights legislation signed by President Lyndon B. Johnson in 1965 mandated

   (A) a Constitutional amendment guaranteeing equal rights for women

   (B) that Latinos and Asians have the same employment rights as African Americans

   (C) the protection of the voting rights of southern African Americans

   (D) that affirmative action programs be established in all state universities

   (E) that in light of national security, Vietnam War protesters be denied the right to demonstrate publicly

The era in this question is the 1960s, and it concerns civil rights. You should immediately think that the answer must say something about the civil rights of African Americans and racial discrimination. Choice (A) should be eliminated because the issue of women's rights reflects the feminist movement of the 1970s, not the Civil Rights movement of the 1960s. (Also, the Equal Rights Amendment has never been added to the Constitution.) Choice (E) should be eliminated because, although many people protested the Vietnam War, which did not make the police and the government happy, the protesters were not legally denied their freedom of speech.

So, of the remaining choices (B), (C), and (D), which one of these is most closely identified with the era of 1965? To some extent, all three choices reflect that era's concerns, but if you think about it, choice (B) is off the mark because the Civil Rights movement was largely about guaranteeing the rights of African Americans in the face of racial injustice, even though there were other ethnic minority groups also protesting injustices that they experienced. Choice (D) misses, because affirmative action represents moving beyond basic rights to compensate for past injustices, but the Civil Rights era was more about protecting basic rights. Therefore, (C) is the best choice, because the movement's major aim—after desegregating public accommodations—was defending the basic right of Southern African Americans to vote. The movement hoped that once Southern African Americans were protected when they sought to vote—from police dogs, hoses, lynch mobs, and poll taxes—they would gain the political power necessary to secure the respect and resources that they previously had been denied.

This example sounds like a specific question, but you really didn't have to know a great many details about civil rights legislation in order to answer it. You had to think only about the era of the 1960s, remember generally what was happening at that time, and then choose the best answer to fit the era.

PACING YOURSELF

Any standardized test is an endurance test, the academic equivalent of running a two-mile race over hurdles. The SAT Subject Test in U.S. History consists of 90 multiple-choice questions to be completed in 60 minutes. That leaves you with about 40 seconds per question. The fact is, you may run out of time and not be able to finish all of the questions.

Don't worry. It's okay to run out of time, but you must pace yourself. Pacing means balancing speed with accuracy. You need to get to as many questions as you can, but not so many that you get them all wrong because you are working too quickly. Use the Two-Pass System to choose which questions to answer and which questions to skip for the time being. Pacing may also mean that you spend a few extra seconds on a question you think you can get right. Basically, it means choosing questions to answer according to your own strengths and weaknesses, not according to how the writers of the SAT Subject Test in U.S. History happen to lay them out on your particular test.

Use the Two-Pass System
Answering 90 questions in 60 minutes— are they kidding? Give yourself a break; approach the test with the Two-Pass System. On your first pass through the questions, skip any questions along the way that you can't answer or that you think will take some time. Then, take a second pass through the test to do the remaining questions. The Two-Pass System will keep you from getting bogged down and losing time!.

You certainly want to finish the test, but you want to do so on your own terms. To get you started, we've provided you a pacing chart for the SAT Subject Test in U.S. History. But be careful: When the pacing chart suggests that you leave up to ten questions blank, those ten should not necessarily be the last ten on the test. There could be several easy questions among the last ten, so be sure you get to them. Of those hypothetical ten questions, you want to leave blank only those questions that have you completely stumped. For each of the other questions, if you can safely eliminate even one answer choice, you should guess; we'll explain why in the section on scoring a little later. Maybe you'll skip five questions in the first 80, and then quickly decide which of the five or so out of the last ten questions to come back to if there is some time left.

The pacing chart shows you how many questions you need to get right and how many you can afford to miss in order to achieve your target score. Tailor this chart to your own test-taking style as much as possible. When you take the practice tests in this book, pay attention to your strengths and weaknesses:

- Do you start out great and then lag in the middle of the test? You may be losing focus.

- Do you tend to get stuck on a question and spend too much time on it? Be more aware of when you do this so you can make yourself move on.

- Did you misread the question? You may have been moving too quickly.

- Did you pick a choice that didn't make sense within the era of the question? You may need to review certain eras.

After you take any practice test, be sure to spend some time analyzing what questions you missed and asking yourself, "Why?" This way you can concentrate on not making the same mistakes on the real SAT Subject Test in U.S. History.

The chart will help you target the score you want on the test you are taking. But remember that it is only a guide. Even if it tells you that you can safely skip ten questions, it is to your advantage to guess smartly on as many questions as possible.

Pacing Chart for the SAT Subject Test in U.S. History									
		Questions 1–35			Questions 36–70			Questions 71–90		
Score on Practice Test	Shooting for	Time spent	Must Answer	Guess or skip	Time spent	Must Answer	Guess or skip	Time spent	Must Answer	Guess or skip
200–390	450	35 min	25	15	25 min	15	10	0 min	0	0
400–460	520	30 min	27	8	20 min	24	11	10 min	9	11
470–540	600	25 min	27	8	20 min	27	8	15 min	11	9
550–600	660	25 min	30	5	20 min	30	5	15 min	15	5
610–660	700	20 min	31	1	20 min	30	2	20 min	23	3
670–800	740+	20 min	33	0–2	20 min	33	0–2	20 min	24	0

TIME IS OF THE ESSENCE

In order to pace yourself correctly, you must be aware of the time and where you are in the test at any given point. It's easy to do. In your mind, separate the total number of questions roughly into thirds. For the first third give yourself 20 to 25 minutes. The middle third should take you about 20 to 25 minutes. Finally, for the last third (actually a bit less), target about 15 minutes. A little more time per question is allowed in the first and second thirds of the test. This is because you are likely to be more alert at the start of the exam, so it pays to spend time on these questions. In the last third, you may be a little more tired, stressed, or even panicky. Your goal in the last third is to read the questions so that you can make quick, educated guesses, even if you have only 10 minutes left. If you have been pacing yourself well, and happen to have 15 to 20 minutes left for the last third, you will be able to maintain your pace and answer the questions with the same relative speed you used in the previous sections.

To accurately keep track of the time, you may want to jot a time frame down at the top of your Scantron sheet near your name. For example, if the test starts at 11:20 a.m., jot down 11:40, 12:05, and 12:20. Then you can refer to these times to quickly see that you must complete the first third by approximately 11:40, the middle third by 12:05, and the rest by 12:20. (Be sure to either erase your notes or write only in a designated area, like where you put your name. Stray marks elsewhere can cause the College Board computers to malfunction.)

Questions	Minutes per Section	Total Time into Test
1–35	20–25	20–25 minutes
36–70	20–25	40–50 minutes
71–90	10–20	60 minutes (exam ends)

Use these time guidelines in conjunction with the pacing chart.

Pressed for time? Our free, customized study guides can help you break up the content in this book into manageable chunks depending on how much time you have available. Register your book online and download them right away!

SCORING: WILD GUESSES VERSUS SMART GUESSES

The SAT Subject Tests are scored on a scale of 200 to 800. This score, the one that is reported to you and to colleges, represents a translation of the raw score you actually acquire in taking the test. The raw score is tabulated by adding one point for each question you answer correctly and subtracting a quarter of a point for each question you answer incorrectly. Each blank gives you zero: no points either way. Think about this mathematically: One correct guess balances four incorrect guesses.

Now that you know about the guessing penalty, you can safely ignore it. Why? Using era-based thinking, you will always be able to make educated guesses, and every educated guess wipes out the negative effect of the penalty. If you can safely eliminate one answer choice out of five, and then guess on the remaining four, you have a one-in-four chance of getting the question right. At first sight, one-in-four odds may not sound so great, but over the whole test, these numbers are significant. If you pace yourself and follow the era technique carefully and thoughtfully, you are likely to make many more correct guesses than incorrect guesses.

> By using Process of Elimination (what we like to call POE) and guessing intelligently, you place the guessing odds in your favor. When you eliminate choices, there is no guessing penalty—only a guessing reward!

A TALE OF THREE STUDENTS

Let's look at how three hypothetical students approached their SAT Subject Test in U.S. History. Scaredy Sam is a good student but a bad test taker; he took the test slowly and carefully, correctly answering most of the questions that he tried, but he ran out of time around question 80. Guessing Geena is an okay student, a great tester, and an aggressive guesser; she finished the test by working carefully on the questions she knew and quickly guessing on the harder questions. And finally, Average Andy is an average student and an average test taker; he took the test as he would any other, without any real concern about pacing; he guessed on a handful, and he ran out of time at the end.

In the following chart, remember that correct answers receive 1 raw point and incorrect answers result in a loss of one-quarter raw score point. Blanks result in 0.

	Scaredy Sam	Guessing Geena	Average Andy
Answered Correctly	60 (+60)	50 (+50)	50 (+50)
Answered Incorrectly	20 (−5)	15 (−3.75)	16 (−4)
Guessed Right	0 (0)	14 (+14)	4 (+4)
Guessed Wrong	0 (0)	11 (−2.75)	12 (−3)
Left Blank	10 (0)	10 (0)	8 (0)
Total Raw Score	55	57.5 = 58	47
Final Score	620	640	570

Get valuable advice about the college application process, including tips for writing a great essay and where to apply for financial aid, when you register your book online!

On this chart, "Answered Correctly" means that they knew the answer with their own history knowledge and got the question right. "Answered Incorrectly" means that they thought they knew the answer but got the question wrong. "Guesses" mean that they didn't know the answer and they knew they were guessing.

These scores are calculated from the genuine SAT Subject Test scoring system. Yet it doesn't seem quite fair that Geena got a better score than Sam even though Sam knew more. Too bad he didn't get to finish the test. And compare Geena to Andy; they both "knew" the right answer to 50 questions, and they both answered wrong on similar numbers of questions—yet their scores differ by 70 points! Why? Because Geena was a better guesser—she guessed right 14 times, while Andy guessed right only 4 times.

The key, therefore, is in the guessing. Geena was simply a better guesser—more aggressive and better able to narrow down the choices when guessing. Using Process of Elimination can make all the difference!

> If you're good at POE, you don't have to know the right answer to a question. You just have to be able to identify the wrong answers, which leaves you with the correct answer by default.

REVIEW: ERA-BASED THINKING AND GUESSING

1. Think of history not just as a collection of a billion tiny facts (or "factoids") such as exact dates and names, but also as a series of eras: the colonial era, the Reconstruction era, the post–World War II era, and so on.

2. For any question you do not absolutely know the correct answer to, start by defining in your own mind what era that question refers to. Sometimes the wording of the question will actually state the era, although often it will not.

3. Read all of the answer choices and see which of them clearly, definitely do *not* relate to the era. Eliminate those choices.

4. Of the remaining choices, choose which one most closely relates to the era.

5. If you can't eliminate down to just one answer choice, eliminate what you can and then guess from the choices you have left. In the long run, you'll gain more points than you lose.

Chapter 3
Cracking the Test

THE TEST

The SAT Subject Test in U.S. History focuses primarily on the history of the United States from just after the adoption of the Constitution to the present day (80 percent of the test). Within this broad period, about half the questions refer to the late eighteenth century and the nineteenth century, and the other half refer to the twentieth century. The remaining 20 percent of the questions are based on pre-Revolution colonization, with a smattering of questions regarding indigenous Native American peoples and precolonial history.

<table>
<tr><td colspan="2" align="center">90 Questions
1 hour</td></tr>
<tr><td>Pre-Columbian history to 1789</td><td>20%</td></tr>
<tr><td>1790–1898</td><td>40%</td></tr>
<tr><td>1899–Present</td><td>40%</td></tr>
</table>

THE SYSTEM

History as Eras, Not as Isolated Facts

The SAT Subject Test in U.S. History, at first glance, seems like a test of facts. After all, the 90 specific questions cover the important people and events of all of U.S. history. In fact, it is a test of major historical trends or eras. The Princeton Review system of era-based thinking described in Chapter 2 will help you turn these fact-like questions into general questions that you can answer with your basic knowledge of U.S. history.

Look at the big picture. The questions on the test usually require that you know about some major topic or event in U.S. history. But these questions are often written in a way that make them seem harder than they really are. To avoid being confused by any of these questions, we recommend era-based thinking.

Pacing

Pacing is the most important aspect of taking the SAT Subject Test in U.S. History, because it is a long test and you are under strict time pressure to finish it. As we noted, pacing simply means spending your limited time where it is best used. You may pace yourself by spending a few extra seconds on a question that you feel you can get right, or by bailing out and guessing on a question that has you boggled. Overall, pacing yourself means taking control of the testing experience so that you can get your best score possible.

True or False?

Q: Before the Revolutionary War, American colonists were allowed to trade freely with all European nations.

Question Arrangement

Unlike some other standardized tests, the SAT Subject Test in U.S. History is not arranged solely in order of difficulty. Questions on the test are arranged in sets according to a particular time period. Within these sets of questions, which vary in number, there is a rough order of difficulty, with the last question in a set being the hardest. For instance, questions 1–5 might concern the American Revolution, with question 5 being the hardest in the set. Then questions 6–9 might deal with the post–Civil War years, with question 9 being the hardest and question 6 being the easiest in this set. On questions 10–14, the focus may become the twentieth century, and so on. These time period cycles will repeat throughout the test. For instance, questions 50–53 might also be about the American Revolution.

This format actually works perfectly with the era-based approach. If one question gets you thinking about the Civil War, it's likely that you will get to answer a few questions about this same era. Just be sure to switch out of that thinking as soon as you are presented with a new era. This could also help you with fact-based questions, because these would probably be the hardest, or the last, in a question set. If a question gives you no clue about the era in which it is set, quickly look to the era of the questions you just answered, the ones just preceding this question. It may help to place the era of the factoid and help you eliminate anti-era choices.

Your best tactic when dealing with this strange question set-up is to have no tactic at all. Because this format is not standard (sometimes there are two questions per set, sometimes five, sometimes one), it will cost you more effort to worry about it than to just go with the flow. Bear in mind that the eras will keep flip-flopping, and use their pattern to help you if you can. Otherwise, don't sweat it.

A Sample Question

Let's take a close look at a question.

> Many Americans viewed the War of 1812 as the "second war of independence." Which of the following best explains this sentiment?

This question seems pretty specific when you look at it standing alone, but the trick to answering it is to figure out what you are really being asked. You are not being asked anything specific about the War of 1812. You are being asked something very sweeping about it: "Why would people compare this war to the War of Independence, that is, the American Revolution?" Now, the question seems pretty general. You want to find the answer choice that has something to do with the American Revolution.

True or False?

A: False! During the colonial era, England wanted exclusive rights to all the goods and services produced by the American colonies. To this end, it placed heavy taxes, called duties, on just about everything, which made it very expensive for the colonists to trade with any country other than England.

So let's look at the question with its answer choices.

Many Americans viewed the War of 1812 as the "second war of independence." Which of the following best explains this sentiment?

(A) The war forced Europe to accept the Monroe Doctrine.

(B) The national anthem, "The Star-Spangled Banner," was written during this war.

(C) The war established the independence of Latin American republics from the colonial powers of Europe.

(D) Despite some military successes by the British forces, the United States was able to protect itself against a dominant power.

(E) The war was a contributing factor in the defeat of Napoleon at Waterloo.

Common Sense POE

Q: Which group of voters was a deciding factor in the 1860 presidential election? What do you think of this answer choice? (C) Women who held abolitionist views

Answer choices (A), (C), and (E) might seem logical if you weren't thinking about the question, or if you were thinking about other American wars. But these answer choices have nothing in common with the American Revolution and so they can't be the link between it and the War of 1812. Choice (B) may seem correct because an anthem reflects and glorifies a nation as an independent entity. Still, an anthem is merely symbolic; it is not a major issue or development of war. Therefore, the correct answer is (D), and the only thing you had to know to get this question right was that America fought Great Britain in both the American Revolution and the War of 1812.

Era-based thinking will help you on most of the questions on the SAT Subject Test in U.S. History. Your primary strategy of attack is as follows:

1. Read the Question—Connect the Era

Read the question and connect it to a particular era.

2. Eliminate Anti-Era or Non-Era Answer Choices

Even if the correct answer doesn't immediately jump out at you, you will be able to eliminate two or three answer choices that are "non-era" or "anti-era."

There are five steps to this strategy.

Use Era-Based Common Sense

Common sense is a powerful tool on the history subject tests, but you must always be thinking about the era of the question. Would it make sense for Andrew Jackson to support the Native Americans? Would it make sense for Lyndon B. Johnson to support Native American groups? Did Thomas Jefferson own slaves? Did Abraham Lincoln own slaves? (The corresponding answers would be No, Yes, Yes, and No.)

The SAT Subject Test writers commonly use wrong answer choices that make sense within current thinking, but are ludicrous statements if you are thinking within the era of the question. For example, if someone said,

"Person X believes that women should have the right to vote,"

you'd say, "Sounds reasonable." But if a SAT Subject Test answer choice read,

"George Washington was an advocate of women's rights…"

you would want to say, "No way." George was a great guy in many respects, but always think about the era (in this case, not the E.R.A.). Women's rights were not in vogue back then. What might be reasonable today could be ridiculous when placed in a different historical era.

The "politically correct" answer will be applicable only to questions concerning the last century. The political response to the "Indian problem" in Andrew Jackson's days was a federally legislated policy supporting the decimation of Native American tribes. But Lyndon B. Johnson favored improvements in the education of Native American youth and increased tribal self-reliance through the reservation system. Although some bits of history may not jibe with our modern sense of morality, always consider the era when answering these test questions. Your own contemporary perspective can lead you to incorrect answer choices.

Similarly, ETS loves to provide you with answer choices containing true, but irrelevant, information. Always be sure that the choice you select answers the question: Just because something is true doesn't mean it's the right answer!

The SAT Subject Test Never Criticizes Our Forebears

Using era-based common sense, you can eliminate unlikely answer choices, but you will almost never find questions that put our country's past leaders in a wholly negative light. You will not find the following question:

> Which of the following U.S. presidents was responsible for the Indian Termination Policy of 1830?

Common Sense POE

A: No way! Get rid of (C)! Women couldn't vote in presidential elections in the nineteenth century. They didn't win the right to vote until 1920, after World War I.

It will never happen. But you may find a question like this:

> Andrew Jackson's presidential administrations were known for all of the following EXCEPT
>
> (A) its rejection of the institution of the Second Bank of the United States
> (B) the humanitarian aid given to the Cherokee Indians following the tribe's dispute with the state of Georgia
> (C) a veto of legislation from Congress which proposed the building of roads and other infrastructure in the western states
> (D) the maintenance of the spoils system which allocated federal jobs on the basis of personal and political loyalties
> (E) the willingness to use federal troops to defend federal laws and their precedence over states' laws

The trick to answering this type of question is not knowing whether each of the five answer choices is or isn't true. It's knowing which one is definitely, positively WRONG. Maybe you are saying, "I dunno," to answer choices (A), (C), (D), and (E), but you should be saying "Not at all!" to (B). Back in the time that the nation was beginning its westward expansion, you wouldn't find too many presidents in support of the rights of Native Americans whose lands were being taken. Answer choices (D) and (E) surely don't make Mr. Jackson seem like a great guy, but they are far more likely, given the historical era, than (B). So, (B) is the correct answer.

Notice how the question is phrased. It is not stating anything blatantly negative about Andrew Jackson, and the SAT Subject Test never would. It is your job to decipher what cannot be true about a person (e.g., that Andrew Jackson helped Native Americans). If you're thinking about the era of a question and using era-based common sense, this isn't too difficult. You must be on your toes in order to translate the knowledge you have into the power to eliminate wrong answer choices.

3. Assess the Remaining Answer Choices: Translate

The answer choices themselves are usually long, complicated sentences. In order to understand them, you have to pare them down. Translate the test language into your own language. By reading the remaining choices slowly and then translating them into your own words, you get a better idea about what is going on. This may sound time-consuming or complex, but it really isn't. Here's why: First, you will be using this process only with the two or three choices you have remaining; second, you do all the translating in your head. And finally, with practice, this type of thinking will come quickly and more naturally to you.

Let's look at an example:

> Which of the following statements best describes the opinion of the majority of Americans regarding the onset of World War II in Europe?

Answer choices:

(A) They were not concerned with international politics and were indifferent to who would be the victor.

(B) They did not agree with the use of U.S. military force or intervention at the time.

(C) They were enraged by the policies of Hitler and were eager to declare war on the Nazi forces.

(D) They hoped the U.S. could sell supplies and equipment to both sides of the conflict, thereby hastening the end of the Great Depression.

(E) They wanted to remain out of the war so that the participants in the war would be weakened and the U.S. could rise as a world power.

Translations:

(A) Didn't care at all!?
(B) Wanted to stay out.
(C) Raring to go!
(D) Supported both sides.
(E) Wanted to grab power.

Quick translations should get (A), (D), and (E) out of there. Then you have to decide between (B) and (C). But before you do that...

4. Stop, Reread the Question

Once you have eliminated the anti-era answer choices and any others that are clearly wrong, you may have two or three choices remaining. This is the crucial moment because, most likely, one of these answer choices is right. A common mistake is to be very careful up to this point and then carelessly choose the wrong answer. You've spent some time on this question, and it's foolish to let the right answer elude you when you are so close to it. Rereading the question should take a few seconds, at most.

Back to our example question:

> Which of the following statements best describes
> the opinion of the majority of Americans
> regarding the **ONSET** of World War II in
> Europe?

Ah, now you see the word in bold, capital letters. Sure, you know that the United States was in World War II, but this question asks us about the beginning of war. And you should know that the United States didn't enter the war right away. Remember the Pearl Harbor bombing? That's what dragged us into the fray. If you were lazy and tried to answer this question quickly, you might have gone for (C), because you know that eventually the United States went over to Europe belatedly to fight Hitler's forces. But the United States did not enter at the onset of the war and that's what this question is all about. So, the correct answer must be (B).

Maybe this last example was easy for you and you're complaining about this last step, saying, *"But I already read the question. Won't it be a waste of time?"* No; re-reading the question will get you the right answer, especially when you can't decide between two or three choices. And if you can't decide, you should keep working, not sit there staring. Rereading the question lets you keep moving forward.

You see, by the time you get to choosing between the right answer and a couple of straggling wrong answers, you've probably forgotten about the question entirely. You're thinking about that crazy choice (D) (*"Should I have gotten rid of it?"*) and about the next question (*"How much time do I have left?"*). You're not thinking about the current question, and that, of course, is the whole point. Usually, after rereading the question, it's easy to choose between the two or three "translated" answer choices you have left. Reminding yourself of the question makes the answer much more clear. Don't short-change yourself at this critical moment.

5. Last Resort: Guess and Move On!

"What if I still don't get it?" Going through the above process makes it highly unlikely that this will happen very often, but on a handful of questions you may not be able to pin down the correct answer. Don't worry; just guess and move on. Reread pages 14–15 if you are not convinced of the benefits of guessing.

Pop Quiz

Q: If you don't know the answer to a question, and you can eliminate at least one answer choice, you should
(A) look for the answer on the ceiling
(B) stare at the question for ten more minutes
(C) look under your desk
(D) guess and move on

Review: The System

1. Read the question—connect the era.
2. Eliminate anti-era or non-era choices.
3. Assess the remaining choices: Translate.
4. Stop, reread the question.
5. Last resort: Guess and move on!

SPECIAL TYPES OF QUESTIONS

For almost all of the questions on the SAT Subject Test in U.S. History, you can use the era-based approach. But watch out for the following special types of questions on this test.

Quote Questions

A good number of quote questions may appear on the test, but luckily they are easy to spot and easy to do. In these questions, you are given a quote or a short piece of writing and asked to identify either the speaker, the time period, or the general philosophy of the writer/speaker. These questions are general and the answer choices tend to be very different from each other, so the era technique works very well. Sometimes there are two questions for one quote, which makes these questions efficient to do. Sometimes several questions refer to a group of quotes; these may be trickier and a little more time-consuming than the standard quote question.

The biggest danger is spending too much time on these questions. When you're confronted with a quote or short paragraph, if your instinct tells you, "Oh, I'd better read this carefully," it's time to restrain yourself. You want to read quickly and read only as much as you need to get a general idea of who is talking about what. The question that follows the quote will always be something on the order of "Who might have said this?" "This philosophy was popular when?" or "This theory is called what?"

So the most efficient way to approach these questions is to hit them running. **Read the question first** so you know whether you are looking for a who, a what, or a when. **Then read the quote**, always thinking about what you are looking for. As soon as you grasp what the quote is referring to, jump to the answer choices and find it. If, in the first sentence, you figure out that the quote sounds like something a knight would say, go and find that answer. There's no reason to read the whole quote. **If your first impression is not specific enough to get you the answer, go back and finish reading the quote.** All the information to make the right decision is there.

EXCEPT Questions

EXCEPT questions strike fear in the hearts of most students. Now is the time to overcome this fear! There may be up to 25 questions in this format on the SAT Subject Test in U.S. History. Variations include questions that use NOT and LEAST. Here are some examples:

> All of the following are true EXCEPT
>
> Which of the following was NOT a ratified amendment?
>
> Which of the following is LEAST likely to be the cause?

When you approach these questions in the right way, they can be easy. (If you've dealt with SAT Critical Reading EXCEPT questions, forget about them for now. Because of the subject matter, SAT Subject Test EXCEPT questions are not as hard.)

These questions are highly susceptible to the technique of elimination, but you have to remember to eliminate the right choices! It's usually the word EXCEPT that's confusing, not the question itself. So, eliminate the cause of your troubles. To answer EXCEPT questions, get rid of the EXCEPT, LEAST, or NOT word in the question and look at each answer choice as if it were a true-or-false question.

EXCEPT Questions Are True-or-False Questions in Disguise

Literally cross out the word EXCEPT, LEAST, or NOT and answer "Yes" or "No" to each answer choice. The "Yes" answers should be eliminated; true answer choices would not be the exceptions. And the "No" answer is the correct answer; the false answer is the exception. Let's look at an example:

> All of the following were presidents of the United States ~~EXCEPT~~
>
> (A) George Washington   YES! Eliminate.
> (B) Thomas Jefferson   YES! Eliminate.
> (C) Fred Smith   Who? NO! (C's the answer.)
> (D) Ronald Reagan   YES! Eliminate.
> (E) Abraham Lincoln   YES! Eliminate.

Choice (C), "Fred Smith," is a resounding NO! It's the exception and, therefore, the right answer.

These questions are not tricky if you just look at the subject matter. Usually students get confused by the "looking for the opposite" aspect of answering this type of question. You can avoid this entirely by forgetting about the words EXCEPT, LEAST, NOT, and just thinking Yes or No.

There's another trick to answering EXCEPT questions on the SAT Subject Test in U.S. History. It's a trick that stems from way back in your own history—back to kindergarten.

"One of These Things Is Not Like the Others"

Just like the game from your youth, many of the EXCEPT questions have one answer choice that really sticks out from the others. On these questions, you want to find the triangle among the squares. Because you're looking for the exception, the one that's different from the others is the right answer. Let's look at these answer choices:

Blahblahblahblahblahblahblah EXCEPT

(A) **adventurers** blah blah blah
(B) blah blah **explorers** blah blah
(C) **frontiersmen** blah blah
(D) **advance scouts** blah blah
(E) **investors of capital** blah blah

Now, which one of these types is not like the others? If you had been able to read the real SAT Subject Test question, which mentioned American fur traders and the West, getting the answer would have been very easy. "Investors of capital" have nothing to do with "adventurers," "explorers," "frontiersmen," or "advance scouts." So the exception, and the right answer, is (E).

The differences in the answer choices of EXCEPT questions are not always as stark as the ones in this example (especially because you didn't have to decipher the answer choices). Usually, the choice that sticks out does so because it is not in the same era as the rest of the choices. Always connect to the era first—the answer to the EXCEPT question may be the anti-era choice.

Pop Quiz

A: (A), (B), and (D) are part of the "checks and balances" system, which is how different parts of the government keep an eye on each other. But what in the world is (C)? It sounds important, but we just made it up. ETS makes up many of their wrong answers, too. Use your common sense. Don't believe it just because ETS wrote it.

Let's look at another example:

> All of the following were immediate social or economic consequences of the American Revolution EXCEPT
>
> (A) increased opportunities for land settlement in the West
> (B) reform of primogeniture inheritance laws
> (C) expanded voting rights for women
> (D) the opening of many areas of trade and manufacture
> (E) the seizing of Loyalist holdings

First, read the question and connect the era. Then cross out the "EXCEPT" and think "Yes" or "No" for each answer choice. The era is the American Revolution: think late 1700s, the colonies break from Great Britain, main disputes are taxing and trading laws, most people live on the Atlantic coast. Answer choices (A), (D), and (E) are firmly within the era, and a "Yes" means to eliminate the choice. Maybe (B) leaves you a little clueless, but if you had to choose between (B) and (C), which one of these things is least like the others? Which answer choice stretches the era's boundaries? Obviously, choice (C) is the "No," the anti-era exception, and the right answer. Women's voting rights did not become law until more than a century later, in 1919. Remember, on EXCEPT questions, the anti-era choice is usually right.

Charts, Maps, Cartoons, and Paintings

Scattered throughout the SAT Subject Test in U.S. History are questions concerning charts, maps, cartoons, and paintings, which help to break up the monotony of the test. These questions are usually fun to answer, perhaps because they're a little distracting. There will be around 10 to 12 of these questions on the test. While the chart questions tend to be very easy, those related to the maps are often harder. The difficulty of cartoon questions depends on how well you can connect the cartoon to an era. If you can, it's a piece of cake. If not, well…use common sense and guess. Sometimes you are given two questions along with a graph or map. This is helpful, because if you have to spend some time deciphering the darned thing, you might as well get two questions' worth of points for it.

When you approach one of these questions, don't look at the graphic you're given! It's a waste of time to try to interpret the information before you even know what you're looking for.

Read the question first. Sure, it's common sense, but because you usually hit the graph, map, cartoon, or painting before the questions, it's important to keep this in mind. When you finish reading the question, **read the title next**; it will quickly tell you what the graphic is all about. After you figure out what's going on, aggressively use POE to eliminate any choice that does not match up with the object you just examined. You'll find some examples on the following pages.

Charts, Tables, and Graphs

Charts, tables, and graphs are really beautiful things, because they are almost always self-explanatory. They usually (not always) contain everything you need to know to answer the questions based on them. In that respect, they are giveaway points, unlike those on the rest of the test. To answer the question correctly, you often merely have to pull the needed information from the illustration. If you are chart- or table-phobic, the best medicine is practice, practice, practice.

ETS shows you the charts first, but skip over them! Read the question first. Then go back to the chart when you know what to look for.

U.S. INCOME TAX 1930–1950 (in millions)

	Individuals	Corporations
1930	$ 1,147	$ 1,263
1940	$ 982	$ 1,148
1950	$ 17,153	$ 10,854

The chart above gives the gross revenue from income taxes collected by the U.S. government in the years 1930–1950. The chart contains enough information to determine which of the following?

(A) In 1940, corporations paid a smaller percentage of their income to the government than did individuals.
(B) In 1950, the government received a higher proportion of its income from individuals than from corporations.
(C) The reduced rate of income tax in 1940 was caused by the end of attempts to cure the Great Depression.
(D) Corporations did not pay a fair share of taxes in 1950.
(E) The increase in the income tax collected in 1950 was due to programs instituted by Dwight D. Eisenhower.

First, read the question. The question asks you what can be determined from the chart. Then look at the chart. Only choice (B) can be determined from the numbers given in the chart. Choice (A) is tricky, but we do not know what percentage of each group's income went to taxes; we know only the totals. Choice (C) is incorrect because it is impossible to determine from the chart that the Great Depression caused the reduced rate of income tax. We don't even know that the rate of taxation changed (people could have been earning less money). Likewise, choice (E) is incorrect because nothing in the chart indicates the cause of the increase. Choice (D) is a judgment call, and that's never appropriate on chart questions.

Some chart-based questions do require knowledge of information not included in the charts themselves. The following question is an example of this.

PERCENTAGE OF BLACKS IN INTEGRATED SCHOOLS IN 1964

Missouri	42.00%
Tennessee	2.72%
Alabama	0.007%
West Virginia	58.20%
Texas	5.50%

The figures above indicate that the states of Tennessee, Alabama, and Texas would most likely be in violation of which of the following Supreme Court decisions?

(A) *Brown v. Board of Education*
(B) *Roe v. Wade*
(C) *Plessy v. Ferguson*
(D) *Marbury v. Madison*
(E) *Griswold v. Connecticut*

In this question you have to use both chart and era techniques. Although none of the states listed has completely integrated schools, Tennessee, Alabama, and Texas have almost none of their black students attending integrated schools. These states would be in violation of the court decision that outlawed segregation, or (A), *Brown v. Board of Education*. The rest of the cases are from different eras.

Don't get caught wasting time on charts. There are lots of points out there just waiting for you to grab them. If the chart is tricky, guess and keep moving.

Map-Based Questions

Call it talent or call it cruelty, but map questions on the SAT Subject Test in U.S. History are confusing. Unlike questions referring to most graphs or charts, map queries may require you to know something history-based. Again, read the question first; then read the title of the map. If the question and map are self-explanatory, great—go for it. But you may find that the question is era-based and then you can just follow the "connect-to-the-era" steps as usual. The map may also involve geography. Unfortunately, geography is not usually stressed in most high school history courses. Just do your best to eliminate wrong answers and guess.

Most important, don't get trapped into spending too much time on these questions. They can be confusing, and if you don't get the answer right away or if you have no clue what the map is supposed to mean, there is no use spending a lot of time on them. This time is stolen from other, easier questions on which you could do better. Remember, you have a lot of ground to cover in your one-hour time limit, so keep moving.

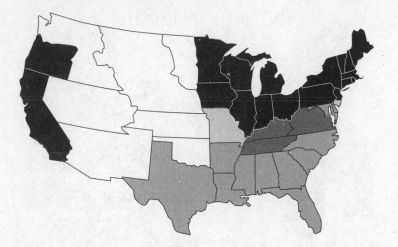

The map above shows the state-by-state results of the presidential election of 1860. Which of the following candidates won the majority of the votes in the states that are shaded in black?

(A) Andrew Jackson
(B) James Monroe
(C) Abraham Lincoln
(D) Stephen Douglas
(E) Ulysses S. Grant

To answer this question correctly, it helps to know that the Civil War happened just after this election. This allows us to eliminate answer choices (A) and (B) immediately. Both Andrew Jackson and James Monroe were presidents in earlier eras. Abraham Lincoln, (C), was president during the Civil War, and the North (the anti-slavery states) supported him in his election. Looks like we have a winner here: The correct answer is (C). Stephen Douglas lost to Lincoln in the election of 1860, and Ulysses S. Grant, though he became president later, was one of Lincoln's generals during the Civil War.

Political Cartoons

The types of cartoons you will encounter on the SAT Subject Test in U.S. History are political cartoons, something like you might find on the editorial page of your newspaper. These are always era-based and will often give you the date that the particular cartoon appeared. More modern cartoons, say from 1972, will probably be easier to recognize and to figure out than older ones, such as those from 1820, mainly because you are more familiar with the humor and the format. Approach cartoon questions just as you would any regular era-based question and let common sense be your guide. Let's look at some examples.

The idea expressed in this nineteenth-century cartoon is that

(A) the Dred Scott decision led to some unusual political alliances in the election of 1860

(B) Dred Scott was an influential statesman who orchestrated peaceful agreements among political rivals

(C) music of the day had become too political to be enjoyed by most people

(D) politicians should heed Dred Scott's example and should be willing to cater to special interest groups

(E) the Dred Scott decision promised a renewed "Era of Good Feelings"

To answer this question, it is essential to connect to the era of the cartoon. Maybe you recall that the Dred Scott decision was a controversy right before the election of 1860. Or maybe you recognize the character of Abraham Lincoln in the upper right-hand corner. If you can connect this cartoon to the pre–Civil War era, you should be able to eliminate choices (B) and (C), because neither of these choices says anything about that era (or any other era). In choice (D), "special interest groups" refers to more contemporary issues, and in choice (E), the "Era of Good Feelings" refers to the period right after the War of 1812; there certainly weren't any good feelings during the era right before the Civil War. Choice (A), the right answer, is most firmly in the pre–Civil War era. To refresh your memory, the Dred Scott decision held that a black man could not be granted freedom even though he had been taken by his own "master" into a free territory. This astounding decision fueled tensions between the North and South, and motivated candidates from very divergent political groups to form alliances in the election of 1860.

Which of the following is the closest to the idea expressed in the cartoon above?

(A) The United States should intervene in the conflict between the working man and business interests.

(B) President Theodore Roosevelt's imperialistic foreign policy caused tension between him and American business interests.

(C) Uncle Sam, representing the American people, looks on disapprovingly as the president attacks a popular form of transportation.

(D) President Theodore Roosevelt is nobly trying to restrain the powerful railroad trusts.

(E) President Franklin D. Roosevelt extended the power of the government so that it could compete with commercial interests.

Again, connect to the era and you will easily solve this question. The man wrestling with the railroad is Theodore Roosevelt. Remember, he was a president in the Progressive Era and one of his many nicknames was "The Trustbuster." He was the first president to try to restrain the railroad monopolies. The American people were sick and tired of the unfair, powerful monopolies during this time, so you can eliminate choice (C). The cartoon itself gives no indication about foreign policy (eliminate (B)), and the drawing is definitely not of FDR (cross out (E)). Choice (A) might look tempting, but the cartoon and the era should lead you to the correct choice, (D).

Factoids—The Bad News

Unfortunately, many questions on the SAT Subject Test in U.S. History are based solely on little factoids, rather than on a general recognition of a particular era. Because they are the toughest questions on the test, your goal with them is damage control. These questions are easy to spot; often the answer choices are just lists of people, states, or countries, or the question is short, asking about a particular book or trial, without giving a date or much information to go with it. Clearly, if you know the fact, these questions are not very hard, but of all the questions on the test, they tend to be the most knowledge-based. They also tend to ask about the more obscure facts in U.S. history. Still, we have ways to reduce your losses on these questions.

Play Your Hunches

These factoid questions are tough for everybody, but some students must get them right or they wouldn't be on the test. This means that it pays to play your hunches. The answer will probably not be something you've never heard of; it might just be about something you never thought was important enough to memorize. On this test, the correct answer will more likely be something you find vaguely familiar than something you've never heard of before. A corollary to this is to...

Go for the Most Famous Person or Thing

The correct answer will more likely be a famous person or thing, rather than someone or something obscure. This does not mean that if a president is listed in a group of choices, you should always select that answer. After all, we've had some pretty forgettable presidents. Again, if you are guessing, just go with your hunches. For instance, Abraham Lincoln may have been more famous than Daniel Webster, but Webster was more famous than Martin Van Buren. Of course, if you know that the famous person in the set is wrong, eliminate that choice and then go for the next most famous person.

Study "The American Legacy"

Some questions may require knowledge of important Supreme Court decisions or the major contributors to American arts and literature. Rather than burying these references in the general history review, we've given them a chapter of their own: "The American Legacy" (Chapter 12). Make sure you're familiar with this information; it could give you just the edge you need on a factoid question.

If You Can Eliminate Any Choice, Guess

But if you can't eliminate any of the choices, skip the question. You don't want to waste time on a question that you have scarcely a chance of getting right. This is a long test and it is more worthwhile to try to finish, and get a crack at some questions that you can get right at the end, than to pull your hair out over hard questions. Check the Pacing Chart (page 12) to see exactly how many questions you can leave out in order to get your target score. (You may be happily surprised

Take a Guess:

A: Even if you've never heard of Joseph Smith, you can still answer this question. If you think about the answer choices, there are good reasons to eliminate (A), (B), and (D). But even if you can eliminate one answer choice, you should still guess. (By the way, the answer is (C).)

at how many you can comfortably guess on or skip.) Remember, it is always better for you to choose the ones you will skip rather than letting the clock choose for you as you run out of time at the end.

Review: The Questions

1. Era questions—Use the system.
2. EXCEPT questions—Turn them into "Yes" or "No" questions or use "One of these things is not like the others."
3. Charts, maps, cartoons, paintings, etc.—Read the question first; read the title second; use common sense.
4. Factoids—Damage control.

If you can eliminate one answer, guess. If you have no idea, then skip the question.

Need help prepping for the SAT? *Cracking the SAT Premium* has all the content review, strategy, and practice you need to help you get a top score.

Part II
Practice Test 1

Chapter 4
Practice Test 1

The Princeton Review Practice SAT Subject Tests in U.S. History

The following is the first practice SAT Subject Test in U.S. History. In order to get a good estimate of your score, you should take it and all other practice exams under test conditions.

- Give yourself one hour to do the test when you are not going to be bothered by anyone. Turn off your phone and tell your parents to tell your friends that you are not home.
- Clear a space to work in. You want no distractions.
- Have someone else time you. It's too easy to fudge the time when you are keeping track of it yourself.
- Tear out the answer sheet provided in the back of the book. This way, you will get the feel for filling in all those lovely ovals.
- Don't worry about the complicated instructions; just pick the correct answer.
- Instructions for grading follow each test.

GOOD LUCK!

U.S. HISTORY
SUBJECT TEST 1

Your responses to the U.S. History Subject Test questions must be filled in on Test 1 of your answer sheet (the answer sheet at the back of the book). Marks on any other section will not be counted toward your U.S. History Subject Test score.

When your supervisor gives the signal, turn the page and begin the U.S. History Subject Test.

U.S. HISTORY SUBJECT TEST 1

Directions: Each of the questions or incomplete statements below is followed by five suggested answers or completions. Select one that is best in each case and then fill in the corresponding oval on the answer sheet.

1. The most important cash crop in seventeenth-century Virginia was

   (A) tobacco
   (B) corn
   (C) wheat
   (D) barley
   (E) grapes

2. The establishment of the Virginia House of Burgesses was significant for which of the following reasons?

   (A) Its members were appointed by the crown.
   (B) Its members were elected by a vote of the large majority of the population of Virginia.
   (C) It was a part of a network of state assemblies that represented a strong, unified system of federal governance.
   (D) Its decisions were not subject to veto by the governor.
   (E) It represented an early step toward representative democracy in the colonies

3. The concept of "virtual representation" is best summarized by which of the following?

   (A) Because colonial governors represented the king of England, they could exercise all the powers of the monarchy.
   (B) British colonists in America were represented in Parliament by virtue of the fact that Parliament represents all British subjects, whether or not they are allowed to vote.
   (C) Native Americans should be allowed to file lawsuits in U.S. federal courts, even though they are not citizens of the United States.
   (D) Wealthy Southern landowners should be allowed to hire others to serve, in their places, in the Confederate army.
   (E) Because a flag stands for the country it represents, the Pledge of Allegiance is, in effect, a loyalty oath to the United States.

4. The election of 1824 is often called the first "modern election" because it was the first

   (A) to occur following the ratification of the Bill of Rights
   (B) that was decided by voters in the western states
   (C) to utilize voting booths
   (D) in which a candidate chosen by party leaders did not win the nomination
   (E) in which African Americans were allowed to vote

5. The first to use the presidential veto extensively was

   (A) George Washington
   (B) Thomas Jefferson
   (C) Andrew Jackson
   (D) William Henry Harrison
   (E) James Buchanan

6. Congress brought impeachment proceedings against Andrew Johnson primarily because

   (A) Johnson sought to block aspects of Congressional Reconstruction
   (B) Johnson's Republican policies had fallen out of favor with the Democratic majority
   (C) Johnson repeatedly vetoed congressional aid packages aimed at reestablishing the South's economic independence
   (D) a congressional committee discovered that Johnson had accepted bribes from western gold speculators
   (E) it was rumored that Johnson was too ill to execute the office of the presidency effectively

GO ON TO THE NEXT PAGE

7. The Supreme Court's decisions in both *McCullough v. Maryland* and *Gibbons v. Ogden* involved questions regarding

   (A) the powers granted the federal government under the Constitution
   (B) the authority of the United States government to curtail civil liberties during wartime
   (C) the constitutionality of the federal income tax
   (D) the legality of slavery in the United States
   (E) the power of the federal judiciary to void congressional legislation

8. "In good time we are going to sweep into power in this nation and throughout the world. We are going to destroy all enslaving and degrading capitalist institutions and recreate them as free and humanizing institutions."

   The statement above best represents the ideology of

   (A) Radical Republicans of the 1870s
   (B) American Socialists of the 1910s
   (C) Isolationists of the 1920s
   (D) New Deal Democrats of the 1930s
   (E) McCarthyites of the 1950s

9. All of the following were cash crops of the early Chesapeake colonies EXCEPT

   (A) corn
   (B) cotton
   (C) tobacco
   (D) rice
   (E) indigo

10. The development of the Interstate Highway System was accompanied by a sizable population shift from

   (A) western states to eastern states
   (B) cities to suburbs
   (C) rural areas to large urban centers
   (D) single-family housing to apartment buildings
   (E) southern states to midwestern states

11. Lyndon Johnson's social programs were known collectively as the

   (A) American System
   (B) Second New Deal
   (C) New Frontier
   (D) Great Society
   (E) 1,000 Points of Light

12. The concept of religious freedom for which the United States is well known, was best exemplified by which of the following?

   (A) Henry David Thoreau
   (B) John Calvin
   (C) William Penn
   (D) William Bradford
   (E) Roger Williams

13. The fundamental difference between the Congregationalist and Separatist wings of the Puritan movement was that

   (A) one group settled in the northern colonies, the other in the southern
   (B) only one group wanted to split from the Anglican Church
   (C) only one group advocated the separation of church and state
   (D) one group believed the Bible was factually accurate the other believed it was not
   (E) one group while emained in England while the other emigrated to the New World

14. All of the following were reasons for exploration of the New World EXCEPT

   (A) the search for allies in international trade and politics
   (B) the search for a shorter trade route to Asia
   (C) the search for raw materials
   (D) the search for gold and other precious metals
   (E) the search for land to settle

GO ON TO THE NEXT PAGE

15. The Sugar Act of 1764 was designed to

(A) encourage colonists to import more sugar from Great Britain

(B) strengthen the colonial economy by increasing the duty England paid on imports

(C) raise revenues to offset the costs of the French and Indian War

(D) improve relations among the English, French, and Spanish colonists in the New World

(E) prevent the impressment of American colonists to the British navy

16. All of the following were acts imposed on the American colonists by Great Britain EXCEPT

(A) the Intolerable Acts

(B) the Taft Hartley Act

(C) the Stamp Act

(D) the Tea Act

(E) the Navigation Acts

17. The transition of the American economy from a subsistence economy to a market economy was largely the result of two inventions by Eli Whitney. Those two inventions were the

(A) automobile and the cotton gin

(B) telephone and the telegraph

(C) repeating rifle and interchangeable machine parts

(D) cotton gin and the electric light

(E) cotton gin and interchangeable machine parts

18. The Embargo Act of 1807 resulted in all of the following EXCEPT

(A) the near collapse of New England's import-export industry

(B) the alleviation of French and British harassment of American ships

(C) the cessation of legal trade with Canada

(D) an increase in smuggling of British goods into the United States

(E) a sharp decrease in the value of American farm surplus

19. Which of the following factors contributed LEAST to the demise of the Federalist Party?

(A) Throughout the early nineteenth century, party leadership shifted from moderates to extremists.

(B) The loss of the presidency in 1800 disrupted the unity of the party.

(C) The resolutions of the Hartford Convention caused those outside the party to view the Federalists as traitors.

(D) The party's power base was New England, a region that grew less powerful politically as more states were added to the Union.

(E) Dissension over the Kansas-Nebraska Act split the party along regional lines.

20. The Compromise of 1850 included all of the following provisions EXCEPT the

(A) admission of California to the Union as a free state

(B) creation of two new territories, Utah and New Mexico

(C) repudiation of the concept of popular sovereignty

(D) prohibition of slave trade in the District of Columbia

(E) strengthening of the fugitive slave law

GO ON TO THE NEXT PAGE

23. The majority of Japanese Americans imprisoned in internment camps during World War II

    (A) were native-born Americans
    (B) were employees of the Japanese government
    (C) lived on Pacific islands
    (D) had expressed their primary allegiance to Japan during the 1940 census
    (E) worked in the munitions industry

24. During World War II, the availability of consumer goods to civilians

    (A) increased greatly, because the war invigorated the economy
    (B) increased slightly, because some citizens were overseas serving in the armed forces
    (C) remained at the same level it had been at prior to the war
    (D) decreased slightly, causing prices to rise; only the poor were substantially affected
    (E) decreased greatly, to the point that the government had to ration most necessities

21. Signs such as the one shown in the photograph represent

    (A) the philosophy of Radical Reconstructionists
    (B) the reforms of the Fourteenth Amendment to the Constitution
    (C) the enforcement of the Taft-Hartley Act
    (D) desegregation efforts by southerners
    (E) the prevalence of Jim Crow laws

22. The Open Door Policy was primarily aimed at increasing sales of American goods in

    (A) Vietnam
    (B) Eastern Europe
    (C) France
    (D) China
    (E) Brazil

25. "I have never been a quitter. To leave office before my term is completed is abhorrent to every instinct in my body, but as president I must put the interests of America first. America needs a full-time president and a full-time Congress, particularly at this time, with the problems we face at home and abroad. Therefore, I shall resign from the presidency, effective at noon tomorrow . . . ."

The speech quoted above was delivered in which year?

    (A) 1944
    (B) 1954
    (C) 1964
    (D) 1974
    (E) 1984

GO ON TO THE NEXT PAGE

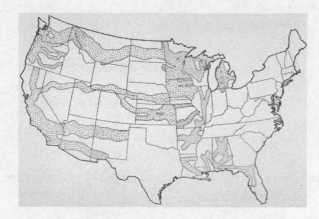

26. The shaded areas of this map from the late 1800s most likely indicate

    (A) fertile river regions of the western states
    (B) Native American reservations
    (C) land grants provided to railroad companies
    (D) pathways of the Underground Railroad
    (E) canal transportation routes

27. During the early seventeenth century, the British valued the American colonies as

    (A) markets for raw goods produced in England's West Indian colonies
    (B) producers of livestock and fresh fruits and vegetables
    (C) manufacturing centers
    (D) population centers from which the British military could draft soldiers
    (E) conduits of trade with Native American artisans

28. The Articles of Confederation were flawed in all of the following ways EXCEPT:

    (A) They did not create a powerful chief executive office of the government.
    (B) They did not empower the government to levy taxes.
    (C) They did not grant the national government the right to regulate commerce.
    (D) They made the admission of new states to the union impossible.
    (E) They required the unanimous consent of the states for most national legislation.

29. Which of the following does NOT describe a beneficial economic result of the construction of the Erie Canal?

    (A) The success of the Erie Canal sparked a boom in canal construction across the country, providing jobs for thousands.
    (B) The canal greatly decreased the cost of moving cargo from the Midwest to New York City.
    (C) The building and maintenance of the canal provided a foundation for the economies of several cities along its banks.
    (D) The availability of the canal greatly eased traffic along the congested Mississippi River, especially in the South.
    (E) By creating greater access to a port city, the canal facilitated more trade with Europe.

30. Which of the following is true of the Indian removal policy pursued by the United States during Andrew Jackson's presidency?

    (A) It met with great popular resistance in the states from which Indians were removed.
    (B) It was implemented with the cooperation of all Indian tribes involved.
    (C) Its implementation violated Indian rights as defined by the Supreme Court.
    (D) It was less harsh than the policy pursued by the previous administration.
    (E) Its focus was the relocation of Indians living in the northeastern states.

31. The United States took control of the Oregon Territory by

    (A) annexing it from Mexico during the Mexican War
    (B) expelling the Russian army, which occupied the territory
    (C) bartering American-held colonies to France, which owned the Oregon Territory
    (D) buying it from the Native Americans who lived there
    (E) negotiating a settlement with Great Britain, which also laid claim to the area

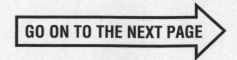

32. The Reconstruction Act of 1867 required Southern states to do all of the following to gain readmission to the Union EXCEPT

    (A) allow African Americans to participate in state conventions and elections
    (B) ratify the Fourteenth Amendment to the Constitution
    (C) pay reparations and provide land grants to all former slaves
    (D) rewrite the state constitution
    (E) submit the state constitution to the U.S. Congress for approval

33. The cartoon above depicts Theodore Roosevelt as

    (A) a militant imperialist
    (B) a laissez-faire economist
    (C) an overseas advocate of American exports
    (D) a trustbuster
    (E) an environmentalist

34. In his book *The Souls of Black Folks*, W. E. B. DuBois challenged Booker T. Washington's views concerning the advancement of African Americans in American society. The difference between the two men's positions can be best summed up as the difference between

    (A) despair and optimism
    (B) violence and pacifism
    (C) religiosity and atheism
    (D) democratic and totalitarian ideals
    (E) confrontation and accommodation

35. Which of the following correctly states Woodrow Wilson's position on Germany's use of U-boats during World War I?

    (A) Wilson demanded that all U-boat attacks be stopped because he believed that they violated international law.
    (B) Wilson opposed the use of U-boats only against British ships.
    (C) Wilson supported the U-boat attacks, because their primary targets were British ships.
    (D) Because the U-boats were built by American manufacturers, Wilson actively campaigned for their use.
    (E) Because the U-boats traveled underwater, their existence was secret and Wilson did not learn of them until after the war ended.

36. "I have no trouble with my enemies. I can take care of my enemies in a fight. But my friends . . . they're the ones who keep me walking the floor at nights!"

    The president who made this statement presided over an administration besmirched by the Teapot Dome Scandal, among other instances of corruption. He was

    (A) George Washington
    (B) Franklin Pierce
    (C) Woodrow Wilson
    (D) Warren G. Harding
    (E) Dwight D. Eisenhower

37. In *Gideon v. Wainwright*, the Supreme Court ruled that the government must

    (A) enforce federal laws guaranteeing African Americans the right to vote
    (B) provide defense lawyers to felony defendants who are too poor to hire attorneys
    (C) prevent businesses from establishing monopolies in essential services, such as food production
    (D) overturn laws aimed at discriminating against unpopular religious groups
    (E) advise criminal suspects of their right not to incriminate themselves

GO ON TO THE NEXT PAGE

38. The sites of colonial cities were chosen primarily on the basis of their proximity to

   (A) gold mines
   (B) coal reserves
   (C) wild game
   (D) mountains
   (E) waterways

39. Which of the following is true of the Townshend Acts?

   (A) They halved the number of English military and government officials in the colonies.
   (B) They did not impose any new taxes on the colonists.
   (C) They stripped the colonial legislatures of the "power of the purse" by altering the method by which tax collectors were paid.
   (D) They offered the colonists direct representation in Parliament if they, in return, would renounce the Declaration of Independence.
   (E) They repealed the Tea Act.

40. Throughout the nineteenth century, United States senators were chosen by

   (A) popular election
   (B) the House of Representatives
   (C) the president
   (D) their state governors
   (E) their state legislatures

41. Which of the following is NOT true of the reform movements of the 1830s?

   (A) Their memberships were dominated by women.
   (B) They were concentrated primarily in the Midwest.
   (C) Many were inspired by the Second Great Awakening.
   (D) Reform groups' alliance with the Whigs was stronger than their alliance with the Democrats.
   (E) Most reform groups were devoted to improving the lots of disenfranchised groups.

42. Which of the following is NOT a nineteenth-century American novel?

   (A) *Moby-Dick*
   (B) *For Whom the Bell Tolls*
   (C) *The Last of the Mohicans*
   (D) *The Adventures of Huckleberry Finn*
   (E) *The Scarlet Letter*

43. During the 1840s, immigrants to the United States were most often born in

   (A) Ireland
   (B) Cuba
   (C) Japan
   (D) Russia
   (E) Canada

44. In the early 1850s, many Northern states passed personal liberty laws in response to the

   (A) political platform of the Know-Nothing Party
   (B) growing popularity of the concept of Manifest Destiny
   (C) Fugitive Slave Act
   (D) Emancipation Proclamation
   (E) Haymarket Square Riot

45. The Populists wanted the government to increase the amount of money in circulation because they believed that doing so would result in

   (A) a recession, which would allow banks to increase the number of mortgage foreclosures
   (B) a drop in the wholesale price index, which would spur international trade
   (C) price stagnation, which would encourage foreign investment in American manufacturing
   (D) inflation, which would make it easier for farmers to repay their loans
   (E) universal employment for adults

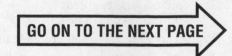

GO ON TO THE NEXT PAGE

46. In the early twentieth century, the U.S. government asserted its right to intervene in Latin American politics if it felt that instability in the region threatened U.S. security. That assertion is known as the

(A) domino theory
(B) Roosevelt Corollary to the Monroe Doctrine
(C) "mutually assured destruction" strategy
(D) Good Neighbor Policy
(E) theory of social Darwinism

47. All of the following contributed to the Senate's defeat of the Treaty of Versailles EXCEPT

(A) President Wilson's unwillingness to compromise with the Senate
(B) the opposition of the British and French governments to the treaty
(C) postwar isolationism among conservatives
(D) widespread skepticism about the potential effectiveness of the League of Nations
(E) criticism that the treaty punished Germany too harshly

48. Members of which of the following groups would have been LEAST likely to switch allegiance from the Republican to the Democratic Party because of the New Deal?

(A) African Americans
(B) The poor
(C) Economic conservatives
(D) City dwellers
(E) Union members

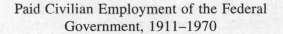

Paid Civilian Employment of the Federal Government, 1911–1970

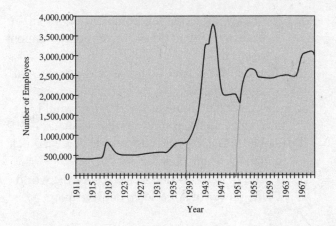

49. Which of the following hypotheses best accounts for the trends in federal employment of civilians shown in the graph above?

(A) The government grows most rapidly during wartime.
(B) Growth in the federal government closely mirrors the growth of the population of the United States.
(C) The growth and reduction of the federal government is primarily a function of which party controls the White House.
(D) By employing those who would have otherwise remained unemployed, the government engineered the country's recovery from the Great Depression.
(E) Increases in the number of rights guaranteed to citizens are always accompanied by an immediate growth in the size of government.

GO ON TO THE NEXT PAGE

50. In deciding to drop atomic bombs on Japan, President Truman was probably LEAST influenced by his

    (A) misconception that the bomb was no more destructive than other conventional weapons of the era
    (B) fear that the Soviet Union would join the war against Japan
    (C) certainty that an invasion of Japan would result in numerous American casualties
    (D) belief that it was the best way to force a quick Japanese surrender
    (E) desire to demonstrate to the rest of the world the power of America's new weapon

51. The difference between a "cold war" and a "hot war" is that, during a "cold war,"

    (A) neither side publicly acknowledges its animosity toward its enemy
    (B) United Nations armed forces are used to maintain treaties
    (C) the opponents differ over religious, rather than political, ideals
    (D) the opposing sides are military superpowers
    (E) the opposing sides do not engage in military combat

52. Anne Hutchinson was banished from the Massachusetts Bay Colony because she

    (A) campaigned for women's suffrage
    (B) argued that all colonists should have the right to bear arms
    (C) believed that one could communicate with God without the assistance of the clergy
    (D) organized a boycott of British goods
    (E) sold provisions and weapons to local Native Americans

53. Most historians regard the First Great Awakening as a response to

    (A) Enlightenment ideals
    (B) the English Civil War
    (C) the Industrial Age
    (D) World War I
    (E) the Great Depression

54. "I hold it that a little rebellion, now and then, is a good thing, and as necessary in the political world as storms in the physical."

    The statement above was made by Thomas Jefferson in response to

    (A) Bacon's Rebellion
    (B) the War of 1812
    (C) the Louisiana Purchase
    (D) Shays' Rebellion
    (E) the Embargo Act of 1807

55. The XYZ Affair resulted in

    (A) a reversal of American public sentiment toward France
    (B) an American declaration of war against English settlers in Canada
    (C) the mass relocation of Southwestern Indians
    (D) the establishment of the First National Bank
    (E) the Missouri Compromise

56. Although Texas petitioned for admission to the Union in 1836, the United States did not annex the territory until 1845. Of the following issues, which two were most responsible for that delay?

    I. Concern for the rights of Native Americans in the region
    II. Slavery
    III. Widespread popular antagonism toward expansion of any type
    IV. Fear of provoking war with Mexico

    (A) I and III
    (B) I and IV
    (C) II and III
    (D) II and IV
    (E) III and IV

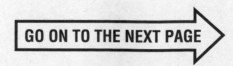

57. The site of the photograph above is most probably

    (A) Rhode Island in the 1830s
    (B) Ohio in the 1850s
    (C) Nebraska in the 1880s
    (D) Illinois in the 1910s
    (E) Louisiana in the 1940s

58. A historian wanting to analyze quantitative data concerning how Americans earned their livings during the 1880s would probably find the most useful information in which of the following sources?

    (A) The diary of a man who worked several jobs during the decade
    (B) U. S. census reports
    (C) Employment advertisements in a large city newspaper
    (D) Letters from a mid-level government bureaucrat to a friend overseas
    (E) Lyrics to popular songs from that era

59. The American takeover of the Philippines after the Spanish-American War was immediately followed by

    (A) the establishment of democratic self-rule on the islands
    (B) a transfer of control of the islands to Japan
    (C) a Philippine referendum calling for admission to the United States
    (D) a protracted armed insurgence by Philippine nationalists
    (E) a second war, between the United States and England, for control of the islands

60. The Progressive movement received the greatest support from which of the following constituencies?

    (A) Middle-class city dwellers
    (B) Land-owning farmers
    (C) Migrant farm workers
    (D) Southern Democrats
    (E) Western cattle ranchers

GO ON TO THE NEXT PAGE

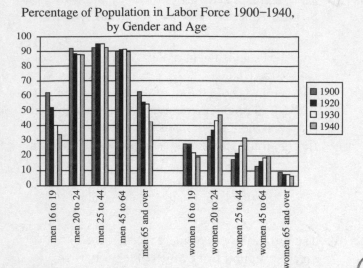

Percentage of Population in Labor Force 1900–1940, by Gender and Age

Legend: 1900, 1920, 1930, 1940

61. The data presented in the chart above best supports which of the following conclusions?

(A) Preparations for the United States' entry into World War II increased employment rates for all segments of the American population.

(B) Young people chose to pursue full-time education in increasing numbers between 1900 and 1940.

(C) Child labor laws enacted during the Progressive era essentially put an end to the employment of people under the age of 16.

(D) Between the years 1920 and 1930, most men left agricultural jobs to pursue work in manufacturing.

(E) Between 1900 and 1940, men between the ages of 25 and 64 who did not work simply did not look hard enough for jobs.

62. Which of the following novels does NOT take African American alienation from the cultural mainstream as one of its central themes?

(A) Ralph Ellison's *Invisible Man*
(B) Richard Wright's *Native Son*
(C) F. Scott Fitzgerald's *The Great Gatsby*
(D) Zora Neale Hurston's *Their Eyes Were Watching God*
(E) James Baldwin's *Go Tell It on the Mountain*

63. Most historians believe that Franklin Roosevelt decided to run for an unprecedented third presidential term primarily because he

(A) was convinced that the United States would soon enter World War II

(B) hoped to establish a precedent of three-term presidencies

(C) believed that only he could prevent the Communist takeover of Cuba

(D) wanted Harry Truman to succeed him but believed Truman was not yet ready to take over the presidency

(E) knew that he would die within weeks of his reelection

64. In response to a 1957 court order to integrate Little Rock public high schools, the state of Arkansas

(A) closed the city's high schools for two years
(B) initiated the nation's first state-funded school busing program
(C) integrated schools in the city of Little Rock, but not in smaller towns
(D) allowed blacks and whites to attend the same schools, but held segregated classes
(E) negotiated a compromise with the court, allowing the state ten years to complete the integration process

65. Which of the following states the central idea of the 1963 book *The Feminine Mystique*?

(A) The United States military, having succeeded at racial integration, should also integrate by gender.

(B) Cultural forces conspire to discourage women from pursuing careers and to encourage them to seek fulfillment in domestic life.

(C) Mentally, psychologically, and physically, women are fundamentally no different from men.

(D) Those who pursue abortion rights do so in support of a larger, politically subversive agenda.

(E) The economic circumstances that, in many families, require both spouses to work full-time are bringing about the destruction of the American family.

GO ON TO THE NEXT PAGE →

66. The primary purpose of the War Powers Resolution of 1973 was to

    (A) provide the U.S. Army with enough funding to win the Vietnam War
    (B) allow the president to suspend the writ of habeas corpus during times of war
    (C) empower military leaders to overrule presidential orders
    (D) pardon all Americans who had refused military service during the Vietnam War
    (E) make it more difficult for the president to unilaterally commit American troops overseas

67. Bacon's Rebellion is one of the earliest examples of

    (A) a potentially violent conflict resolved through peaceful negotiation
    (B) armed conflict between French and British colonists
    (C) an act of pacifist civil disobedience
    (D) a populist uprising in America
    (E) a colonial protest against unfair tariffs imposed by the British

68. Of the following, which did mercantilists consider most important to a country's economic well-being?

    (A) Full employment
    (B) A favorable balance of trade
    (C) The establishment of a large national debt at moderate interest rates
    (D) Free trade
    (E) The extension of civil liberties to as many people as possible

69. Which of the following argued for a "broad constructionist" interpretation of the Constitution?

    (A) Thomas Jefferson
    (B) Alexander Hamilton
    (C) James Madison
    (D) Benjamin Franklin
    (E) Thomas Paine

70. The "Lowell system" was established for the primary purpose of

    (A) clearly defining and distinguishing the roles of the local, state, and national governments
    (B) promoting abolitionism in the Southern states
    (C) calculating the net worth of the United States' gross national product
    (D) rehabilitating nonviolent criminals
    (E) enticing rural New England women to work in textile mills

71. In the years immediately following the declaration of the Monroe Doctrine, the doctrine's goals were achieved primarily because

    (A) the American military imposed a blockade on all European ships traveling to the Western Hemisphere
    (B) American merchants reinforced the doctrine with a boycott of goods produced in countries that violated its goals
    (C) the British navy prevented Spain and Portugal from retaking their colonies in Central and South America
    (D) American and European diplomats negotiated a treaty reiterating the Monroe Doctrine's objectives
    (E) a prolonged European economic depression made it impossible for any European nation to intervene in the Western Hemisphere

GO ON TO THE NEXT PAGE

72. Andrew Jackson opposed supporters of the doctrine of nullification for all of the following reasons EXCEPT:

(A) He believed they had misinterpreted the Virginia and Kentucky Resolutions, on which their doctrine was based.
(B) Jackson feared that nullification, if accepted, would threaten the stability of the Union.
(C) Nullification supporters believed the states could unilaterally interpret the Constitution; Jackson disagreed.
(D) The nullification movement was led by Jackson's political enemy, John C. Calhoun.
(E) Jackson believed that the federal government, not state governments, should exert the most influence over the lives of citizens.

73. Settlement houses were established as a means of combating problems caused by

(A) migrant farming
(B) the Dust Bowl
(C) strip mining
(D) nuclear radiation
(E) urban poverty

74. "[The wealthy man is required]…to consider all surplus revenues which come to him simply as trust funds, which he is called upon to administer…in the manner which…is best calculated to produce the most beneficial results for the community—[he is] the mere trustee and agent for his poorer brethren…doing for them better than they would or could do for themselves."

The ideas above are most characteristic of

(A) transcendentalism
(B) socialism
(C) the doctrine of nullification
(D) black separatism
(E) the Gospel of Wealth

75. The Platt Amendment of 1901 primarily concerned United States' relations with

(A) Great Britain
(B) Germany
(C) China
(D) Cuba
(E) Australia

76. Before the Sixteenth Amendment to the Constitution established a federal income tax, the national government collected its greatest revenues from

(A) customs duties
(B) a national sales tax
(C) fines levied in federal court
(D) rent and lease income from federal properties
(E) the confiscation of property from convicted felons

77. Harry Truman reversed the momentum of his 1948 reelection campaign when he began using his campaign speeches to criticize

(A) the "unnecessary" Marshall Plan
(B) his opponent's "lack of moral decency"
(C) the "do-nothing" Eightieth Congress
(D) the "militant" feminist movement
(E) the "trouble-making" labor unions

78. The following quote about Great Britain's colonial policies most matches which of the types of people below?

"But if it was thought hard that charter privileges should be taken away by act of parliament, is it not much harder to be in part, or in whole, disfranchised of rights, that have been always thought inherent to a British subject, namely, to be free from all taxes, but what he consents to in person, or by his representative? This right, if it could be traced no higher than Magna Charta, is part of the common law, part of a British subjects birthright, and as inherent and perpetual…."

(A) A colonist in North America
(B) A slave in North America
(C) The King of England
(D) A member of the British Parliament
(E) A colonial governor

79. Which of the following does NOT correctly pair a Native American tribe and region in which that tribe lived during the seventeenth century?

(A) Powhatan, Chesapeake
(B) Doegs, Western Virginia
(C) Pequots, Connecticut Valley
(D) Pokanokets, Cape Cod
(E) Sioux, Florida

80. The British established vice-admiralty courts in the colonies primarily to

(A) prevent the colonists from organizing legislatures
(B) try Native Americans and French settlers who threatened British colonists
(C) make it easier to prosecute colonists who violated the Navigation Acts
(D) protect the rights of free blacks in areas where slavery was permitted
(E) process Loyalist property claims after the Revolutionary War

81. The ideals stated in the Declaration of Independence are most similar to those expressed in which of the following?

(A) Machiavelli's *The Prince*
(B) Plato's *Republic*
(C) Thomas Hobbes's *Leviathan*
(D) John Locke's *Two Treatises on Government*
(E) St. Augustine's *City of God*

82. Which of the following best describes the general impact of the War of 1812 on the United States' economy?

(A) The war permanently altered America's trade alliances, allowing France to supplant England as the country's chief trading partner.
(B) The disappearance of the English market for tobacco caused an economic collapse that affected the entire South.
(C) The war quarantined the United States from European technological advances, stalling America's industrial revolution for almost a decade.
(D) By isolating the United States from Europe, the war had the advantageous effect of promoting economic independence.
(E) War expenses bankrupted the First National Bank, halting the construction of the national railroad and putting thousands out of work.

83. Although the Mormon Church established its first headquarters in Ohio, the church's followers eventually relocated to Utah, primarily because

(A) the region's isolation offered the church protection from its enemies
(B) the federal government recruited church members to settle the area
(C) a prolonged drought left much of Ohio's farmland unusable
(D) the Shakers, who had already relocated to Utah, invited the Mormons to join their religious community
(E) Mormon theology required the Mormons to live in complete isolation from the non-Mormon world

GO ON TO THE NEXT PAGE

84. The English colonial system in North America during the seventeenth and eighteenth centuries was most closely based on which economic system?

   (A) Laissez-Faire
   (B) Free Trade
   (C) Salutary Neglect
   (D) Mercantilism
   (E) Bartering

85. According to the cartoon, the relocation of the textile industry to the South was facilitated primarily by the region's

   (A) availability of slave labor
   (B) access to cheap coal
   (C) proximity to European trade routes
   (D) abundance of skilled fashion designers
   (E) favorable weather conditions

86. Which of the following was the most likely reason that President Taft fell out of favor with many Progressive Republicans?

   (A) He passed legislation which lowered tariffs only slightly.
   (B) He supported regulation of railroads.
   (C) He was opposed to legislation involving taxes.
   (D) He was anti reform.
   (E) He passed legislation allowing for the direct election of senators.

87. Which of the following contributed LEAST to the economic factors that resulted in the Great Depression?

   (A) Technological advances that allowed farmers and manufacturers to overproduce, resulting in large inventories
   (B) Concentration of wealth in too few hands, guaranteeing that business failures would have widespread ramifications
   (C) A steadily widening gap between the cost of consumer goods and the buying power of the average consumer
   (D) Wild speculation by stock investors, producing an unstable and volatile stock market
   (E) Interventionist economic policies from the federal government, resulting in overly conservative behavior on the part of private investors

88. Which of the following actions would most likely be taken by the government if it wished to slow the rate of inflation?

   (A) The Treasury Department would increase the amount of currency in circulation.
   (B) The president would order the creation of new jobs within the federal government.
   (C) The Federal Reserve Board would increase the prime interest rate.
   (D) Congress would lower the rate at which businesses are taxed.
   (E) The president's trade commissioner would lower export tariffs.

GO ON TO THE NEXT PAGE

89. In 1932, Herbert Hoover ordered the army against protesters who had camped in the streets of Washington, D.C. throughout the summer. Those protesters were

   (A) farmers demanding that the government buy their surplus crops
   (B) former civilian government employees who had been laid off in the wake of the Depression
   (C) Communist agitators calling for a constitutional convention
   (D) African Americans demonstrating against civil rights abuses in the South
   (E) World War I veterans demanding early payment of their benefits

90. This image by Joseph Riis was most likely intended to

   (A) document the living habits of specific races
   (B) criticize immigration policies that led to overcrowding in urban areas
   (C) expose urban poverty to wealthy benefactors
   (D) encourage the use of contraception to prevent overcrowding
   (E) advocate for lower taxes in urban areas

STOP

**If you finish before time is called, you may check your work on this test only.
Do not turn to any other test in this book.**

Chapter 5
Practice Test 1:
Answers and
Explanations

16   minus incorrect

PRACTICE TEST 1 ANSWER KEY

Question Number	Correct Answer	Right	Wrong	Question Number	Correct Answer	Right	Wrong	Question Number	Correct Answer	Right	Wrong
1.	A	✓		31.	E	✓		61.	B		✓
2.	E	✓		32.	C	✓		62.	C	✓	
3.	B	✓		33.	D	✓		63.	A	✓	
4.	D		✓	34.	E	✓		64.	A		✓
5.	C	✓		35.	A	✓		65.	B		✓
6.	A	✓		36.	D	✓		66.	E		✓
7.	A	✓		37.	B	✓		67.	D	✓	
8.	B	✓		38.	E	✓		68.	B	✓	
9.	A	✓		39.	C		✓	69.	B	✓	
10.	B	✓		40.	E		✓	70.	E	✓	
11.	D	✓		41.	B	✓		71.	C		✓
12.	E	✓		42.	B		✓	72.	E	✓	
13.	B	✓		43.	A	✓		73.	E	✓	
14.	A		✓	44.	C	✓		74.	E	✓	
15.	C	✓		45.	D	✓		75.	D	✓	
16.	B	✓		46.	B	✓		76.	A		✓
17.	E	✓		47.	B	✓		77.	C	✓	
18.	B		✓	48.	C	✓		78.	A	✓	
19.	E		✓	49.	A	✓		79.	E		✓
20.	C	✓		50.	A	✓		80.	C	✓	
21.	E	✓		51.	E	✓		81.	D	✓	
22.	D	✓		52.	C	✓		82.	D	✓	
23.	A	✓		53.	A	✓		83.	A	✓	
24.	E	✓		54.	D		✓	84.	D		✓
25.	D	✓		55.	A	✓		85.	B		✓
26.	C	✓		56.	D	✓		86.	A	✓	
27.	A	✓		57.	C	✓		87.	E	✓	
28.	D	✓		58.	B	✓		88.	C	✓	
29.	D	✓		59.	D	✓		89.	E		✓
30.	C	✓		60.	A	✓		90.	C	✓	

PRACTICE TEST 1 EXPLANATIONS

1. **A** No, you don't have to memorize the entire agricultural history of the United States! This question asks you to remember a Big Picture fact about the colonial South: namely, that its economy was based on tobacco sales to England.

2. **E** The Virginia House of Burgesses was the first elected body of legislative representatives in North America. While the Governor retained ultimate veto authority over the Burgesses' decisions, the body gave Virginia's settlers a voice in government and was a significant early step on the road toward self-government in the United States.

3. **B** The concept of "virtual representation" was put forward by the British in the aftermath of colonial complaints about the Stamp Act. The colonists protested the Stamp Act, which imposed a tax on government seals, pointing out that they had no representation in Parliament and were, therefore, subject to "taxation without representation." According to the theory of "virtual representation," however, members of Parliament represent all British subjects regardless of who elects them. Thus, the British argued, the colonists were represented and the tax was fair.

4. **D** Prior to 1824, party leaders selected their presidential candidate through congressional caucuses. Each year, however, more states allowed their citizens to vote directly for presidential candidates, and by 1824, enough states were doing so that the caucus system could no longer control the nomination process. The Democratic-Republican (the party that later became today's Democrats) caucus chose William H. Crawford as its nominee. Challengers included John Quincy Adams, Henry Clay, and Andrew Jackson. Ultimately Adams won, bringing about the demise of the caucus system and ushering in the age of "modern elections."

5. **C** George Washington (A) used the veto sparingly, hoping to establish a precedent for others to follow. Thomas Jefferson (B), who, like Washington, feared a too-powerful presidency, followed Washington's lead. Andrew Jackson did not; a popular leader faced with a contrary Congress, Jackson often wielded the veto as a means of getting his way. William Henry Harrison (D) died after one month in office, and so had no time to use the veto extensively. Both he and Buchanan (E) postdate Jackson.

6. **A** In the years following the Civil War, President Andrew Johnson vehemently disagreed with Congress over the course Reconstruction should follow. Johnson favored a lenient approach toward the South; Congress, which was dominated by Northern Republicans, wanted to punish the South for seceding. Because the Republicans had a huge majority in Congress, they could override Johnson's many vetoes. When Congress passed a law forbidding Johnson from firing members of his own staff (the Tenure of Office Act), Johnson ignored it and fired Secretary of War Stanton (a Radical Republican who favored Congress's Reconstruction plan). Although his violation of the Tenure of Office Act was the official reason for Johnson's impeachment, the true reason was that Congress was sick of Johnson's opposition. Congress was dominated by Republicans (B) during Johnson's term; Johnson sought to bring the South quickly back into the union and so would not have vetoed aid packages for the region (C); and answers (D) and (E) simply have no basis in fact.

7. **A** In *McCullough v. Maryland*, the Marshall Court heard a case wherein the state of Maryland had passed a law intending to interfere with the function of the Second Bank of the United States. The court invalidated the Maryland law, establishing two important Constitutional principles in the process: first, that the Constitution granted to Congress implied powers in order to execute those powers specifically given to it under the Constitution—the so-called Necessary and Proper Clause—and second, that no state may impede the federal government from the lawful exercise of its power. *Gibbons vs. Ogden* was a similarly significant ruling dealing with the scope of the federal government's authority under the Constitution. The ruling in the case established that the Commerce Clause of the Constitution empowered the federal government to regulate interstate commerce.

8. **B** Of the five groups listed in the answer choices, only the socialists had any desire to "destroy all enslaving and degrading capitalist institutions." Radical Republicans (A) sought to punish the South after the Civil War; isolationists (C) wished to avoid military and political involvement in Europe; New Deal Democrats (D) sought to resuscitate the economy by means of aggressive government intervention; and (E) McCarthyites crusaded against the "Communist menace."

9. **A** Cotton, tobacco, indigo, and rice were all cash crops of the Chesapeake colonies. Corn did not become a cash crop in the United States until the middle of the nineteenth century.

10. **B** During the Eisenhower administration, the government began developing the Interstate Highway System. Interstates were initially developed to assist in troop mobilization in the event of war; however, their most important benefits were to the civilian population. The new roads sped interstate commerce, thus lowering the cost of goods. They also facilitated speedy travel in and out of cities, allowing city workers to move to the suburbs.

11. **D** The American System (A) was an 1820s program designed to strengthen the national government; the Second New Deal (B) was implemented in 1934 by Franklin Roosevelt; the New Frontier (C) was the name of John F. Kennedy's agenda; and the 1,000 Points of Light (E) was George H. W. Bush's social program.

12. **E** Roger Williams founded the city of Providence in the colony of Rhode Island after being banished from the Massachusetts Bay Colony for his religious beliefs. Williams believed that church and state should be separate and that all religions, including Judaism, should be tolerated. He also believed in the prohibition of slavery and of the need for fair treatment of Native Americans.

13. **B** As their name implies, the Separatists wanted to split completely with the Anglican Church. The Congregationalists, on the other hand, wanted to reform the Anglican Church but did not want to leave it. They hoped to purge the church of corruption and sought greater autonomy as a means of distancing themselves from the central church's failings.

14. **A** European nations explored the New World for raw materials, land to be settled, a shorter trade route to Asia, and for precious metals such as gold. They did not, however, search for trading partners among the previously existing inhabitants of North and South America. Most European nations saw Native Americans as obstacles to colonialism, and at best, as people to take advantage of in terms of trade.

15. **C** All the taxes imposed on the colonies between the end of the French and Indian War and the American Revolution were designed to offset the costs of the war. The British argued that the war had served to protect the colonists and that therefore the colonists should bear some of its cost. All of the incorrect answers contradict the Big Picture for the era. Choice (A) implies that the colonies enjoyed free trade, but they did not—even without the Sugar Act, they were dependent on England for such staples as sugar. Choice (B) states that the Sugar Act placed a tax on England, when in fact it taxed the colonies, to the English government's benefit. The English, French, and Spanish (D) were enemies in the New World land grab, none of whom took major diplomatic or economic action to improve their relations (at least not that you would have to know about on the SAT). Choice (E) refers to a practice common in the years leading up to the War of 1812 and thus refers to the wrong era.

16. **B** The Taft Hartley Act is a United States federal law that restricts the activities and power of labor unions. It is also known as the Labor Management Relations Act of 1947.

17. **E** The cotton gin, invented in 1793, revolutionized Southern agriculture by making it easier to remove the seeds from cotton plants (the machine was 50 times more efficient than a human being). The machine made it much cheaper to use cotton for textiles, and as a result the demand for cotton grew very rapidly in the late 1700s and early 1800s. Cotton soon became one of the foundations of the U.S. market economy. Whitney's second innovation was the use of interchangeable parts in manufacturing. Whitney originally struck on the idea while mass-producing rifles for the U.S. Army. Prior to Whitney's breakthrough, manufacturers had built weapons (and other machines) by hand, custom-fitting parts so that each weapon was unique. The process was costly, time consuming, and inconvenient, because replacing broken parts was extremely difficult. Soon his idea was being applied to all aspects of manufacturing. Interchangeable parts gave birth to the machine-tool industry, which produced specialized machines for such growing industries as textiles and transportation. (Without interchangeable parts, such machines would have been impractical because they would be too expensive to build and too difficult to fix.) Whitney's advances also helped promote assembly line production, another essential component of a market economy.

18. **B** In reaction to British and French harassment of U.S. merchant ships, the government passed the Embargo Act of 1807, which forbade trade with both nations. The law devastated America's import and export business by banning trade with the nation's two biggest trade partners. New England's economy collapsed, farmers had nowhere to sell their surplus, and smuggling became widespread. The law failed, however, to end the harassment of U.S. ships on the high seas. Confrontations over this issue eventually led to the War of 1812.

19. **E**   This is an easy one if you remember your dates. The Federalist Party dissolved after the War of 1812. Remember the Era of Good Feelings (1820)? Its name refers to the fact that, for a brief time, the nation had only one political party (the second party, the Federalists, having recently collapsed without another party taking its place). Each of the incorrect answers refers to something that occurred during the early 1800s, the era of the Federalists' demise. The Kansas-Nebraska Act (E) was passed in 1854, long after the Federalists had disappeared from the political landscape.

20. **C**   Far from repudiating popular sovereignty, the Compromise of 1850 reinforced the concept of popular sovereignty by leaving the slave status of Utah and New Mexico up to residents of the territory (popular sovereignty allowed territories themselves to decide, by vote, whether to allow slavery within their borders).

21. **E**   Jim Crow laws, passed by many Southern states in the era following Reconstruction, mandated forced racial segregation in the South. The Supreme Court essentially endorsed the laws by ruling that the Fourteenth Amendment did not protect African Americans from discriminatory state laws, and that blacks would have to seek equal protection from the states, not from the federal government. By accepting the "separate but equal" principle in its infamous *Plessy v. Ferguson* decision, the Court ensured more than a half-century of legal segregation in the South. Radical Reconstructionists (A) sought to integrate the South quickly after the Civil War; the Fourteenth Amendment (B) was designed specifically to guarantee the rights of African Americans; and the Taft-Hartley Act (C) was passed after World War II and was intended to curb the growing power of labor unions. Choice (D) is the opposite of what the picture shows—forced segregation.

22. **D**   In the late 1890s, President McKinley sought an Open Door Policy for all Western nations hoping to trade with Asia. During this period, Europe controlled international trade with China; McKinley and Secretary of State John Hay suggested that the United States be given better trade opportunities in the region. The European nations that had colonized China were not so keen on the idea; to their way of thinking, they had fought for those markets and they did not intend to share. The policy failed, although the United States eventually gained access to Chinese markets after providing military support to suppress a Chinese rebellion.

23. **A**   Believe it or not, the government imprisoned a large number of its own citizens during World War II. Paranoia that Japanese Americans, even those born in the United States, would help the Japanese war effort led to the drastic measure, which relocated West Coast residents with Japanese ancestry to prison camps, primarily in the South. Most lost their homes and possessions as a result of the internment. A 1944 lawsuit concerning the internment, *Korematsu v. United States*, reached the Supreme Court. The Court upheld the government's right to take such drastic measures during wartime.

24. **E**   For obvious reasons, the U.S. government declared the war effort the nation's chief priority. As part of the effort, the economy was retooled to support the war. Manufacturers and producers of raw materials gave top priority to military shipments, resulting in a sharp decline in consumer goods for those at home. The situation grew so bad that the government had to ration such items as gasoline and meat.

25. **D**   The key line from this quote is the last one: "I shall resign from the presidency, effective at noon tomorrow." To date, there has been only one president to resign from office, President Richard Nixon. Connect him to the era of the 1970s and you should be able to pick the right date, 1974 (D).

26. **C**   In the 1800s, the federal government granted land to several railroad companies to encourage the building of cross-continental railroad systems. This map, with its long east-west ribbons of shaded area, represents those land grants (C). Although all the answer choices could be within the era of this question, the geography of the shaded areas should help you eliminate wrong answer choices. Choice (A) should be eliminated because the United States does not have any long-running, east-west rivers; choices (D) and (E) would be correct only if the shaded areas were in the eastern part of the country. Finally, choice (B) can be eliminated because Native American reservations can also be found in New England, and the shaded areas in this map do not extend into New England.

27. **A**   The correct answer describes the colonies' role in Britain's mercantilist economy. Throughout the colonial period, most European economists subscribed to a theory called mercantilism. Mercantilists believed that economic power was rooted in a favorable balance of trade (that is, exporting more than you import) and the control of specie (hard currency, such as coins). Colonies, they felt, were important mostly as economic resources. That is why the British considered their colonies in the West Indies, which produced sugar and other valuable commodities, more important than their American colonies. The American colonies were seen primarily as markets for British and West Indian goods, although they also were valued as sources of raw materials that would otherwise have to be bought from a foreign country. Several answer choices can be eliminated using common sense. The length and difficulty of the trip from the colonies to England makes it unlikely that England could have depended on the colonies for livestock, fresh fruit, and fresh vegetables (B); the colonial economy was based in agriculture, not manufacturing (C); and the market for "primitive" art, such as that created by Native Americans (E), did not develop until the twentieth century.

28. **D**   Under the Articles of Confederation, it was possible for the nation to add new states. The procedure for doing so was laid out in the Northwest Ordinance, passed by the government under the Articles of Confederation.

29. **D**   The Erie Canal linked the Great Lakes to New York City, creating a major trade route from the midwest to the northeast. It had no appreciable effect on traffic along the Mississippi, however, because the two waterways serve two entirely different regions. The Mississippi runs from the midwest to the deep south.

30. **C**   In two separate decisions (*Cherokee Nation v. Georgia* and *Worcester v. Georgia*), the Supreme Court protected Native American rights to their land. Jackson ignored these decisions, forcibly evicting tribes from the Georgia area if they would not leave voluntarily. He supported the Removal Act of 1830, which set in motion the events that resulted in the Trail of Tears, a brutal 1838 forced march of Cherokees that resulted in thousands of deaths from sickness and starvation.

31. **E** Although James Polk had promised during his presidential campaign to go to war for the Oregon Territory (the slogan "Fifty-four Forty or Fight" refers to latitude of the nation's desired northern border), Congress ultimately negotiated a treaty with Great Britain for the region. Their reasoning was simple: The United States did not have the manpower to fight two wars at once, and war in the Mexican territories was imminent.

32. **C** Ironically, Reconstruction called for many harsh and punitive measures, but it did not require the South to pay reparations to the party most deeply hurt by slavery.

33. **D** The cartoon shows Theodore Roosevelt "taming" several lions, each clearly emblazoned with the word *trust* on its back. The lions represent business trusts, corporate mergers undertaken with the purpose of artificially raising prices or controlling markets. Roosevelt took on National Securities, Standard Oil, and several other powerful trusts, earning him the nickname "The Trustbuster."

34. **E** Booker T. Washington was a southern African American educator in the late 1800s. Among his many achievements is the founding of Tuskegee Institute, a vocational institution for African Americans. Washington believed that economic success would provide African Americans their quickest route to equality in American society, and Tuskegee was created with that goal in mind. A Southerner who had lived through the slave era, he harbored no illusions that the South would soon grant African Americans equal social and legal status. Because Washington did not demand an immediate end to legal discrimination, he has sometimes been portrayed as an accommodationist. He is often compared with W. E. B. DuBois. DuBois, a Northerner of the generation following Washington's, took a more aggressive, confrontational approach, demanding immediate equality under the law for African Americans. He was a founder of the National Association for the Advancement of Colored People (NAACP).

35. **A** As part of its World War I strategy, Germany used its U-boats—submarines in modern language—to attack ships providing supplies to its enemies (the attacks were meant to counter a British blockade of trade to Germany). According to international law at the time, an attacker had to warn civilian ships before attacking. Submarines could not do this, because doing so would eliminate their main advantage (i.e., the enemy doesn't know where they are). To address this legal issue, Germany issued a blanket announcement stating that it would attack any ship it believed to be carrying military supplies to the enemy. President Wilson was not satisfied, demanding a specific warning before each and every such attack. When the German submarines sank the passenger ship *Lusitania* in 1915 (killing 1,200 passengers), the action provoked the condemnation of both the government and the public. At the time, most Americans did not know that the *Lusitania* was carrying many tons of ammunition to the British. It knew only that the attack had resulted in the loss of 1,200 innocent lives. Anti-German sentiments naturally grew as a result of the event.

36. **D** This is a Trivial Pursuit question, yes, but one that asks you to recall a Big Picture issue for the 1920s: the fact that Warren G. Harding's administration was rife with corruption. By all accounts, Harding was an honest man who had the misfortune of surrounding himself with corrupt advisers; several of his cabinet members wound up in prison. The most infamous incident of his administration was the Teapot Dome scandal, in which oil companies bribed the secretary of the interior, in return for which he allowed them to drill on public lands.

37. **B** In *Gideon v. Wainwright*, the Supreme Court ruled that a defendant in a felony trial must be provided a lawyer for free, if he or she cannot afford to hire a lawyer. The Court based its decision on the Sixth Amendment, which guarantees defendants the right "to have assistance of counsel," and the Fourteenth Amendment, which guarantees due process at the state level. If (E) sounded particularly familiar, it's because it refers to another important case concerning the rights of criminal defendants. That case, *Miranda v. Arizona*, established the right of defendants to be informed of their rights before questioning.

38. **E** This question tests a basic principle of geography: Cities are nearly always located near a major source of water. At the time colonial cities were established, waterways provided the best means of long-distance travel. Cities also needed water for drinking and bathing and to power whatever manufacturing plants they might have. In short, to build a successful city, you must have plenty of water.

39. **C** This question asks you to remember that the passage of the Townshend Acts is among the events that led up to the American Revolution. The Townshend Acts taxed goods imported directly from Britain. It was the first tax of its type in the colonies. Mercantilism, the British economic philosophy, approved of duties on imports from other European nations but not on British imports. Some of the tax collected under the Townshend Acts was set aside for the payment of tax collectors, meaning that colonial assemblies could no longer withhold government officials' wages in order to get their way (the "power of the purse"). The Townshend Acts also created more vice-admiralty courts and several new government offices to enforce the Crown's will in the colonies. The colonists ultimately pressured the British into repealing the Townshend Acts by organizing a successful boycott of British goods.

40. **E** Senators were not chosen by popular election (the current method) until 1913. Under the provisions of the original Constitution, senators were chosen by the legislatures of their home states. The framers of the Constitution did not want to vest all political power in the general electorate; hence, only House members were chosen by direct election (the president, remember, was chosen by electors in the electoral college). The Seventeenth Amendment changed the system by which senators are chosen.

41. **B** Reform movements of the 1830s were inspired by the problems of urban living: poverty, disease, poor education, and the like. Naturally, reform groups sprung up in the nation's urban areas, nearly all of which were located in the Northeast. Usually, the most active members of reform groups were women, particularly those of the middle and upper classes. They targeted drinking and gambling, both perceived as root causes of larger societal problems. Reform societies also helped bring about penitentiaries, asylums, and orphanages, by popularizing the notion that society is responsible for the welfare of its least fortunate.

42. **B** Another Trivial Pursuit question, alas. *For Whom the Bell Tolls* was written by Ernest Hemingway in 1940. More to the point, its subject was the Spanish Civil War, which took place between 1936 and 1939. Each of the other books is a famous work by a great American nineteenth-century author: Herman Melville (*Moby-Dick*), James Fenimore Cooper (*The Last of the Mohicans*), Mark Twain (*The Adventures of Huckleberry Finn*), and Nathaniel Hawthorne (*The Scarlet Letter*).

43. **A** This question asks you to remember the Big Picture on American immigration. In the mid-1800s, most immigrants came from Ireland, England, and Germany. Immigrants from Cuba (B) and Canada (E) have always been relatively small in number, certainly not enough to make up "the greatest number of immigrants" during any given period. Russian immigration (D) was greatest in the late 1800s and again in the 1980s and 1990s; the Japanese (C) made up a large portion of immigration to the West Coast in the late 1800s.

44. **C** The Fugitive Slave Act of 1850 was designed to make it much easier to retrieve escaped slaves by requiring free states to cooperate in their retrieval. Abolitionists considered it coercive, immoral, and an affront to their liberty. In response, many Northern states passed laws weakening the Fugitive Slave Act. These laws, called personal liberty laws, required trial by jury for all alleged fugitives and guaranteed them the right to a lawyer. The intent was to slow or even halt the process by which slaves were returned to the South. The Know-Nothings (A), who were active during this era, organized around an anti-immigration policy; Manifest Destiny (B), also contemporaneous with the era tested by this question, proclaimed the right of the United States to expand to the West Coast; the Emancipation Proclamation (D), which freed the slaves, was issued in 1861; and the Haymarket Square Riot (E), a key event in labor union history, occurred well after the 1850s.

45. **D** The Populist Party sought a "loose money" policy in an effort to spark inflation. The party primarily represented farmers, who were experiencing hard economic times. Their biggest problem was that many owed large amounts of money in mortgage payments for their farms. However, produce prices were falling due to overproduction, making it difficult for the farmers to make ends meet. The farmers hoped to persuade the government to mint more money. If more money were put into circulation in the economy, they reasoned, inflation would result. Inflation would increase the price of farm goods and, therefore, make their debts easier to pay off. Because silver was cheap and plentiful, the Populists called for a liberal policy toward the minting of silver coins. That is how the Populists came to be associated with the "silver issue."

46. **B**   The Roosevelt Corollary to the Monroe Doctrine set the stage for Teddy Roosevelt's interventionist foreign policy in the Western Hemisphere. The Roosevelt Corollary was invoked by the government to justify military interventions in Nicaragua, Cuba, Haiti, the Dominican Republic, and Mexico. It was later overturned by Franklin D. Roosevelt's Good Neighbor Policy (D). The domino theory (A) holds that communist expansion, even into small countries like Vietnam, must be prevented at all costs, because once communists take over one country, the others surrounding it fall quickly, like dominoes. "Mutually assured destruction" (C) described the U.S.–Soviet nuclear relationship throughout much of the Cold War; neither was willing to use nuclear weapons because an attack by either would guarantee the destruction of both. The "doctrine of social Darwinism" (E) was invoked by late nineteenth-century capitalists to explain why they were so rich while others were so poor.

47. **B**   Both the British and the French supported the Treaty of Versailles; indeed, they signed the treaty (the United States, on the other hand, did not). President Wilson supported the treaty despite its weaknesses (while he had hoped for an equitable settlement, the treaty imposed harsh punishments on the losers of the war). Wilson favored the treaty primarily because it created the League of Nations, which he believed could prevent such wars in the future. The Senate, however, opposed the treaty. At war's end, most Americans quickly favored a return to isolationist foreign policy. They particularly wanted to steer clear of European conflicts, which most Americans considered to be the problem of the Europeans. Thus, the Senate was particularly wary of the League of Nations. Wilson lost the resulting stalemate, and the treaty was never signed.

48. **C**   Franklin Roosevelt's New Deal altered the political landscape by attracting many traditionally Republican constituencies to the Democratic Party. Roosevelt's progressive social programs attracted African Americans (formerly loyal to the Republican Party because it was the party of Lincoln), city dwellers (prior to Roosevelt, the Democratic Party was the party of rural Americans), the poor, and union members, all of whom benefited from the New Deal. Economic conservatives, however, opposed government interference with the economy. Accordingly, they bristled at Roosevelt's aggressive economic policies.

49. **A**   According to the chart, the size of the federal government grew during World War I (1917–1919), World War II (1941–1945), the Korean War (1950–1953), and the Vietnam War, particularly as it progressed (mid-1960s–1974). Although Democrats were in power during each of these wars, lending some credibility to (C), the graph shows a large reduction in federal employment in 1946–1947, when the Democrat Harry Truman was president. If one party could preside over both a large increase and a large decrease in federal employment, then the employment level would not be dependent on the party in office, making choice (C) incorrect.

50. **A**   Truman knew that the atomic bomb was considerably more powerful than conventional weapons of the era, although he and many others were surprised to discover exactly how much more powerful it was. His reasons for dropping the bomb included a fear that the Soviets would enter the war in the Pacific (B) and thus become a political power in the region; certainty that a ground invasion of Japan would result in heavy casualties (C); the belief that the devastating effect of the weapon would force an immediate surrender (D); and the desire to establish a leadership role in the postwar era (E).

51. **E** A "cold war" is one in which two countries do not engage in military battles but are nonetheless clearly enemies. During a cold war, the prospect of military engagement is never far off. During the Cold War, the United States and the Soviet Union battled in every way except on the battlefield. They plotted against each other politically, denounced each other repeatedly, and poured billions into weapons research and development in an effort to gain the upper hand on the other.

52. **C** Anne Hutchinson (1591–1643) preached a personal, devotional brand of Christianity that relied on direct communication with God. Her teachings challenged Puritan beliefs and the authority of the Puritan clergy. The fact that she was an intelligent, well-educated, and powerful woman in a resolutely patriarchal society also turned many against her. She was tried for heresy, convicted, and banished. She moved to Rhode Island, the colony founded by Roger Williams (another religious exile from Massachusetts), and then later relocated to New York.

53. **A** Between the 1730s and 1760, the colonies experienced a wave of religious revivalism known as the First Great Awakening. Two men, Congregationalist minister Jonathan Edwards and the Methodist preacher George Whitefield, came to symbolize the period. Edwards preached the severe, pre-deterministic doctrines of Calvinism and became famous for his graphic depictions of hell in sermons as "Sinners in the Hands of an Angry God." Whitefield preached a Christianity based on emotional spirituality, which today is most clearly seen in Southern evangelism. The First Great Awakening is often described as the response of devout people to the Enlightenment, a European intellectual movement that borrowed heavily from ancient philosophy and that emphasized rationalism over emotionalism or spirituality. The colonist who typified Enlightenment ideals in America, incidentally, was Ben Franklin. Franklin was self-made and self-educated, a printer's apprentice who, through his own ingenuity and hard work, became a wealthy printer and a successful and respected intellectual. His *Poor Richard's Almanack* was extremely popular and remains influential to this day (it is the source of such pithy aphorisms as "a stitch in time saves nine" and "a penny saved is a penny earned"). He did pioneering work in the field of electricity. He invented bifocals, the lightning rod, and the Franklin stove, and he founded the colonies' first fire department and first public library. Franklin espoused Enlightenment ideals of education, government, and religion.

54. **D** In 1787, an army of 1,500 farmers marched on Springfield, Massachusetts, to protest a number of unfair policies, both economic and political. They were armed and very angry, and gave the elite classes this wake-up call: The revolution may not be over yet. Shays' Rebellion was interpreted differently by the nation's political factions. To those favoring a strong central government, the rebellion was proof that the Articles of Confederation were inadequate to govern the new nation. For others (like Jefferson, who opposed a strong central government and preferred to reserve most rights to the state), the rebellion demonstrated that governments must either heed the will of the people or risk political turmoil. A little chronology would have helped you eliminate one of the incorrect answers here: Bacon's Rebellion (A) occurred in the 1670s, long before Jefferson was born. Each of the other three incorrect answers refers to events of Jefferson's presidency; however, none refer to a "rebellion" and, therefore, are unlikely subjects of the quotation cited.

55. **A**   During the 1790s, France began seizing American ships on the open seas. Adams sent three diplomats to Paris to negotiate an end to this practice. French officials demanded a huge bribe of the delegation before they would even allow negotiations to begin. The diplomats refused and returned home, where Adams published their written report in the newspapers. Because he deleted the French officials' names and replaced them with the letters X, Y, and Z, the incident became known as the XYZ Affair. As a result of this debacle, popular sentiment toward the French reversed; formerly pro-French, the public became vehemently anti-French, to the point that a declaration of war seemed possible.

56. **D**   When Mexico declared its independence from Spain in 1821, the new country included Texas and much of the Southwest, including California. The Mexican government established liberal land policies to entice settlers, and tens of thousands of Americans (many of them cattle ranchers) flooded the region. In return for land, the settlers were supposed to become Mexican citizens. They never did; instead, they ignored Mexican law, including—and especially—the one prohibiting slavery. When Mexico attempted to regain control of the area, the settlers rebelled and declared independence from Mexico. It was during this period that the famous battle at the Alamo was fought (in 1836). For a while Texas was an independent country, called the Republic of Texas. The region applied for statehood, but the existence of slavery in the area guaranteed a congressional battle over Texas's statehood. Wariness of the inevitable war with Mexico that statehood would provoke further slowed the move toward statehood. Accordingly, Texas did not become a state until 1845. As expected, war with Mexico soon followed.

57. **C**   The photograph shows a rudimentary home dug into a mound, typical of those built by prairie settlers in the 1800s. Note also the cow in the background, another tip-off that the photograph depicts a ranching region. Each of the incorrect answers identifies an area that had been more fully developed and settled during the period cited. Finally, check out the next question: It asks about the 1880s, so this question shouldn't be asking about a later period. Remember that the questions rotate through eras in a repeating pattern.

58. **B**   This question asks you to assess the usefulness of various historical documents. Note that the question asks you to focus specifically on quantitative data about all American labor during the 1880s. This should help you eliminate (A), which would provide anecdotal evidence about a single individual only; (C), which provides information about one city only and, therefore, might not provide a representative sample for the entire nation; (D), which, like (A), is anecdotal and would provide information about too small a group of workers; and (E), which provides no quantitative data whatsoever. In fact, none of the incorrect answers would likely provide any useful quantitative data, meaning that (B) must be the correct answer by Process of Elimination.

59. **D**   The American takeover of the Philippines sparked a debate among foreign policy leaders: Should the United States control the Philippines, or should it grant the country independence? Proponents of annexing the Philippines argued that, if the United States granted the islands independence, they would simply be conquered by another European nation, with the only result being that the United States would lose a valuable possession. Opponents felt that the United States should promote independence and democracy, both noble national traditions. To control the Philippines, they argued,

would make the United States no better than the British tyrants the colonists had overthrown in the Revolutionary War. In the end, the Senate voted to annex the Philippines. Filipino nationalists responded by waging a three-year-long guerrilla war against the United States. Although the United States eventually gained control of the country, the Philippines remained a source of controversy for decades to come. The United States granted the Philippines independence in 1946.

60. **A** The Progressives of the early 1900s followed in the wake of the Populists of the preceding decade, but the second movement succeeded where its predecessor had failed. One of the reasons populism faltered is that its constituents were mostly poor farmers, whose struggle for daily survival made political activity difficult. The Progressives achieved greater successes in part because theirs was an urban, middle-class movement. Its proponents started with more economic and political clout than did the Populists; furthermore, Progressives could devote more time to the causes they championed. Also, because many Progressives were northern and middle-class, the Progressive movement did not intensify regional and class differences, as the Populist movement had.

61. **B** The chart shows a steady decrease in the number of young people entering the workforce during each succeeding decade between 1900 and 1940. Although this data does not prove that more young people pursued full-time education during this period, it does support the conclusion, which is all the question requires. Choice (A) is contradicted by the data in the chart; each of the other incorrect answers draws a conclusion that simply cannot be supported by the data because it draws a generalization outside the scope of the data. Choice (C), for example, discusses the work situation of Americans under the age of 16; the chart, however, provides no data for this age group, making it impossible to draw any conclusions about it.

62. **C** Each of the incorrect answers cites a novel by an African American about the African American experience in the United States. In Fitzgerald's *The Great Gatsby*, a bootlegger rises to the upper echelons of all-white high society.

63. **A** From the outset of World War II until the United States' entry in 1941, Franklin Roosevelt was convinced that America would, and should, eventually enter the war. In fact, he angled the country toward participation, particularly after Poland fell to Germany, by extending aid to the Allies. The strong possibility that America would soon enter the war convinced Roosevelt to run for an unprecedented third term, breaking the two-term tradition established by Washington and honored by all other presidents. After Roosevelt's death, the government formalized the two-term limit with a constitutional amendment.

64. **A** That's right: Arkansas chose to close down its public schools rather than integrate them. That's how bad race relations were in the South a half-century ago.

65. **B** Betty Friedan's *The Feminine Mystique* was a widely popular book of the early 1960s that challenged many Americans' assumptions about the roles women serve in society. Friedan particularly bristled at the conventional presumption that all women wanted nothing more than to marry and raise families. The book called for reform to make it easier for women to join the professional ranks that, at the time, were the near-exclusive domain of men (white men, to be even more specific). Friedan was a co-founder of the National Organization of Women (NOW), an organization that has led the assault on laws allowing gender discrimination.

66. **E** Before the United States can go to war, the Constitution requires a declaration of war approved by Congress. Congress made no such declaration concerning the Korean and Vietnam wars, however; officially, the United States was not at war in either situation. In reality, of course, the nation was at war; the executive branch had merely executed an end-run around the necessary declaration of war by declaring both conflicts "police actions." The unpopularity of the Vietnam War led Congress to pass the War Powers Resolution, which requires the president to seek periodic approval from Congress for any substantial troop commitment. President Nixon vetoed the bill, claiming it limits the president's Constitutional power as commander-in-chief. Congress overrode the veto, and the law still stands.

67. **D** Bacon's Rebellion is often cited as an early example of a populist uprising in America. It took place on Virginia's frontier during the 1670s, and it concerned westward expansion. As the farmable land to the east filled up, settlers looked to the western portion of the colony. Many settlers were willing to chance the dangers of frontier life in return for an opportunity to "strike it rich," but as they were encroaching on land already inhabited by Native Americans, those dangers were great. The pioneers soon believed that the colonial government was not making a good-faith effort to protect them, and that, furthermore, the government was using them as a "human shield" to protect the wealthier colonists to the east. Rallying behind Nathaniel Bacon, these settlers first attacked both the local Doeg and the Susquehannock tribes, and then turned their attentions toward the colonial governor. The rebels marched on Jamestown and burned it to the ground, but when Bacon died of dysentery, the rebellion dissolved. The war Bacon almost instigated between the colonists and Native American tribes was averted with a new treaty.

68. **B** Mercantilists believed that economic power is rooted in a favorable balance of trade (that is, exporting more than you import) and the control of specie (hard currency, such as coins).

69. **B** "Broad constructionists" (sometimes called "loose constructionists") believe that the Constitution should be interpreted loosely when determining what restrictions it places on federal power. Broad constructionists emphasize the importance of the elastic clause, which allows Congress to pass laws "necessary and proper" to the performance of its duties. Alexander Hamilton was a leader of the broad constructionist school, advocating the formation of a National Bank and other economic policies spearheaded by the national government. Hamilton justified each of his proposed programs by citing the elastic clause of the Constitution. Of the men cited in the answer choices, Jefferson (A) and Madison (C) were adamant opponents of broad constructionist views, favoring instead a strict interpretation of the Constitution (hence their moniker, "strict constructionists"). Thomas Paine (E) had left America and returned to Europe before the Constitution was enacted and so played little role in the debate over the Constitution. Benjamin Franklin (D) died in 1790, also before the debate between broad and strict constructionists had been framed.

70. **E** During the era following the War of 1812, the textile industry in New England grew rapidly, resulting in a labor shortage. As a result, textile manufacturers had to "sweeten the pot" to entice laborers (almost all of whom were women from nearby farms) to their factories. The most famous worker-enticement program was called the Lowell system (also called the Waltham system), so named after the Massachusetts town in which many mills were located. The Lowell system guaranteed employees housing in a respectable, chaperoned boarding house, cash wages, and participation in cultural and social events, organized by the mill. The system was widely copied throughout New England. It lasted until the great waves of Irish immigration in the 1840s and 1850s made factory labor plentiful, at which point mills stopped offering such benefits to employees.

71. **C** During James Monroe's presidency, international tensions increased as a result of a series of revolutions in Central and South America. All involved native inhabitants revolting against, and declaring independence from, European imperial regimes. Ultimately, events compelled Monroe to recognize the new nations. At the same time, Monroe decided that America should assert its authority over the Western Hemisphere. The result was the Monroe Doctrine, a policy of mutual noninterference. You stay out of North America, Monroe told Europe, and we'll stay out of your squabbles. The Monroe Doctrine also claimed America's right to intervene anywhere in its own hemisphere, if it felt its security was threatened. No European country tried to intercede in the Americas following Monroe's declaration, and so the Monroe Doctrine appeared to work. No one, however, was afraid of the American military; Spain, France, and others stayed out of the Western Hemisphere because the powerful British navy made sure they did. The British were already establishing a powerful empire in Asia; this, coupled with their prevention of Spanish and French intervention in the Americas, assured England's supremacy in Europe.

72. **E** Jackson, like the supporters of nullification, supported states' rights and believed that the federal government should exercise only those powers necessary to maintain national security. Nullification was a central issue of the Jackson presidency. The doctrine of nullification, first expressed by Jefferson and Madison in the Virginia and Kentucky Resolutions, holds that the individual states have the right to judge the constitutionality of federal laws and to disobey those laws if they find them unconstitutional. The Tariff of 1828 (also known as the Tariff of Abominations), although passed during the Adams administration, did not develop into a national crisis until 1830 (during Jackson's administration), when some states started to consider nullifying the tariff. Jackson was a strong supporter of states' rights, but also thought nullification endangered the Union and was thus too extreme. The 1830 nullification movement failed, but it laid the groundwork for opposition to the Tariff of 1832, which South Carolina nullified. Jackson threatened to call in troops to enforce the tariff, but in the meantime worked behind the scenes to reach a compromise that would diffuse tensions. Although the crisis subsided with the compromise, no resolution was reached over the question of nullification, and it would continue to be an issue until the Civil War.

73. **E**   Settlement houses provided some of the first public services for America's urban poor. These houses became community centers, providing schooling, childcare, and cultural activities. In Chicago, for example, Jane Addams founded Hull House to provide such services as English lessons for immigrants, day care for children of working mothers, child care classes for parents, and playgrounds for children. Addams also campaigned for increased government services in the slums. She was awarded the Nobel Peace Prize for her life's work in 1931.

74. **E**   Wealthy industrialists of the late 1800s opposed government assistance to the needy, government support of the arts, and other such government activities that we today take for granted. These men argued that they were perfectly capable of providing these services to society, proclaiming a "Gospel of Wealth" that in fact required them to do so. According to this secular gospel, the concentration of wealth among a few powerful men was the natural and most efficient result of capitalism. Further, this great wealth brought with it a responsibility to give back to society. The chief proponent of the Gospel of Wealth was Andrew Carnegie, a steel tycoon who funded many public works in New York City, Pittsburgh, and elsewhere. Transcendentalism (A) was a mid–eighteenth century philosophy championed by Ralph Waldo Emerson, Henry David Thoreau, and Herman Melville, among others; socialism (B) is the belief that the state should own and control major industries; the doctrine of nullification (C) is described in the explanation for question 72, above; and black separatism (D) is the belief held by some African Americans that their community would be best served by removing itself from white society.

75. **D**   Another Trivial Pursuit question; the Platt Amendment concerned Cuba. In 1903, the Roosevelt administration strong-armed Cuba into accepting the agreement underlying the Platt Amendment, which essentially committed Cuba to American semi-control. Under Platt's stipulations, Cuba could not make a treaty with another nation without U.S. approval; furthermore, Cuba granted the United States the right to intervene in its affairs if Cuban domestic order dissolved. The result was a number of invasions and occupations by the Marines. For ten of the years between 1906 and 1922, the American military occupied Cuba, arousing anti-American sentiments on the island. By considering era, you should be able to eliminate Australia (E) from among the answer choices. The rest of the incorrect answers, alas, are within the realm of possibility (although China (C) is a longshot; the only thing you need to know about American relations with China during this era concerns the Open Door Policy). This is a tough question.

76. **A**   Answer this question by considering era and using Process of Elimination. Remember that, compared to today's government, the national government of the era was very weak. A national sales tax (B) is the policy of a strong central government; even with the strong modern national government, we don't have one. Eliminate this answer choice. Similarly, relatively few cases were tried in federal courts (C) during this time; most cases worked their way through the state courts. Furthermore, the government of the day rarely imposed large fines on businesses (the only entities large enough to fund government operations). Eliminate this answer choice as well. How much property do you think most convicted felons (E) have? Usually, not much. This answer contradicts common sense: Get rid of it. That leaves you with answer choices (A) and (D). If you're stumped here, you have a fifty-fifty shot, so you should definitely guess. Under the Homestead Act, the government basically gave away federal land, but beyond that, rents on such property have not ever been a major source of funds in the twentieth century, so cross out (D) and pick (A).

77. **C** By the time 1948 rolled around, many Democratic constituencies—among them labor, consumers, southerners—were, for various reasons, angry at President Truman. His defeat in the election seemed certain. Truman's popularity, however, received an unintentional boost from the Republican-dominated Congress. The staunchly conservative legislature passed several anti-labor acts too strong even for Truman, who had previously supported some anti-union measures; the Taft-Hartley Act, passed over Truman's veto, prohibited closed shops (which require union membership as a prerequisite to hiring), restricted labor's right to strike, prohibited the use of union funds for political purposes, and gave the government broad power to intervene in strikes. The same Congress then rebuked Truman's efforts to pass health-care reform; increase aid to schools, farmers, the elderly, and the disabled; and promote civil rights for blacks. The cumulative effect of all this meanness made Truman look a lot better to those he had previously offended. Still, as election time neared, Truman trailed his chief opponent, Thomas Dewey. He then made one of the most brilliant political moves in American history: He recalled the Congress, whose majority members had just drafted an extremely conservative Republican platform at the party convention, and challenged them to enact that platform. Congress met for two weeks and didn't pass one significant piece of legislation. Truman then went out on a grueling public appearance campaign, everywhere deriding the "do-nothing" Eightieth Congress. To almost everyone's surprise, Truman won reelection, and his coattails carried a Democratic majority into Congress.

78. **A** This quote by Massachusetts politician James Otis, Jr. elucidates the concept of taxation without representation which the colonists were attempting to remedy. Parliament felt that virtual representation gave it the right to pass laws for the good of all its citizens while the colonists felt their needs could not properly be heard unless they had actual representatives in Parliament; therefore, the answer is choice (A).

79. **E** The Sioux occupied a large portion of the Midwest and the West. Did you confuse the Sioux and the Seminoles? The Seminoles currently have five reservations in Florida.

80. **C** Vice-admiralty courts are military courts in which defendants are not tried by a jury of peers. Why did the British see the need for such courts in the colonies? When the British tried to prosecute violators of its tax law before colonial juries, the jurors regularly ignored the law and acquitted the defendant. Jurors sympathized with the defendants, after all, because they too hated the British taxes. In order to convict violators, the British were forced to establish vice-admiralty courts. The colonists, of course, objected, further building momentum for the American Revolution.

81. **D**   Locke's *Two Treatises on Government* includes several key arguments that greatly influenced the Declaration of Independence. Among them are the notions that people are born with "natural rights" to life, health, liberty, and property; people create governments to protect these rights; because governments can accomplish this, people agree to obey their governments. Locke called this agreement "the social contract." Locke proposed that the people have the right to overthrow their government when it fails to serve this fundamental purpose. Machiavelli's *The Prince* (A) is a primer for devious political leaders; Plato's *Republic* (B) outlines a utopia in which philosopher-kings rule autocratically; Hobbes's *Leviathan* makes the case for autocracy by arguing that humans are too evil to participate in any more liberal form of government; and St. Augustine's *City of God* (E) is primarily a theological treatise.

82. **D**   The War of 1812 had one clear, indisputably positive result: It spurred American manufacturing. Cut off from trade with Europe from the time of the 1807 embargo until the end of the war, the states became more self-sufficient by necessity. New England became America's manufacturing center during the war, and after the war the United States was less dependent on imports than it had been previously. Several incorrect answers can be eliminated based on the era covered by the question. The American Industrial Revolution (C) did not begin until the late 1800s, much later than the era tested. Similarly, construction of a national railroad (E) occurred at a much later date.

83. **A**   The Mormon Church of Jesus Christ of Latter-day Saints was formed in Western New York's "Burned Over" District in 1830. The church is based on the revelation of Joseph Smith, a revelation that Mormons believe to be divinely inspired. Smith's preaching, particularly his acceptance of polygamy, drew strong opposition in the East and Midwest, and Smith was killed by a mob while imprisoned in Illinois. The Mormons, realizing that they would never be allowed to practice their faith in the East, made the long, difficult trek to the Salt Lake Valley, which they settled and transformed from desert into farmland through extensive irrigation. The Mormons' success was largely attributable to the settlers' strong sense of community and selflessness, and through their communal efforts they came to dominate the Utah territory.

84. **D**   Mercantilism was an economic theory and system common in Europe from the sixteenth through eighteenth centuries that promoted governmental regulation of a nation's economy for the purpose of increasing a nation's power and wealth. It included a national economic policy aimed at accumulating monetary reserves through a positive balance of trade, especially of manufactured goods. Mercantilism dominated Western European economic policy during the age of exploration and led to the founding of colonies throughout the New World.

85. **B**   The Southern gentleman pictured in the cartoon has a bucket of coal at his feet. It's just that simple: There's nothing tricky about this question. Process of Elimination should have helped you get rid of some answer choices: European trade routes (C) are more easily accessed from the North; the North is also home to big cities, more likely locations in which to find skilled fashion designers (D); and, because textile industries do their work indoors, weather conditions (E) are not a major consideration in their location. Last, but not least, (A) is wrong, since the relocation of the textile industry happened *after* the Civil War (after the abolition of slavery).

86. **A** William Howard Taft was a Progressive; however, he was not as outspoken or as effective as his predecessor Roosevelt. The passage of the Payne-Aldrich Tariff during his presidency caused Taft to lose favor with Republicans who hoped for much lower tariff rates. Choices (B) and (E) are true, but would not have alienated Progressive Republicans. Choices (C) and (D) are not true.

87. **E** When the Great Depression began in the late 1920s, Herbert Hoover was president. A conservative Republican associated with the laissez-faire philosophy of government, Hoover did not launch any "interventionist" economic policies until the 1929 crash had already occurred, and his reaction to this catastrophe was measured and restrained compared to the later New Deal spearheaded by President Roosevelt. Choice (E) is also wrong, since "conservative" behavior on the part of private investors did not lead to the stock market crash of 1929. On the contrary, investors took reckless risks that tended to exacerbate their losses.

88. **C** Inflation—the rapid increase in prices—results when the economy grows too rapidly. To slow economic growth, the Federal Reserve Board increases interest rates. This makes it harder to borrow money and thus makes it more difficult for businesses to grow. Each of the four incorrect answers describes an action that would increase the rate of economic growth.

89. **E** In what may have been the greatest mistake of his presidency, Herbert Hoover ordered federal troops to drive protesting war veterans from Washington, D.C. At the time, Congress was considering early payment of benefits to World War I veterans; the payments were intended to lessen the impact of the Depression on at least one segment of the population. One thousand impoverished veterans and their families, calling themselves the Bonus Army, came to Washington in May to lobby for the bill. By mid-June, their numbers had grown to 15,000. When the bill was narrowly defeated, many refused to leave. They squatted in empty government offices or built shanties, and they stayed through the summer. In July, Hoover ordered the army to expel them, which the army did, with great force. Employing the cavalry and attacking with tear gas, army forces drove the veterans from D.C. and then burned their makeshift homes. One hundred people died during the attack, including two babies who suffocated from exposure to tear gas. It's not the type of thing an astute politician does during an election year, to say the least; Franklin Roosevelt was later heard to quip that he won the 1932 election the day Hoover ordered the attack. An interesting side note: The troops that evicted the Bonus Army were led by none other than Douglas MacArthur.

90. **C** Joseph Riis was a muckraking journalist and photographer who chronicled the lives of the urban poor in his book *How the Other Half Lives*. He used these images to encourage middle- and upper-class people to help the poor through charity work and political change.

HOW TO SCORE PRACTICE TEST 1

When you take the real exam, the proctors will collect your test booklet and bubble sheet and send your answer sheet to the processing center where a computer looks at the pattern of filled-in ovals on your answer sheet and gives you a score. We couldn't include even a small computer with this book, so we are providing this more primitive way of scoring your exam.

Determining Your Score

STEP 1 Using the Answer Key at the beginning of this chapter, determine how many questions you got right and how many you got wrong on the test. Remember, questions that you do not answer don't count as either right answers or wrong answers.

STEP 2 List the number of right answers here.

(A) _____

STEP 3 List the number of wrong answers here. Now divide that number by 4. (Use a calculator if you're feeling particularly lazy.)

(B) _____ ÷ 4 = _____

STEP 4 Subtract the number of wrong answers divided by 4 from the number of correct answers. Round this score to the nearest whole number. This is your raw score.

(A) _____ – (B) _____ = (C) _____

STEP 5 To determine your real score, take the number from Step 4 above and look it up in the left column of the Score Conversion Table on the next page; the corresponding score on the right is your score on the exam.

PRACTICE TEST 1
SCORE CONVERSION TABLE

Raw Score	Scaled Score	Raw Score	Scaled Score	Raw Score	Scaled Score
90	800	52	620	14	420
89	800	51	620	13	420
88	800	50	610	12	410
87	800	49	610	11	410
86	800	48	600	10	400
85	800	47	600	9	400
84	800	46	590	8	390
83	800	45	590	7	390
82	800	44	580	6	380
81	800	43	580	5	380
80	790	42	570	4	370
79	790	41	570	3	370
78	780	40	560	2	360
77	770	39	550	1	360
76	770	38	550	0	350
75	760	37	540	−1	350
74	750	36	540	−2	340
73	740	35	530	−3	340
72	740	34	530	−4	330
71	730	33	520	−5	320
70	720	32	520	−6	320
69	720	31	510	−7	310
68	710	30	510	−8	300
67	700	29	500	−9	300
66	700	28	490	−10	290
65	690	27	490	−11	280
64	690	26	480	−12	280
63	680	25	480	−13	270
62	670	24	470	−14	280
61	670	23	470	−15	260
60	660	22	460	−16	250
59	660	21	460	−17	250
58	650	20	450	−18	240
57	650	19	450	−19	240
56	640	18	440	−20	230
55	640	17	440	−21	220
54	630	16	430	−22	210
53	630	15	430		

Part III
Content Review

Chapter 6
A Nation Is Born

INTRODUCTION

Contrary to popular belief, the United States of America was not born on July 4, 1776, with the signing of the Declaration of Independence. It did not spring up instantaneously, as if American colonists woke up one morning and decided that they were no longer British citizens. The War for Independence (1775–1783) was the end result of a long process of gradual independence. Indeed, after living for 150 years in the Americas (thousands of miles away from Europe), many colonists began to develop the characteristics that would go on to define the nation: a strong, independent work ethic, a keen eye for business opportunities, and above all, a belief in divinely ordained human rights.

The following pages offer a brief introduction to the major eras in American history. The SAT Subject Test in U.S. History covers a fairly wide range of time, so prepping for this test can seem quite daunting. Begin by studying the colonial period in the 1700s, with the establishment of the first English colony at Jamestown, Virginia. Then continue through the span of the 1800s and 1900s, with their social upheavals and ideological swings, up to history you might even remember happening within your (or probably your parents') lifetimes. Along the way you will refresh your memory about Jeffersonian versus Jacksonian Democracy, the bloody clash between the North and South, Westward Expansion, the Industrial Revolution, two World Wars, the Great Depression, and the Cold War. Remember, these descriptions are merely outlines, offering the key markers of each era to help you master the SAT Subject Test questions. They are intended only as guides, not as substitutes for more comprehensive readings. If you have completed a full year of high school U.S. History, you should have covered most of this material. This text will help you sharpen your understanding of the most key concepts as well as teach you how to tackle the various question types and pace yourself, both of which will help you earn a better score.

ERA: THE COLONIAL PERIOD

1600s to Early 1700s

Most historians believe that the first Native American people migrated from Asia to North America across a land bridge more than ten thousand years ago. Native American civilizations achieved many technological advancements, such as a complex calendar, agriculture, and irrigation. In the eleventh century, a Norse (Viking) sailor, **Leif Eriksson**, reached North America. While the **Vikings** chose not to settle the new world they had "discovered," the search for shorter trade routes to Asia would lead other Europeans to "discover" this land, several hundred years later. As you know from elementary school, in 1492, Columbus sailed the ocean blue. Columbus, under the **patronage** of **King Ferdinand and Queen Isabella of Spain**, journeyed West on what he believed would be a brief journey to Asia. Since Columbus believed that he had landed in India, he called the native peoples that he encountered **"Indians."** After he and other explorers reached the Americas, many of the natives perished from diseases (like **smallpox**) carried by the Europeans (and, later, by African slaves). The transfer of disease from Europeans to Native Americans, as well as that of plants and animals between the New World and Europe, was called the **Columbian Exchange.**

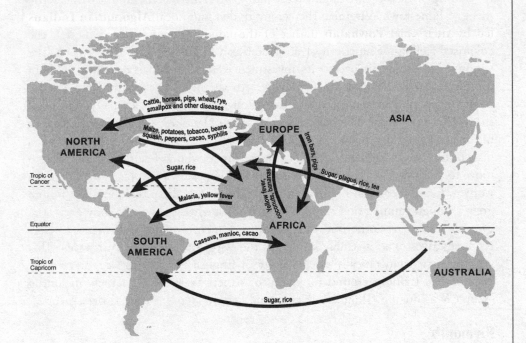

While European explorers became less sure of their abilities to find the **Northwest Passage**, their discoveries spurred many European nations to explore and invest in North and South America. Reasons for exploration range from searching for gold and natural resources, to creating colonies, which would alleviate overpopulation in Europe and provide the outlets for manufactured goods on which **mercantilism** depended. While pre-colonial history is not featured as often as other sections, you should know that Spanish rule included Florida and that the Spanish explorers often intermarried with the natives. American colonial history in the United States starts in the early 1600s with the English colony at **Jamestown, Virginia**. Although technically the first English colony was **Roanoke, Virginia**, this colony was abandoned in the 1580s and the settlers were never found. Colonies of this time period were generally established for two reasons: **commercial gain** and/or **social and religious freedom**. You'll find a list of the reasons that many colonies were founded at the end of this section. Commercial colonies, like Jamestown, were established by trading companies. Other types of colonies were initiated with **royal charters**, also known as **proprietary grants**.

Life in the Early Colonies—South vs. North

Jamestown

In 1607, the **Virginia Company**, founded by English investors hoping to get rich by trading with the natives and discovering precious metals, founded the settlement of Jamestown, Virginia. The colony traded with local **Algonquian Indians**, led by their chief **Powhatan** (father of the famous **Pocahontas**), although the colonists' feelings of superiority would later lead to conflict with the Natives. The Virginia Company discovered its investment return in tobacco, which brought prosperity to the Virginia colony, along with the need to encourage more settlement. In order to attract settlers to the colony, the Virginia Company developed the **headright system**, which promised 50 acres of land to every new arrival paying his or her own way. This new system encouraged both small farmers, who owned little or no land in England, as well as large farmers who were already profitable, to move to Virginia. As a largely **agrarian** colony, Jamestown had far more men than women. Combined with high **infant mortality** rates, the population of Virginia grew through immigration rather than natural increase. As the colony grew, the Virginia Company authorized the landowning men of major settlements to elect representatives to an assembly known as the **Virginia House of Burgesses**. This was the first democratically elected body in English North America, and would become the training ground for many of America's founding fathers including George Washington, Thomas Jefferson, and Patrick Henry, among others.

Plymouth

In contrast to the Jamestown settlement, which was founded as an economic venture, the second English colony at **Plymouth, Massachusetts**, was founded by the **Pilgrims** to escape **religious persecution**. The Pilgrims were a group of religious **Separatists**, who felt that the **Church of England** (the church founded by **King Henry the VIII** after the **Catholic Church** refused to grant him a divorce) was too corrupt to be salvaged. This group believed that in order to practice its religion without interference, it had to move to the New World. The Pilgrims are remembered for designing the **Mayflower Compact**. This agreement was drafted to determine what the colony's civil laws would be once the pilgrims landed.

Although both groups fell under the **Protestant** faith, in contrast to the Separatists, the **Puritans** wanted to reform, or purify, the church. Many Puritans settled in the New England area, which later became the **Massachusetts Bay Colony**. Most immigrants to the northern colonies came within family groups and sought to create close-knit communities based on **mutual consent**. This led to the founding of a colonial legislature and a land distribution system based on towns rather than individual plots of land. New England settlers, free from the tropical diseases of the southern colonies, had much longer life expectancies and lower infant mortality rates. The resulting strong family structures and the pious nature of their religion, led the Puritans to create strict rules to govern their religious community.

Economics

In colonial America, the local climate in many ways determined what each colony could and could not do to develop its economy. The New England terrain and climate were poorly suited for farming, so **New England** settlers primarily practiced **subsistence farming**, growing just enough food to feed themselves and their families. Boston was a major port city, and much of New England's economy developed around sea trade and fishing. **Southern colonies** could support **large-scale agriculture** because of their good soil and climate. **Plantation systems** developed to produce single crops, such as tobacco, rice, indigo, and, later, cotton—also known as **cash crops**, because they were sold as well as consumed by the growers. This type of farming was labor-intensive and was at first done by **indentured servants**, people who had agreed to provide several years of labor in exchange for passage to North America. Later, the system of indenture on plantations turned out to be insufficient to meet the demand for labor. Also, **Bacon's Rebellion** in 1676 highlighted the precarious nature of the relationship between indentured servants and Virginia elites. This opened the door for the inhumane **slave trade**, which had been carried on by English merchants since at least the sixteenth century, and which increased steadily throughout the seventeenth, eighteenth, and the first half of the nineteenth centuries.

The economic differences between the northern and southern colonies would have far-reaching effects, particularly in terms of the sectional conflicts that led to the Civil War.

Religion

Religion was at the center of colonial life for many of the settlers. The established church groups were the **Anglicans**, who followed the Church of England, and the Puritans, who followed **Calvinist** teachings. In addition to these, many other religious sects flourished, each practicing different versions of **Protestantism** (the one colony founded by Catholics was Maryland). The **Massachusetts Bay Company**, founded by Puritan merchants in England, moved its headquarters to New England in 1628, in order to handle its affairs, both secular and religious, without interference from the English King. **John Winthrop**, a middle-class settler from England, was elected governor of **Massachusetts Bay Colony** and preached a famous sermon that included his idea of a "**City on a Hill.**" Winthrop used this phrase to warn the Puritans that their community in New England would be used by God to set an example of righteousness to the world, and that they should act for the good of the whole rather than the individual.

Even though many groups came to the New World to practice their religions freely, they were not necessarily tolerant of other people's religions. **Roger Williams,** a Separatist who immigrated to Massachusetts Bay in 1631, quickly discovered this. Williams argued that England had no right to grant settlers land already occupied by Indians, that church and state should be kept separate, and that Puritans should not impose their religious beliefs on others. Puritans believed that society depended upon **consensus**, so they could not allow someone to disagree with their **doctrines**, and banished Williams from the colony. Roger Williams eventually founded the city of **Providence** on land he actually purchased from local Indian tribes. His colony, which would eventually become **Rhode Island**, had complete separation of church and state and tolerated all religions, including Judaism. Williams's idea of **religious freedom** would become one of the hallmarks of the United States. Later, another religious dissenter, **Anne Hutchinson**, who diminished the importance of ministers and claimed to have spoken to God directly, was also banished from Massachusetts and moved to Rhode Island.

In addition to Puritans and Separatists, the **Quakers** sought religious freedom in the New World. **William Penn**, a close friend of **King Charles II** of England, was granted the region between New York and Maryland. This area, later called **Pennsylvania**, promised toleration of all religions, the right to bail and trial by jury, and pledged to establish a representative assembly. **Philadelphia**, founded on the Delaware river, drew Quakers from around the world and became a trading post soon able to rival Boston.

Although much of New England was settled by devout Puritans, their descendants were sometimes less religious. The **Halfway Covenant** (1662) was passed to make it easier for the less religious children of the Puritans to become baptized members of the Puritan church. During the early 1700s, there was a wave of religious fervor called the **Great Awakening**. Preachers like **Jonathan Edwards** and **George Whitefield** emphasized Calvinist teachings about eternal damnation, the mercy of God, and salvation by faith.

Despite their economic and religious differences, the American colonies before the Revolution were very English in character. The advances in science, politics, and writing that occurred during the Enlightenment period in Europe greatly influenced the colonists.

The Dominion of New England

One of the first causes of conflict between the colonies and the mother country was the **Dominion of New England**. The English set up an autocratic government under Edmund Andros and consolidated the New England colonies in an attempt to stop rampant smuggling. After the **Glorious Revolution** in Britain (1688), the Dominion was thrown out and Massachusetts became a royal colony. England then left the colonies alone for a while, a policy known as **salutary neglect**.

Reasons for the Founding of Selected Colonies

Virginia (1607):   Economic gain
Plymouth (1620):   Religious freedom (Separatist Pilgrims)
Massachusetts (1629):   Religious freedom (Nonseparatist
                            Puritans); later merged with Plymouth
Maryland (1633):   Religious freedom (Catholics)
Connecticut (1636):   Religious differences with Puritans in
                            Massachusetts
Rhode Island (1636):   Religious freedom from Puritans in
                            Massachusetts
New York (1664):   Seized from Dutch
New Jersey (1664):   Seized from Dutch
Delaware (1664):   Seized from Dutch, who took it from
                            Swedes
Pennsylvania (1682):   Religious freedom (Quakers)
Georgia (1732):   Buffer colony and alternative to
                            debtors' prison

Geography = Destiny?
A good general guide for remembering which colonies were established for what reasons: The northern colonies were mostly established for religious reasons, the southern for commercial

ERA: TENSIONS LEADING TO THE AMERICAN REVOLUTION

Early 1700s to 1775

Mercantile Laws and Early Conflicts

England, like other European countries, believed strongly in the practice of **mercantilism**. Mercantilists believed that a state's power was based on its ability to minimize the importation of foreign goods, thus maintaining a favorable balance of trade. Mercantilists also wanted to increase specie (gold or silver coin). Great Britain recognized that the colonies were good sources of both goods and services. Therefore, it monopolized the colonial trade, restricting the colonies from trading with other nation-states (France, Spain, the Netherlands, and their colonies) through passage of the **Navigation Acts** and similar laws. These acts raised money by placing heavy taxes, called **duties** or **tariffs**, on colonial goods traded with anyone outside the Empire. Such policies angered the colonists, who had been mostly self-governing during the period of salutary neglect. Colonists couldn't make as much money with limited trade as they could with free trade, and as a result the colonists often disobeyed the laws.

In addition to disagreements about trade, the colonists began to push back against British rule in North America. Colonial leaders sought to increase the powers of elected **assemblies** relative to the powers of the **colonial governors** and other officials appointed by the British government. Colonists viewed governors and appointed officials as threats to colonial ways and later, as puppets of the monarchy, while assemblies were viewed as protectors and representatives of the people.

Some colonies even attempted to influence British appointees by threatening to withhold salaries or by refusing to follow colonial directives. A famous case involving a conflict between a colonial governor and a colonist was that of **John Peter Zenger**, a colonial newspaper editor. Zenger accused New York's colonial governor (William Cosby) of staffing the State Supreme Court with royalist judges, and of causing trouble with the colony over his salary. Cosby had Zenger arrested for **seditious libel** and imprisoned him for eight months before trial. Zenger's lawyer defended his right to print critical statements as long as they could be proven true, and Zenger was found innocent by a jury. This case showed the growing discontent of the colonists with colonial rule, and served as the precedent for the First Amendment of the Bill of Rights, which protects freedom of speech and the press.

The French and Indian War (1754–1763)

By the mid-1700s, American colonists felt threatened by the **colonial settlements of France** in the interior of the continent (Ohio Valley) and Quebec. France and Britain were long-time rivals, fighting numerous wars over the centuries. Now, they fought wars in North America over such prizes as dominance over the fur trade, rights to the North Atlantic fisheries, and possession of the **Ohio-Mississippi Basin**. French colonists did not force Native Americans to assimilate to their religion or culture, and therefore had a much better relationship and ability to trade with the Native Americans of North America. As smaller conflicts between the French and English colonists escalated, the French enlisted various Native American groups, including the Algonquin and Shawnee to fight alongside them against the English colonies and Britain, and later against the British allies, the **Iroquois Confederacy**.

English colonists, who feared the French would take control of more land or access to trade routes, sent delegates from seven colonies to Albany, New York in 1754 to discuss the crisis. Under the leadership of Benjamin Franklin, **The Albany Congress** had two goals, to persuade the powerful Iroquois Confederacy to side with the English, and to coordinate defense of the colonies. The Iroquois chose to remain neutral (until later when it became clear that Britain would win), and the **Albany Plan of Union**, which would have established an elected inter-colonial legislature with the power to tax, was rejected by the colonies who feared a loss of **autonomy**. Although the Congress did not achieve either of its goals, it does represent an early example of the cooperation between the colonies that would become essential during the American Revolution.

After the English colonists endured massive losses to the French, Britain declared war on the French, thus beginning the **French and Indian War**, or **The Seven Years' War** as it was called in Europe. While the British spent the first three years of the war losing to the French, the British, led by Prime Minister **William Pitt**, (for whom the French Fort Duquesne was renamed Pittsburg) changed its military strategy and agreed to reimburse the colonists for wartime expenses and placed recruitment in the colonists' hands. These new policies led the colonists to provide greater support for the war. The resulting British victory changed the boundaries of the two empires' worldwide possessions. The French lost much of their territory on the North American continent, including Quebec and the Ohio Valley to

Britain. The French retained only a few of their islands in the West Indies (prized for their sugar production) and fishing rights off Nova Scotia.

The war had been enormously expensive, and the British felt that the American colonists did not share equally the burden of the war costs. On the other hand, as American colonists no longer needed the strong defense against the French that the British provided, the colonists began to reconsider their roles as subjects within the colonial system. The **Proclamation of 1763**, which forbid colonists from settling on land west of the Appalachian Mountains (which was still inhabited by French settlers and Native Americans), further angered the colonists who hoped to settle on or profit from the territory they had gained from the French after the war.

Taxation Without Representation

Directly following the French and Indian War, a new prime minister, **George Grenville**, was appointed. He sought tighter control over the American Colonies in order to raise revenues for Great Britain. In addition to stricter enforcement of existing trade laws, Grenville passed other unpopular laws. The **Sugar Act** (also known as the Revenue Act), which placed new duties on certain foreign goods (not just sugar), basically forced the colonies to conduct all trade through England. Although the Sugar Act resembled the Navigation Acts, by which the colonists had long abided, the fact that it was explicitly designed to raise revenue upset the colonists, who felt as if the mother country was trying to take advantage of them. Colonial legislatures sent petitions to Parliament, arguing that the act would hurt trade for Britain as well as the colonies and that the colonists had not consented to the act's passage. Grenville ignored the colonists' pleas as he proceeded with his plans to increase Britain's revenue. The **Stamp Act** decreed that all legal and commercial documents, newspapers, and pamphlets should bear a stamp. The stamps were sold only by Grenville's Treasury—at a cost that virtually doubled the colonists' tax burden—and could be paid for only in hard currency, which was extremely rare in the colonies. Apart from the financial burden, the Stamp Act required that violators be tried in **Vice-Admiralty Courts**, in which judges alone rendered decisions. Colonists denounced the Stamp Act as another attempt to make revenue solely for the Empire, and as an attempt to take away the colonists' right to trial by a jury of their peers.

These laws generated uproar, not only because people thought that they were generally unfair, but also because the colonists were not represented in the British Parliament when these laws were passed. The British government believed in the practice of **virtual representation**, which meant that Parliament saw itself as representing the entire country and acted in the best interests of all citizens. The British government also operated on the belief that by being part of the British Empire, the colonies' consent to acts of Parliament could be presumed. Thus arose the revolutionary cry, "**No taxation without representation**." Many groups organized to protest the strict enforcement of these taxes. The **Sons of Liberty** were a particularly radical group that took to burning stamps and terrorizing British officials. Britain responded by repealing most of Grenville's Acts, but passed the **Declaratory Act** in an attempt to prevent future protests by the colonists. The Declaratory Act stated that the mother country could tax colonists in any way it

"These are the times that try men's souls. The summer soldier and the sunshine patriot will, in this crisis, shrink from the service of their country; but he that stands it now, deserves the love of men and women."
—Thomas Paine in *The Crisis*, 1776

saw fit. While some colonists celebrated their victory with the repeal of the Stamp Act, others worried that the Declaratory Act opened the door to a new wave of British taxation.

A few years later, the Chancellor of the Exchequer (a top treasury official), Charles Townshend, worked to raise colonial taxes again. The **Townshend Acts** levied taxes on goods such as paper, glass, and tea, but even more troubling, the acts applied to items that were imported from Britain rather than those from other countries, which went against mercantilist theory. What colonists found even more upsetting was that these new acts were meant to pay the salaries of royal officials in the colonies, which meant that the colonists could no longer influence these people by threatening their salaries. Rather than complain again about the lack of consent, colonists contended that Parliament could regulate colonial trade but could not exercise that power to raise revenue for the mother country alone, thereby avoiding the issue of consent.

Protests began again, and this time, even more boycotts and violence accompanied the new taxes. In the **Boston Massacre**, British soldiers who had been sent to the colonies to protect tax officials got into a brawl with colonial protestors, and the soldiers shot into a crowd, killing five civilians. Also at Townshend's behest, Parliament passed the **Tea Act**, which removed mercantilist duties on tea exported to America by England's politically powerful but financially troubled **East India Company**. This act drastically lowered the cost of that company's tea, which flooded the colonial market and undercut the price of tea sold by colonial merchants. These merchants still had to pay duties on other teas or smuggle tea (and risk imprisonment) to avoid the tax. Colonial resistance leaders also felt that this new act was the first step in the creation of an East India Company **monopoly** of all colonial trade and prepared to address what they felt was a new threat to their freedom. After failed negotiations between the colonial governor of Massachusetts, tea agents, and colonists, sixty men dressed as Native Americans assembled in Boston Harbor where they boarded the ships carrying the tea shipments and threw hundreds of chests of tea into the harbor. While the **Boston Tea Party**, as it came to be known, brought a new series of restrictive measures down upon the colonies, it also served as an example of bravery and patriotism that inspired colonists throughout America.

Needless to say, Britain was not amused by Boston's idea of a tea party and decided to punish the whole colony of Massachusetts with the **Intolerable Acts** (known in Britain as the **Coercive Acts**). Great Britain closed Boston Harbor until the city paid for the lost tea. The charter of Massachusetts was revoked, and all of its elected officials were replaced with royal appointees. Town meetings were forbidden, and Bostonians were forced to feed and lodge the soldiers who would implement these policies with the passage of the **Quartering Act**.

These strict actions infuriated colonists, who believed that Great Britain had begun a plan of deliberate oppression, and they were spurred to action. The **First Continental Congress** of 1774 was a gathering of representatives from all the colonies. The participants agreed to join together in a boycott of English goods. In addition, the Congress wrote up a list of grievances to present to the king.

Few colonists thought that these actions would ultimately lead to a military conflict. They also did not yet anticipate the complete separation of the colonies from England in the American War of Independence.

British Acts for the Colonies

Name of Act (Year)	Description
Navigation Acts (1651–1673)	Placed protective tariffs on imports that might compete with English goods; colonists could buy goods only made in England or imported via English ports
Proclamation Act of 1763	Forbade settlement west of the Appalachian Mountains
Sugar Act (1764)	Levied new duties on sugar, molasses, and similar products
Currency Acts (1764)	Prohibited colonies from printing paper money
Stamp Act (1765)	Instituted a tax for raising revenue on all legal documents and licenses; caused a huge uproar in the colonies and the formation of "Sons of Liberty" organizations
Declaratory Act (1766)	Asserted the British government's right to tax the colonies
Townshend Acts (1767)	Taxed goods imported from Britain and used the money to pay tax collectors (formerly paid by the colonial assemblies)
Tea Act (1773)	Gave the nearly bankrupt East India Company an unfair advantage in the tea trade in the colonies; colonists responded with the Boston Tea Party
Intolerable Acts (1774)	Closed Boston Harbor until the tea from the Boston Tea Party was paid for; revoked the charter of Massachusetts and replaced the commonwealth's elected officials. Soldiers were quartered in civilians' houses. One of these laws, the Quebec Act, expanded Quebec's territory and gave rights to Catholics.

Two Types of Laws
One way to think of the unpopular laws imposed on the colonies in the years leading up to the Revolution is to divide them up into two types: restriction laws and taxation laws.

Restriction:
Navigation Acts
Proclamation Act
Currency Acts
Tea Act
Intolerable Acts

Taxation:
Navigation Acts (yes, this one was a double whammy!)
Sugar Act
Stamp Act
Declaratory Act
Townshend Acts

ERA: INDEPENDENCE AND THE NEW UNITED STATES

1775 to 1800

The American Revolution

A **Second Continental Congress** was scheduled to meet a year after the first one. Before it could meet, however, skirmishes broke out between the colonists and the British soldiers, known as the **Redcoats**, in **Lexington and Concord**, Massachusetts. In April of 1775, British General **Thomas Gage** sent an expedition to confiscate colonial military supplies that were being stockpiled at Lexington. When the British arrived, they were greeted by less than one hundred local militiamen, who quickly retreated once they realized they were outnumbered. As the colonists fled, a shot rang out (from which side is still debated), and the British proceeded to fire on the Americans. After killing and wounding several men, the British moved on to Concord where they encountered a much larger militia presence. The colonial militiamen, who were largely untrained farmers or workers, did not follow traditional military strategy, choosing to shoot from behind trees or from windows rather than in the open field. By the end of the day, the British had suffered 70 deaths and even more casualties.

As these local conflicts began to escalate, both Britain and the colonists extended separate plans of reconciliation. The **Olive Branch Petition**, sent to **King George III** from the colonists, affirmed American loyalty to Great Britain and entreated the king to prevent further conflict. Both sides were unable to reach a compromise, however, and in July 1775, Britain acknowledged an open rebellion in the colonies. This acknowledgement occurred while the Second Continental Congress was meeting in Philadelphia. While the delegates originally met to consider the colonists' situation and possible next steps, they quickly realized the need to prepare the colonies for war. The Congress authorized the printing of money, established a committee to supervise relations with foreign countries, and most important, it created the **Continental Army** and appointed its generals.

The decision to break with Great Britain was not one that the colonists made lightly. At the beginning of the war, many Americans were torn between their desire for freedom and their loyalty to England. Some colonists were reluctant to break away from Great Britain because they shared a common language and culture. Others worried that the British Empire's superior military would crush the rebellion and make things even worse for the colonists. It was also difficult for colonial leaders to build consensus between the colonies on war goals alone, which made some colonies feel like the connection to England was all that they had in common with other colonies.

On the other hand, many colonists expressed arguments in favor of separating from the mother country. A recent immigrant from England, **Thomas Paine**, summed up many of these arguments in his pamphlet ***Common Sense***, which criticized the monarchy and urged the colonists to form a better government. Paine advocated the establishment of a republic, a government by the people with no king or nobility. He wrote in common language and referenced the Bible, selling tens of thousands of copies to the colonists and inspiring radical action among the colonial leaders, who were still meeting at the Second Continental Congress.

The **Declaration of Independence** was adopted by Congress on July 4, 1776. The document, written mostly by **Thomas Jefferson**, accused the King of England of oppressing Americans through excessive use of force and of attempting to destroy representative government in the colonies. The declaration's long-term importance, however, was not its criticisms of George III, but rather its statements of equality and the rights of the people. These concepts have shaped the American ideal since the nation's founding. As the founding fathers signed the Declaration of Independence, the **American Revolution** had officially begun.

General George Washington led the American troops against great odds. He was chosen because he had experience in the French and Indian War, and because he could draw his home state of Virginia (the largest state) into the war. The British forces were larger in number, better trained, and supported by the wealth of England, the richest and most powerful nation in the world at that time. Washington's skills were invaluable in keeping the American forces alive during the war's early years. While American soldiers were untrained, Washington used the fervor of the revolution to inspire his men and employed unorthodox military strategies to defeat the British, who were used to fighting organized battles in the open field. One such technique was using the element of surprise. After winning several battles and taking most of New Jersey, the British stopped to celebrate Christmas. Washington and his men took boats across the icy Delaware river at night and surprised the **Hessians** (**mercenary soldiers**) and the British forces. The Americans captured 900 men and killed 30, but more importantly, they buoyed American spirits. Later, while the Continental Army was forced to winter at **Valley Forge**, where they suffered from cold, disease, and lack of food and supplies, Washington continued to motivate his troops and paid the wives and children of the soldiers to work as laundresses and nurses. Washington used this time to train his army, aided by **Baron Friedrich von Steuben**, who had come from Prussia by way of France. The Baron helped Washington train his army and instituted policies of organization and sanitation of the camp that helped limit the spread of disease. In the spring of 1778, the American troops emerged from Valley Forge strong in their commitment to independence and now equipped with the training to achieve it.

France was a decisive ally for the Americans. From the beginning of the war, France had secretly supplied weapons and goods to the colonists. After the American victory in **Saratoga**, in upstate New York, France—along with Spain and Holland—formally declared war against Great Britain. In addition to providing the colonists with a navy crucial for their final victory at **Yorktown** (1781), by joining with America, France raised the possibility that Britain might have to fight a war at home as well. Another factor in America's favor was that the British greatly overestimated the American's **Tory**, or **Loyalist**, support. The British had approached the war as if they merely had to suppress a few radicals. Fighting an entire nation of people, united in their quest for freedom, was more than the British had bargained for.

At the Movies

Watching movies and TV isn't a substitute for studying (really!) but it can help make history more memorable. Two films that bring the Revolutionary Era to life are

1776 (1972)
About the days leading up to the signing of the Declaration of Independence

The Patriot (2000)
Shows the Revolution as it happened in the South

You may also want to check out the following seven-part TV miniseries:

John Adams (2008)
Based on the Pulitzer-winning biography by David McCullough

After years of fighting and the loss of life and expenditure of wealth, Great Britain no longer thought it worthwhile to fight the American colonies, especially as other European nations placed military pressure on Britain. American independence was established in the **Treaty of Paris** (1783), two years after the final battle at Yorktown. The treaty established the boundaries of this new nation: to the north, the present-day boundary with Canada, the south, at the northern border of Florida, and to the west at the Mississippi River, but most significantly, it granted the Americans the unconditional independence they so deeply desired.

True or False?

Q: All of the American colonists wanted to start a war with England to win their independence.

Major Battles of the Revolutionary War

Battle	Date	Location	Significance
Lexington-Concord	April 1775	Massachusetts	First armed conflict. British destroy supplies at Concord but suffer numerous casualties on way back to Boston. Propaganda victory for U.S. Casualties: U.S.—95. British—273.
Fort Ticonderoga	May 1775	Lake Champlain	Ethan Allen and Benedict Arnold captured the fort and 60 cannons, which were later dragged 300 miles and used in defense of Boston.
Breed's Hill (Bunker Hill)	June 1775	Boston	British succeed but suffer huge losses (1,000 casualties.) One-sixth of all British officers killed in war die here. Americans lose 400 dead and wounded. Only battle in long siege of Boston.
Invasion of Quebec	Winter 1775–76	Maine/Canada	Gens. Arnold and Montgomery attack Quebec prematurely and fail in invasion attempt of Canada.
Dorchester Heights	March 1776	Boston	British forced to evacuate New England after cannon put in place.

Battle	Date	Location	Significance
New York (Brooklyn Heights— Long Island, White Plains)	August 1776	New York	U.S. Army forced to retreat to Manhattan, then New Jersey. British General Howe offered generous terms of surrender to the Americans, but they demanded independence and talks broke down.
Trenton	December 1776	New Jersey	Hessian army crushed in Washington's raid across the Delaware River. Casualties: U.S.—4, British—900 captured, 30 killed.
Princeton	January 1777	New Jersey	U.S. recovers New Jersey from British in 10 days. British retreat to New York, where they remain for the war.
Brandywine Creek Germantown	September 1777 October 1777	Pennsylvania	British seize Philadelphia after these victories.
Saratoga	October 17, 1777	Upstate New York	Turning point of war. Convinced French of U.S. strength. Burgoyne surrenders 5,800 men.
Monmouth	June 1778	New Jersey	U.S. Army almost captured British but cowardice allowed British forces to escape.
Savannah	December 1778	Georgia	Beginning of British push in the South. British are at first welcomed in Savannah and colonial government is restored.
Kaskaskia and Vincennes	February 1779	Western territories	Clark captures British forts, which proved important in negotiations with British after the war.

True or False?

A: False! Not all of the colonists were eager to fight a revolution. Some colonists, known as Loyalists or Tories, stayed loyal to the British crown. Many colonists were unhappy with the way they were being treated by England, but didn't necessarily want to be independent. Some also believed that England would win the war because it was more powerful, and feared the consequences to the rebels if

Battle	Date	Location	Significance
Charleston	December 1779	South Carolina	British gain control of South with victory here. 5,000 Americans surrender in the single largest loss of troops until the Philippines in 1942.
King's Mountain	October 1780	South Carolina	Bloody victory for U.S.
Cowpens	January 1781	South Carolina	Gen. Greene divided his forces and scored a victory over Cornwallis, who had a larger army.
Guilford Court House	March 1781	North Carolina	In fierce fighting, Americans frustrate British, who control Southern cities, but not the rural areas. While winning the field, Cornwallis finally gives up attempt to defeat Greene's army and plans to link up with British supplies and reinforcements in Virginia.
Yorktown	October 19, 1781	Virginia	With 7,800 French soldiers and the French fleet in the harbor, Washington accepts Cornwallis' surrender as major fighting ends.

Source: Feldmeth, Greg D. "Revolutionary War Events," *U.S. History Resources* faculty.polytechnic.org/gfeldmeth/chart.rev.html

ERA: FROM WASHINGTON TO JEFFERSON

Constitution 1.0: The Articles of Confederation

The colonies did not wait to win their independence from England before setting up their own governments. As soon as the Declaration of Independence was signed, states began writing their own constitutions. In 1777, the Continental Congress sent the **Articles of Confederation**, the first national constitution, to the colonies for ratification. The colonists intentionally created little to no central government since they were afraid of ridding themselves of Britain's imperial rule only to create their own tyrannical government. The articles contained several major limitations, as the country would soon learn. For one, the Articles gave the federal government no power to raise an army (which hurt the colonies during **Shays' Rebellion**). The Articles also curtailed the government's ability to levy taxes, regulate international trade, enforce treaties, and perform other tasks necessary to international relations.

Federal Government Under the Constitution

In 1787, the newly independent nation convened a Constitutional Convention during which the U.S. Constitution, the foundation for the government of the United States, was written. The Constitution established the three branches of government: the **Executive**, or the Presidency; the **Legislature**, or the **Congress** (including both the Senate and the House of Representatives); and the **Judiciary**, or the Supreme Court and the lower federal court system. The branches were set up with a system of **checks and balances** so that none of the three branches could attain too much power. For example, the president has the power to veto a bill to stop it from becoming a law, and Congress has the power to override a president's veto. Originally, the Congress was the strongest element of the government because, with the **power of the purse**, Congress can raise and spend revenue. Also, Congress has the power to make laws. In the twentieth century, however, the Executive Branch developed into perhaps the strongest branch, with presidents like Franklin D. Roosevelt pushing for a broader interpretation of the U.S. Constitution.

The Constitution was in many ways a difficult compromise among the various states' interests. One stumbling block to its formation concerned the way each state would be represented in the national legislature. Large states wanted legislative delegations based on state population. This proposal, called the **Virginia Plan**, would have given large states many more legislative representatives than the small states. Small states argued that each state should be represented equally. This plan was called the **New Jersey Plan**. The two sides compromised and created

> ### Separation of Powers
> The framers of the Constitution believed no one faction of the government should be able to become too powerful. To prevent this, they borrowed the concept of **separation of powers** from political philosopher Charles de Montesquieu. The framers delegated different but equally important tasks to the three branches of government. In practice, we call this system "checks and balances." Separation of powers also prevents a person from serving in more than one branch of the government at the same time.

Vocab Time!
"Bicameral legislature" means a legislature that is divided into two houses. The system began in England in the 1600s with the two houses of Parliament: the House of Commons and the House of Lords. (Funnily, the House of Lords has no real power in British government now.)

a bicameral legislature, with the House of Representatives apportioned by state population and the Senate apportioned equally (two delegates for each state). This compromise is often referred to as the **Great Compromise**, or the **Connecticut Compromise**.

Another area of contention was the question of representation among slave states. Each state had two senators, but representation in the House of Representatives was based on the number of people who lived in each state. The dilemma was this: How could you count slaves as both property (for taxation purposes) and people (for representation purposes)? The problem was "solved" with the **Three-Fifths Compromise**, which mandated that each slave be counted as three-fifths of a person when establishing the population of a state for representation.

The **Bill of Rights**, the first ten amendments to the Constitution, was also a compromise to urge states to ratify the document. Federalists, including **Alexander Hamilton** and **James Madison** (watch out—he won't be a Federalist for long!), rallied for a strong national government that would have the necessary power to superseded some state powers. **Anti-Federalists**, those opposed to the Constitution, refused to ratify the Constitution until they were promised a Bill of Rights to ensure that the new federal government would not infringe on people's rights.

The Bill of Rights in a Nutshell

1. Freedom of religion, speech, press, assembly, and petition
2. Right to bear arms in order to maintain a well-regulated militia
3. No quartering of soldiers in private homes
4. Freedom from unreasonable search and seizure
5. Right to due process of law, freedom from self-incrimination, double jeopardy (being tried twice for the same crime)
6. Rights of accused persons; for example, the right to a speedy and public trial
7. Right of trial by jury in civil cases
8. Freedom from excessive bail, cruel and unusual punishment
9. Rights not listed are kept by the people
10. Powers not listed are kept by the states or the people

The Constitution was ratified and passed in 1788. The Bill of Rights was added after ratification in 1791.

Although the Constitutional Convention successfully provided a framework of law that the United States has used for more than 200 years, many of the compromises sowed the seeds of discontent that later plagued the growing Union and helped lead to the Civil War. The issues of slavery and the balance of states' rights and national interests continued to be sources of major political tension from 1789 to the 1860s. The expedient compromises of the Constitutional Convention, namely the Three-Fifths Compromise and the Bill of Rights, were not enough to settle the disputes.

The Rise of Political Parties

George Washington was elected the first president in 1789. With others, he worked to formalize the structures described in the Constitution. Because of the financial difficulties faced by the new nation, Alexander Hamilton's position as the Secretary of the Treasury was especially important. Hamilton worked quickly to establish a financially sound federal government. He urged Congress to pass legislation that would dictate the repayment of the national debt in order to encourage foreign investment and would establish a national bank. Many, including James Madison, one of the original framers of the Constitution, felt that these powers were not explicitly mentioned in the Constitution and were therefore unconstitutional. This first conflict regarding the Constitution led to the political definitions of a "loose" (Hamilton) versus a "strict" (Madison) interpretation of the document.

The **Whiskey Rebellion** was similar in many respects to the earlier Shays' Rebellion, and was the first internal threat to the new government. Farmers, who were also whiskey producers, violently protested a large tax on whiskey, and Washington dispatched 15,000 troops to squelch the uprising. Although it demonstrated the effectiveness of a strong federal government, many felt that this use of power was excessive and revealed a bias toward the large, wealthy speculators who had lent the government money. These speculators were to be paid back from the proceeds of the whiskey tax. This unrest, coupled with ideological divisions over constitutional interpretation, inspired the new Democratic-Republicans, led by Madison and Thomas Jefferson, to challenge Federalist control of the government. At the time, Democratic-Republicans, or Anti-Federalists, favored farmers and agricultural interests, while the Federalists leaned toward manufacturing and commercial interests.

Early Political Parties

Party	Federalists	Democratic-Republicans
Qualities	Not all the same Federalists who supported the Constitution's ratification	Also known as Anti-Federalists (not all the same Anti-Federalists who opposed the Constitution's ratification), Jeffersonians, and Republicans
Leaders	Alexander Hamilton, John Adams	Thomas Jefferson, James Madison, James Monroe
Values	• Loose (broad) interpretation of the Constitution • Favored merchants • Wanted a strong national government and a national bank • Wanted to repay the debt • Opposed to the War of 1812 • Pro-British	• Strict (narrow) interpretation of the Constitution • Favored farmers • Opposed to the national bank • Pro-French

The Federalist Papers

After the Constitutional Convention ended, Alexander Hamilton, James Madison, and John Jay wrote a series of newspaper articles supporting the Constitution. The articles were designed to persuade the states of the wisdom of a strong central government combined with autonomous political power retained by the states. Today, these essays are the primary source for understanding the original intent of the framers of the Constitution.

Know Your Rights!

The government now provides affordable housing, free education, and health care to many people, but these things aren't mentioned in the Constitution. Many rights that you may think are in the Constitution are actually laws that were passed much later.

As the United States struggled to establish itself as a nation, its leaders had to contend with various threats from Great Britain, France, and Spain. Washington had been a strong advocate of **neutrality**, even before his **Farewell Address of 1796**, because he felt that the young nation could not withstand a war. Still, it was difficult for American diplomats to reach agreements with, say, Great Britain, without angering France. One infamous incident during John Adams' presidency was known as the **XYZ Affair** (XYZ stands for the code letters of the three French agents who demanded bribes from the American diplomats). Americans were indignant about the French agents' treatment of American representatives; the affair threatened to lead to war between the United States and France.

Also during Adams's administration, the **Alien and Sedition Acts** were passed, which (1) allowed the deportation of foreigners who seemed to be a threat to national security, and (2) designated fines or imprisonment for persons who wrote "falsely and maliciously" against the laws of the government. Although the "sedition" aspect of this law violated the First Amendment in the Bill of Rights, it was used to arrest and otherwise suppress Democratic-Republicans who had been sympathetic to French interests. In an attempt to repeal these laws, Madison and Jefferson wrote the **Virginia and Kentucky Resolutions** (1798–1799). These resolutions would have given states the power to repeal unconstitutional laws. Although these resolutions did not gain national acceptance, they helped strengthen the Democratic-Republican Party and platform.

In the watershed **election of 1800** (what is known as the Revolution of 1800), Thomas Jefferson, leader of the Democratic-Republican Party, won the presidency, signaling the first transfer of power from one party to another. The new nation achieved this with much verbal infighting and mudslinging, but without bloodshed.

ERA: JEFFERSONIAN REPUBLICANISM, 1800–1816

Jefferson surrounded himself with loyal Democratic-Republicans and stood up to the Federalist appointees in the judiciary branch. The Democratic-Republicans wanted to restrain the large federal government that had been built up by the Federalists in the preceding years. Part of Jefferson's philosophy was that agriculture represented the noblest and most democratic aspects of American life. Often his policies favored their interests over the interests of business, trading, and manufacturing. Jefferson's presidency is best known for the **Louisiana Purchase** (1803), which virtually doubled the size of the United States. Also during his term as president, Jefferson sent marines to Tripoli in North Africa to fight pirates in what became known as the **First Barbary War.**

During Jefferson's term, **John Marshall**, a Federalist, helped mold the judiciary into a powerful constitutional branch when he presided as the Supreme Court's Chief Justice. Marshall's long-running Marshall Court (1801–1835) maintained an ideology of a strong federal government even when that clashed with the Jeffersonian Democrat's emphasis on states' rights. The **Marshall Court** is best known for establishing the practice of **judicial review**, by which the Supreme

Court has the authority to declare laws unconstitutional. This power was not explicitly granted in the Constitution, but the precedent was set in the case of *Marbury v. Madison* (1803), which has helped secure the system of checks and balances. In *McCulloch v. Maryland* (1819), the Marshall Court affirmed the power of the federal government over state governments.

The Louisiana Purchase

So, why did the French sell all that land? Well, Napoleon Bonaparte was in a bind: He had an empire to establish and he needed funds. The French wanted to sell the land to get money to fight their enemies in Europe. Plus, a slave revolt in Haiti, ably led by **Pierre Toussaint L'Ouverture**, had depleted Napoleon's troops and supplies to a point at which it seemed impossible for France to retain the island. When Jefferson sent emissaries to France, his primary concern was control of the Mississippi River and the port of New Orleans, invaluable trade routes for the Ohio Valley and western territory. Although Jefferson was concerned about the constitutionality of such a large land purchase (remember, philosophically he was a "strict" interpreter of the Constitution, and nothing in it explicitly gave the president the power to buy land), he agreed with the expansionist interests of the nation and supported Congressional approval of the deal.

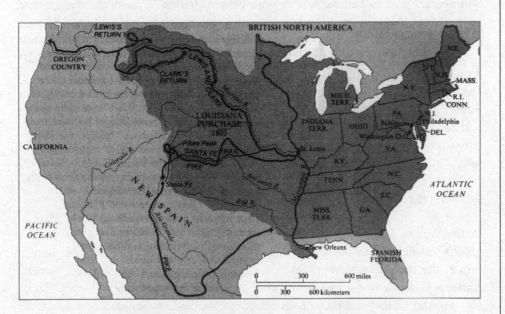

The United States After the Louisiana Purchase

The **Lewis and Clark Expedition** (1804–1806) was funded by Congress soon after the Louisiana Purchase. These explorers, helped by Native American guides, traveled from St. Louis to the Pacific Ocean in a year and a half. Their expedition helped establish U.S. claims to the disputed Oregon territory.

The War of 1812

During the early 1800s, Great Britain and France were at it again, fighting wars that affected the United States. The British were stopping U.S. ships and searching them for British naval deserters. This was particularly troublesome because the British would often seize native-born or naturalized American citizens as well as runaway British sailors. The **Chesapeake Incident** was the most widely publicized episode of this "sailor kidnapping," formally known as **impressment**. The French also violated American neutrality rights by restricting trade and seizing U.S. ships and their cargoes while they rested in French harbors.

Jefferson tried to avoid hostilities with these two world powers by issuing an **embargo**, which prohibited all foreign countries from trading with the United States until they respected national sovereignty. This embargo had a dramatic effect on the Americans, especially New England merchants. Because the policy seemed to penalize Americans more than foreign interests, the embargo was repealed and replaced with the **Nonintercourse Act** (1809). Although symbolically different, the result was pretty much the same. The embargo had restricted all foreign trade, whereas the Nonintercourse Act restricted trade with Great Britain and France only, but these countries were the largest traders in the world.

Jefferson's successor, Democratic-Republican **James Madison**, continued Jefferson's policies. The driving force for a war declaration in 1812 was the mood of public opinion rather than a specific event. The **War Hawks**, a group of Westerners and Southerners who rallied for war against Britain, felt their national integrity had been compromised by the illegal searches and seizures of American ships, and were concerned about the safety of the national borders. Madison, then president, was swayed by the War Hawks' popularity and asked for a declaration of war in 1812.

The United States was largely unprepared for war with a world power. The Republicans had been reducing the federal government, and military expenditures had been the first to go. Thus, the lack of a standing armed force led to some early embarrassments on the battlefield. Later, American ships had some success on the water. In the end, a crucial factor was that Britain was still fighting France and trying to subdue Napoleon in Europe. The **Treaty of Ghent** (1814) ended the war, by declaring it a stalemate.

In the War of 1812, only battle of consequence for the SAT Subject Test in U.S. History occurred after the war had officially ended. The technology of communication at the time delayed word that a treaty had been signed. Meanwhile, General **Andrew Jackson** won a resounding military victory at the **Battle of New Orleans**. News of this victory and the announcement of the peace treaty reached major cities at about the same time. Thus, it was popularly misunderstood that the United States had "won" the war with its military prowess. Jackson, the leader of the "victory" battle, went on to become a folk hero and president. (Just think, if CNN had been around...)

The War of 1812 caused significant regional division within the states. New Englanders opposed the war from the outset, because their livelihood was based on trade with Britain and other world powers. As noted before, the War Hawks consisted of mainly Westerners and Southerners. As the war pressed on and there were no significant victories, the Federalist Party held a meeting, known as the **Hartford Convention**, to formulate and submit their grievances to Madison's administration. The Federalists announced their demands in Washington, D.C., just as news of Jackson's victory and the signing of the Treaty of Ghent reached the capital. The Federalist Party was denounced as traitorous, and its leaders returned to New England in disgrace. The Federalist Party's impact on the national scene **collapsed** because, politically, they were on the wrong side of the war's outcome. A major consequence of the War of 1812 was the decline of Northeastern (Federalist) influence in national politics, coupled with the rising power of Southern and Western interests.

Reform Movements

During the early part of the nineteenth century, many people challenged religious and social institutions, often in attempts to lead what they considered a more moral life. These **reform movements** were enhanced by an optimistic mood at least partially inspired by the expanding western frontier.

Leaders of the religious movements, which are often referred to as the **Second Great Awakening**, were often **fire-and-brimstone** evangelists who preached that individuals had to purge sin from their lives and actively seek salvation rather than depend upon the local church or religious leaders. But the followers of one movement, **Transcendentalism**, believed that God created people without evil and with the capacity to be perfect. Many intellectuals embraced this theory, the most influential being **Henry David Thoreau** and **Ralph Waldo Emerson**.

Some religious groups stressed values contrary to the dominant materialist culture, and this compelled them to congregate in isolated settlements. The **Shakers** valued simplicity and hard work. One can see this reflected aesthetically in their minimalist, functional furniture. Another group, the **Mormons**, settled the state of Utah in the 1840s to escape persecution for their beliefs. (The term "Mormon" comes from the name of a prophet believed to have compiled the Book of Mormon, the scripture of the Mormon Church, which is officially called the Church of Jesus Christ of Latter-day Saints.)

Chapter 6 Drill

Turn to Part IV for answers and explanations.

1. Which of the following most strongly influenced the economic and political principals of the English colonial system?

   (A) Monarchism
   (B) Salutary Neglect
   (C) Communism
   (D) Mercantilism
   (E) Laissez-Faire

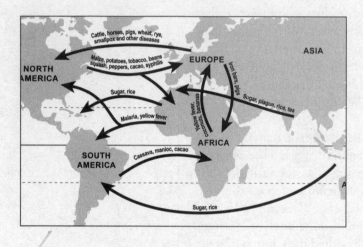

2. The image above represents what concept from U.S. history?

   (A) The Great Migration
   (B) Triangular Trade
   (C) Columbian Exchange
   (D) Free Trade
   (E) Command Economy

3. All of the following were reasons for exploration of the New World EXCEPT

   (A) the search for allies in international trade and politics
   (B) the search for a shorter trade route to Asia
   (C) the search for raw materials
   (D) the search for gold and other precious metals
   (E) the search for land to settle

4. The "Indian Territory" shown in the image below was barred from colonial settlement by which of the following?

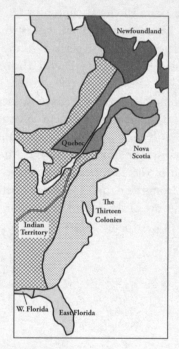

   (A) Seward's Folly
   (B) Dunmore's Proclamation
   (C) Proclamation of Neutrality
   (D) Gadsden Purchase
   (E) The Proclamation of 1763

5. The First Continental Congress met in order to

   I.   Draft a list of grievances to send to England
   II. Organize boycotts of British goods
   III. Coordinate colonial militias

(A) I only
(B) II only
(C) I and II only
(D) I, II, and III
(E) None of the above

did not consider military actions yet

6. Which of the following LEAST contributed to the colonists' desire to be free from Great Britain's control?

(A) Being forced to pay taxes specifically designed to generate revenue
(B) Being forced to quarter British soldiers
(C) Desire to overthrow the monarchy
(D) Increased feelings of self-sufficiency on the part of colonists
(E) Lack of actual representation in Parliament

7. "Small islands, not capable of protecting themselves, are the proper objects for kingdoms to take under their care; but there is something absurd, in supposing a continent to be perpetually governed by an island."

The above quote is most likely taken from which of the following?

(A) *Poor Richard's Almanac*
(B) *Common Sense*
(C) The Olive Branch Petition
(D) *Civil Disobedience*
(E) The Declaration of Independence

8. Which of the following had the LEAST influence on the American victory in the Revolutionary War?

(A) The Americans formed an alliance with France.
(B) The Americans fought on home ground.
(C) The Americans fought for a cause that was personal to them.
(D) The American military was better trained than the British military.
(E) The Continental Army employed nontraditional military practices.

9. Which statement about the movement for independence in the American colonies is most accurate?

(A) British colonial policies led to conflict between the colonists and England, and later, to demands for independence.
(B) The King of England wanted to push the colonists toward independence as they were a financial drain on the British empire.
(C) The northern colonies advocated revolution while the southern colonies refused to abandon the Mother Country.
(D) The French Revolution inspired the Americans to break with Great Britain.
(E) Colonists wanted to break with England as soon as they settled in America.

Chapter 6 Summary

Here are the most important concepts to remember from Chapter 6:

- The Spanish, French, Dutch, and British had different styles of interacting with Native populations.

- The Columbian Exchange revolutionized both European and Native cultures by expanding trade and technology and creating a racially mixed New World, stratified by wealth and status.

- African slavery started in this period, gradually replacing Native slavery and European indentured servitude.

- The belief in European superiority was a key rationale for the colonization of North America.

- Europeans and Native Americans vied for control of land, fur, and fishing rights.

- Britain's increased attempts to control the colonies and impose burdensome taxation led to the colonists' desire for revolution.

- France, Britain, Spain, and the new United States vied for control of land; the borders of the new United States were constantly expanding.

- The common people had changed their view of government. The belief in egalitarianism and democracy replaced trust in monarchy and aristocracy.

- The new United States struggled to define its ideals as boundaries changed and regional opinions clashed.

- New developments in technology, agriculture, and commerce built wealth and infrastructure, transforming America from a wilderness to a developed society.

- Relationships with Britain and France were problematic, each country playing one off the other. After the War of 1812, relationships stabilized.

- The Second Great Awakening was a catalyst for various reform movements which would continue until the early twentieth century.

Chapter 7
From Sea to Sea

ERA: THE BEGINNINGS OF EXPANSION

1816 to 1825

The era following the War of 1812 has come to be known as the "**Era of Good Feelings**." Coinciding with the Presidency of **James Monroe**, the "good feelings" were due to the prosperity of a booming cotton market, the lack of political opposition to Democratic-Republican policies (due to the demise of the Federalist Party), and the afterglow of a seeming war victory. But, in light of the militarism of westward expansion, conflicts with Indians, and the continued inequities of slavery, the phrase isn't without irony.

Adaptations to Expansion

During this time, great numbers of people were drawn westward by an abundance of cheap land and stories of plentiful natural resources. This ongoing westward expansion influenced many of Monroe's domestic and international policy decisions. His administration negotiated the **acquisition of Florida** from Spain in the Adams-Onís Treaty of 1819 and settled the boundary issue with Great Britain over the Oregon Territory with the signing of the Treaty of 1818. In order to protect expanding American territorial interests and as a validation of the spirit of Republicanism sweeping many former European colonial holdings in North and South America, Monroe asserted what has come to be known as the Monroe Doctrine (1828) during a message to Congress. In his address, he declared that any European interference in the Western hemisphere would be regarded as a hostile act. The **Monroe Doctrine** proved greatly influential in nineteenth- and twentieth-century international affairs, subsequently being reinterpreted by Theodore Roosevelt in the "Roosevelt Corollary," his Latin American policies, and by John F. Kennedy in his policies on communist Cuba and Soviet involvement there.

The rapid growth of Southern and Western populations also fueled the **transportation revolution**. Because Republicans did not believe in federal involvement at the state level or in potential private enterprises, many of the spate of road and canal building and improvement projects that were undertaken during the period were completed with state funding. The **Erie Canal** (1825) of New York became the model for other states eager to reap the financial rewards of improved transportation infrastructure. The invention of the steamboat also contributed to the transportation revolution, fueling interstate trade and thus interstate dependence. **Regional specialization** become more pronounced. New England developed a concentrated manufacturing base, while the South deepened its existing plantation system of cash-crop agriculture.

Sectional Compromises

The Constitution was drafted to include a mixture of provisions that balanced the interests of slave and non-slave states, but as westward expansion raised the issue of the entry of new states, the weakness of the constitutional compromise balancing those interests grew. Northern interests pushed for the admittance of western territories as "free" states (meaning states where slavery was prohibited) and Southern interests backed their entry as "slave" states (states in which the practice of slavery was protected by law). Admitting a new state as either would have upset the status quo in which the Senate was equally divided between members from free and slave states. So, during this period, **sectional politics**, North versus South (and to some extent versus West), became the principle focus of national politics as the question of how to admit new states loomed.

The **Missouri Compromise** of 1820 was the first settlement of a series of settlements reached to resolve these disputes. Missouri, historically a slave territory, had applied for statehood, but Northerners protested, fearing that its admittance as a slave state would lead to slave states outnumbering and dominating free states in the Senate. Representative James Tallmadge of New York offered the **Tallmadge Amendment**, which allowed for Missouri's entry, provided that all children of slave parents born after Missouri's entry should be free at the age of 25, and provided that no additional slaves were introduced into Missouri. Tallmadge's amendment failed in the Senate, but touched off a heated controversy. The issue was not resolved until the free territory of Maine, then part of Massachusetts, stepped forward for statehood. The compromise accepted the entry of both states, Missouri as slave and Maine as free. In addition to maintaining balance in the Senate, the compromise banned slavery from all parts of the Louisiana Purchase north of the **36° 30' Latitude**. The often heated wrangling that marked the controversy and compromise set the tone for the increasingly heated 40 years leading up to the outbreak of the Civil War.

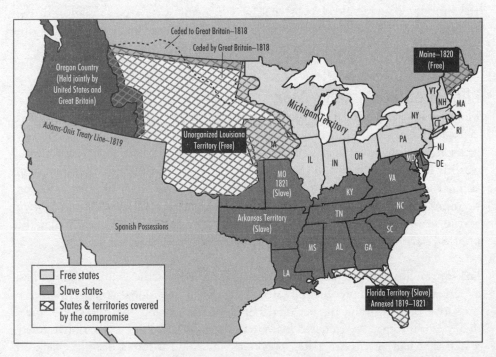

Missouri Compromise, 1820

Party Politics Revisited

As was tradition, James Monroe chose not to run for re-election following the conclusion of his two terms in office in 1824. The presidential election that determined his election was a three-man race between a trio of Republicans: **John Quincy Adams, Henry Clay**, and **Andrew Jackson**. When the results were tallied, Jackson lacked the electoral majority needed for the presidency, despite winning a plurality (the greater number of votes, but less than 50 percent of the votes cast) in the popular vote. Because the Electoral College could not choose a winner, the vote was thrown to the House of Representatives, where Adams was awarded the presidency; he named Henry Clay his Secretary of State. Jackson was angered by what he felt was a corrupt political conspiracy (nicknamed the "**corrupt bargain**") and immediately began campaigning for the next election. This marked the re-emergence of party politics in the previously united federal government of Republicans. Jackson supporters initially included John C. Calhoun, a powerful Southerner and Adams's vice president, and **Martin Van Buren**. They called their political coalition the **Democrats** and campaigned for a return to Jeffersonian ideals. Adams, Clay, and their supporters began calling themselves **National Republicans.**

ERA: JACKSONIAN DEMOCRACY

1828 to 1840

The bitterly contested election of 1828 was in many ways a continuation of the election of 1824, four years later. But, in 1828, it was Jackson, along with his running mate John C. Calhoun, emerging victorious.

Leader of the Common Man

Many political reforms had taken place during the 1820s, and the vote was extended to far more white males than in decades past. The foundation of Andrew Jackson's personal popularity, already the war hero of the Battle of New Orleans, was his image as a "friend to the common man." He was the first president who seemed to be more a figure "of the People" than an aristocrat. In office, Jackson surrounded himself with friends and supporters and advocated what was known as the **spoils system**, as in "to the winner go the spoils." This meant that the political party in power filled government jobs with their own supporters.

Jackson molded his presidency into one of the strongest the young republic had experienced. He set a precedent by stretching the constitutional boundaries of the executive branch, using his personal popularity to expand the role of the presidency. For instance, he exercised his veto power to forcefully shape national policy, a step that had never been taken previously. During his terms in office, Jackson was involved in frequent clashes with a variety of groups, including Native Americans, Southerners, and bankers.

Jackson's Confrontations

Jackson favored selling land cheaply to settlers in order to further expansion into the sparsely settled West. To complement his vision of westward expansion, he advocated the complete "removal" of Indians, blatantly disregarding the provisions of treaties that the U.S. government had entered into with many of the tribes. His signature of the Removal Act of 1830, effectively mandated that the tribes surrender unconditionally to federal forces and move en masse west of the Mississippi River or, if they chose, stand their ground and die in a futile effort to remain on their ancestral lands. Chief Justice John Marshall and the Supreme Court overturned the Removal Act, in a ruling that declared it unconstitutional, but Jackson refused to obey the ruling. If Jackson was indeed a "friend to the common man," that friendship was restricted to white Americans.

Jackson also famously involved himself in the heart of the **nullification crisis**, a conflict between South Carolina and the federal government over the matter of taxation. South Carolina, led by former Jackson support and Vice President John C. Calhoun, defied the much decried (at least in the South) "**Tariff of Abominations**." The tariff placed restrictions on the importation of British goods—goods that gentrified Southern planters relied upon because they were not produced locally. This tariff angered Southerners more broadly, as well, with many in the South fearing a sharp increase in the price of imported goods. Furthermore, they feared retaliation by the British in the form of increased tariffs on Southern cotton exports—the very core of the Southern economy. Consequently, South Carolina declared the tariff null and void in the state. Southerners emphatically argued their "states' rights" (to free commerce, in this case) outweighed any duty to the federal nation, and that they were justified in nullifying any law they felt contravened their state's interests. Jackson, concerned that South Carolina's blatant disregard of the federal law might lead to its secession from the Union, responded quickly to this crisis. Declaring the state's actions treasonous, Jackson asked congress to authorize the **Force Bill** of 1833 to send troops to defend the Union, to defend federal property and to uphold the law levying tariffs. Realizing that South Carolina lacked the support from elsewhere in the South to push the matter further, Calhoun sought a compromise. When Congress voted to lower the tax slightly, South Carolina backed down.

A major issue in Jackson's reelection campaign in 1832 was the re-chartering of the **Second Bank of the United States**, a private bank that held all federal deposits. (The First Bank of the United States had been established by and at the behest of Alexander Hamilton, George Washington's Secretary of the Treasury.) Some historians feel the second bank was financially sound and generally operated in the interests of the nation; others say it engaged in foolish speculation while ruthlessly pressuring its smaller borrowers. Jackson made no secret of his opinion of the bank: He assailed it as a corrupt, unconstitutional tool of the elites. Jackson's stance was an enormous hit with voters. Once re-elected, in a landslide, Jackson sought to destroy the bank by ordering the transfer of federal monies to smaller, state banks, which came to be known as Jackson's "**pet banks**."

"Liberty and Union, now and forever, one and inseparable!"
—Daniel Webster on the Nullification Crisis, 1830

Jackson's strong will and unwavering stance on a host of issues earned him a number of powerful political opponents and the moniker "King Andrew I," a negative reference to his monarchial tendencies—an especially significant allusion in a nation less than 50 years removed from a revolution against a monarchy. Southerners were embarrassed by his actions in South Carolina. Northeasterners were annoyed by his constant berating of businessmen and merchants. The fomenting of such discontent from such diverse corners helped forge a new political party, the **Whigs**. The Whig Party was significant on the national scene for about 20 years, but it could not satisfy the divergent interests successful parties must serve. The party finally splintered as the rift between the Northern and Southern wings of the party deepened over the question of slavery.

Post-Jackson

Jackson stepped down after the customary two terms and his handpicked successor and former Vice President, Martin Van Buren, assumed the Democratic Party mantle in the election of 1836. Van Buren narrowly defeated his Whig opponents who suggested that a Van Buren presidency would be tantamount to a third term for Jackson. In a sense, they were correct, as much of Van Buren's presidency was roiled by the effects of Jackson's earlier banking policies. A boom in economic growth and industrial expansion, suspect lending practices, and the rise of unregulated banks, had grown into a speculative bubble during the Jackson administration. Shortly after Van Buren assumed office, this bubble burst with a financial market crash that was followed by an economic depression known as the **Panic of 1837**.

In the next election, the Whig Party won with a William Henry Harrison-John Tyler ticket. Tyler was not a full-fledged Whig, but found himself on the Whig ticket because of his strong support among Southern voters. The Whigs soon came to regret their decision when Harrison became the first president to die while in office (due to pneumonia caused by an infection likely acquired during a lengthy inaugural address on a frigid day). Harrison was succeeded in office by Tyler, who clashed with Whig politicians regularly during his time in office.

The fiery passions that so consumed Jacksonian Era politics eventually waned and remained subdued for nearly 20 years. The relatively limited political stature of presidents during this time may have been a reaction to the strong (some thought overbearing, if not outright dangerous) presence of Jackson in the White House. But, it was also because of the state of the nation as it precariously avoided the issue of slavery. American politics became progressively more sectional in character and strong presidential figures that could direct a unified, national political life were absent. Not until the election of Abraham Lincoln was this trend reversed.

Pop Quiz

Q: Which one of these is not like the others?
   (A) the spoils system
   (B) dislocation of Native American tribes
   (C) extended power of the Executive Branch
   (D) support of Northern elites
   (E) expansion of voting rights

ERA: SECTIONAL STRIFE—THE PATH TO THE CIVIL WAR

1840 to 1860

During Van Buren's term, Congress indefinitely tabled all discussion about the issue of slavery in a measured known as the **Gag Resolution** (1836). Supporters of the rule felt that such debates were at best a waste of time, and at worst, needlessly divisive. Opponents of the resolution saw it as unconstitutional. The opponents eventually won out; after eight years, the Gag Resolution was overturned.

North vs. South vs. West

The increasing disagreements among these three regions were in large part due to differences in these regions' economic and cultural character. The North was rapidly developing into an **industrialized economy**, where new factories sprung up, using new methods of production such as **interchangeable parts** (parts made to a standard so that they can be easily replaced) developed by **Eli Whitney**. Urban centers grew as people migrated from the farmlands to the cities. Improvements in transportation and communication systems were in demand to keep pace with industrial expansion. Railroad networks were built throughout the North, and the use of the telegraph aided in running this sprawling network. Technological advances in farm equipment, such as the McCormick Reaper, also aided northern agriculture, allowing the North to produce staple crops at unprecedented rates.

The economy of the South, on the other hand, remained largely agricultural. **Large-scale, labor-intensive plantations**, bore much similarity to their appearance in colonial days, and concentrated on **cash crops**, the production of which, plantation owners argued, necessitated the use of slaves. Apologists for slavery called it the "peculiar institution," a euphemism intended to portray slavery as a somewhat unfortunate consequence of the unique conditions present in the South, rather than as a depraved institution. Slavery might have declined naturally in the South if not for the invention of the **cotton gin**, also by Eli Whitney. The efficient removal of seeds from cotton tufts, coupled with enormous English demand for huge quantities of cotton, encouraged the South to continue to focus on cotton production, which in turn fueled increased demand for slave labor.

Meanwhile, the **West** had its own ideology and interests, but its territories were often used as bargaining chips in the political power struggle between Northern and Southern states. Generally, Westerners supported territorial expansion and subscribed to the notion of **Manifest Destiny**, which held that it was America's destiny go beyond its current boundaries until it stretched from the Atlantic to the Pacific Ocean.

Pop Quiz

A: Choices (A), (B), (C), and (E) are connected to the presidency of Andrew Jackson. Choice (D) doesn't belong because Jackson characterized himself as a president of the people, winning popularity as a "friend to the common man."

Texts, Oregon, and War

President Tyler and his successor, **President James K. Polk**, were both supporters of western expansion. Polk had won on a campaign of "re-annexing Texas and re-occupying Oregon." This slogan glossed over the fact that, at the time, Texas was claimed by Mexico and the Oregon territory was jointly held with Great Britain. Despite the potential for these policies to lead to outright war with either power, expansion was popular among voters.

Texas had been colonized by Americans and had recently won its independence from Mexico. Soon after Polk's election as a "dark horse," or surprise candidate, Texans requested annexation as a U.S. slave state. As a result, the importance of adding the Oregon territory as a state to maintain the balance of free and slave states in Congress grew dramatically. The motto "Fifty-four Forty or Fight" was the expansionist rallying cry that complete control of the entirety of the presumptive territory (to the latitude of 54° 40' north) would be acceptable. Yet, because of the very real danger of fomenting war on two borders, Congress and other more rational elements persuaded Polk to settle the dispute with Great Britain, and the two countries compromised, dividing the territory into distinct American and British possessions along the 49th parallel.

Polk, nicknamed "Young Hickory" because of his similarity to "Old Hickory," Andrew Jackson, was, in the view of many historians, determined to fight a war with Mexico, in hopes of pressuring Mexico to surrender substantial tracts of territory, like California and the Southwest. Others, especially Northerners, opposed war with Mexico and feared that additional Southern acquisitions would overtly favor slave states in the perpetually fragile but at least tenable stalemate between Northern and Southern interests. Despite these concerns, the **Mexican-American War** officially began after Mexican troops crossed the Rio Grande into disputed territory, and Polk, over the objection of congressional Whigs, secured a declaration of war. While the progression of the war was neither as easy nor as swift (the war dragged on for more than a year and a half) as Polk had hoped, its outcome was everything that he had desired. With the **Treaty of Guadalupe-Hidalgo** (1848), Mexico acknowledged the Rio Grande as the southern border of Texas and ceded the territories of California and New Mexico to the United States. Soon after the acquisition of California, gold was discovered in "them thar hills" setting off the **Gold Rush of 1849** and an unprecedented migration to the territory.

True or False?

Q: In 1861, the president supported the expansion of slavery into the western territories of the country.

New Territories—New Compromises

These new territories increased the tension between free and slave states in the populace and in Congress. Even as the Mexican-American War was being fought, representatives from the North and the South began disputing how this new territory would be organized, slave or free. The Gold Rush forced the decision; in 1849, California petitioned Congress for admittance into the Union as a free state. President Zachary Taylor, a Whig, supported admittance. Serious talk of secession circulated among Southerners.

Henry Clay, by then an elder statesman, proposed a series of resolutions in hopes of preserving the free/slave state balance and avert the impending threat of Southern secession. Congressional squabbling followed, but included a number of notable Senate floor speeches, **The Great Debate**, by Clay, **Daniel Webster** and **John C. Calhoun**, collectively known as the **Great Triumvirate**. With the help of Stephen Douglas, a senator from Illinois, a deal that became known as the **Compromise of 1850** was struck. The compromise admitted California as a free state and maintained Texas as a slave state. The rest of the territory in question was divided at the 37th parallel into New Mexico and Utah. These two territories would be "unrestricted"—each locality would decide its own status. The compromise also abolished the slave trade in the District of Columbia. But the compromise's most significant resolution (and what kept the slave issue as a touchstone of public debate) was the new **Fugitive Slave Act**, which required citizens of any state—slave or free—to aide in the recovery of runaway slaves; citizens who refused risked fine or imprisonment. This sanction aroused the anger of even moderate Northerners as a blatantly pro-slavery measure. Southerners found their own point of contention with the compromise, as they were angered by being outnumbered by free states in the Senate.

Although some thought that this compromise would settle the slave issue, it proved to be only a temporary truce. In 1854, the **Kansas-Nebraska Act** effectively repealed the (by that time) hallowed Missouri Compromise. Stephen Douglas introduced the legislation, seeking the quick admission of the Nebraska and Kansas Territories as states. (His home state of Illinois was interested in a proposed expansion of the railroad network into these areas.) Douglas suggested that each locality should decide the slave issue for itself. Douglas's bill passed, widening the gulf between already polarized Northern and Southern interests. In the North, opposition to slavery grew and abolitionists felt more justified in speaking out against the status quo. Many local counties passed **personal liberty laws** that undermined the fugitive slave laws by disallowing their jails to be used for slave holding, further enflaming Southern passions.

The Kansas-Nebraska Act helped set the stage for one of the first violent confrontations stemming from the slavery issue. Because the fate of each locality in the Kansas-Nebraska Act hinged on a popular vote, hundreds of pro-slavery and anti-slavery activists poured into the territories in hopes of swaying the outcome of the referendum. Often armed and ready to fight, Kansas became a literal battleground between pro- and anti-slavery factions. "Bleeding Kansas," as the region came to be known, was the site of several prominent attacks on opposing groups' settlements.

True or False?

A: False! In 1861, Abraham Lincoln was president, and we all know that he represented Northern anti-slavery views.

The most famous incident was **John Brown's raid**, in which Brown, a radical slavery opponent, led a group that murdered pro-slavery settlers. Later John Brown led a separate raid on the U.S. arsenal at Harper's Ferry (then in the state of Virginia) hoping to seize a cache of weapons with which to arm a slave uprising. Brown's raid failed and Brown himself was captured by a detachment of Marines under the command of then Col. Robert E. Lee, tried for treason, and hanged.

A further attempt to resolve the slave crisis was made by the Supreme Court when they handed down the *Dred Scott* **decision**, written by **Chief Justice Roger B. Taney**. The decision in effect nullified all of the previous compromises reached on the slavery issue and granted slave owners the unrestricted right to take their "possessions" into any U.S. territory (although this did not yet apply to all states). Antislavery Northerners were livid. Rather than settling the issue as Taney and the justices had hoped, sectional tensions reached a dangerous, new high.

During the **Lincoln-Douglas debates** of 1858, **Abraham Lincoln** appeared on the national scene as an antislavery Republican. (The Republican party to which Lincoln belonged should not be confused with the Democratic-Republican Party of Thomas Jefferson. This Republican Party was founded in the 1850s with a platform that included preventing slavery from spreading to new territories.) He ran against the incumbent Senator Stephen Douglas in the U.S. Senate race in Illinois. Lincoln challenged Douglas to a series of debates in which he deftly explained his belief that the nation's opposition to slavery could not be grounds for compromise, and challenged the fundamental morality of Douglas's Support of the Dred Scott decision and the Kansas-Nebraska Act. Although Lincoln lost the Senate race, he rose to national prominence as an eloquent speaker able to articulate Northern views.

Who Was Dred Scott Anyway?
Dred Scott was a slave whose master had taken him into free territory, whereupon Scott sued for his freedom. In *Dred Scott v. Sandford* the court decided that slaves and their descendents were not U.S. citizens and therefore could not have legal standing. Additionally, Chief Justice Roger Taney ruled that slaves were property and protected as such by the slave owners' constitutional rights. This meant that slaves could not be taken from their masters regardless of a territory's "free" or "slave" status.

Sway of Public Opinion
In the North, there were outspoken crusaders against the evils of slavery, but most Northerners lacked strong feelings regarding the issue. In the years following the Compromise of 1850, broader opposition to slavery began to crystalize as public opinion changed. **Harriet Beecher Stowe** wrote a heart-rending account of slavery called *Uncle Tom's Cabin*, which brought the moral dilemma into focus for many in the North's large middle class. Although not an abolitionist's manifesto, the simple story galvanized antislavery sentiment. Also, blacks and whites organized the **Underground Railroad**, secretly (and at great personal risk) helping transport runaway slaves to freedom in the North and in Canada. Perhaps no single person has come to be so closely associated with the Underground Railroad than has former-slave-turned-abolitionist **Harriet Tubman**. Dubbed "Moses" by William Lloyd Garrison, Tubman shuttled nearly 70 enslaved African Americans from Maryland to safety in Canada during the course of 13 expeditions made over more than a decade. While only a small fraction of the Southern slave population was ever freed by via this network, its symbolism was significant.

As noted previously, presidents prior to Lincoln avoided the slavery question, but in the **election of 1860**, the issue was unavoidable; party platforms were as polarized as the nation writ large. The **Democratic Party** was overwhelmingly pro-South and pro-slavery; the new Republican Party, which nominated Lincoln, opposed slavery in the new territories; and a third party, a remnant of the defunct Whig Party called the Constitutional-Unionists, sought further compromise on the slave question. In the end, Lincoln carried only 40 percent of the popular vote, almost entirely from Northern states, and failed to carry any slave state. Nonetheless, Lincoln's victory gave Republicans control of both the White House and the House of Representatives; Democrats controlled a majority of seats in the Senate. While Lincoln did not explicitly oppose slavery during the campaign, his election and his belief that the question of slavery must finally be decided, brought the country to the brink of civil war.

Believe it!
Harriet Beecher Stowe succeeded in spreading antislavery ideas throughout America and the world when she wrote *Uncle Tom's Cabin*, a novel about the cruelty of slavery.

Chapter 7 Drill

Turn to Part IV for answers and explanations.

1. The primary purpose of the Tariff of 1828 was to

   (A) protect Southern agriculture from foreign competition
   (B) increase the competitiveness of American manufacturing in domestic markets
   (C) increase imports of foreign-made goods
   (D) punish Southern proponents of nullification theory
   (E) increase federal revenues collected from duties on imports

2. The passage of the Fugitive Slave Act of 1850 led to all of the following EXCEPT

   (A) the passage of the first personal liberty laws in the North
   (B) that law enforcement officials in the North were required to arrest persons suspected of being runaway slaves
   (C) the hardening of the views of moderate abolitionists toward slavery
   (D) the continued smuggling of runaway slaves to Canada by members of the Underground Railroad
   (E) heightened fears of a "slave power conspiracy" in the North

3. The nullification crisis that occurred under Andrew Jackson was primarily caused by

   (A) a dispute over Jackson's heavy use of the spoils system in filling government jobs
   (B) Southern demands that white male suffrage be extended
   (C) outrage over Jackson's relocation of Indian groups from their ancestral lands in the South
   (D) passage of a federal law offering safe harbor to fugitive slaves who arrive in the North
   (E) controversy surrounding the highly protective Tariffs of 1828 and 1832

4. The Kentucky and Virginia Resolutions are similar to the South Carolina Ordinance of Nullification in that both

   (A) denounced high protective tariffs
   (B) were intended to balance the entry of new free states with new slave states
   (C) asserted that states have the sovereign right to override federal laws to which they object
   (D) supported the principle of Manifest Destiny
   (E) stated that the Alien and Sedition acts were unconstitutional

United States Historical Population		
Census	**Population**	**%±**
1790	3,929,214	—
1800	5,236,631	33.3%
1810	7,239,881	38.3%
1820	9,638,453	33.1%
1830	12,866,020	33.5%
1840	17,069,453	32.7%
1850	23,191,876	35.9%
1860	31,443,321	35.6%

5. Which of the following data, if available, would be most helpful in determining the impact of immigration on population growth in the United States during the period indicated above?

   (A) Newspaper accounts of the effects of changing immigrant populations in major cities
   (B) A breakdown of employment records indicating employment of new immigrants by sector
   (C) Charts representing the percentage of immigrants to the United States from 1790 to 1860 by nationality
   (D) Graphs with the birth rate as a percentage of total population
   (E) The population growth rates of countries from which immigrants to the United States departed

6. Which of the following events, which were involved in the opening of the West, occurred first?

   (A) The Gold Rush
   (B) The completion of the Transcontinental Railroad
   (C) The passage of the Compromise of 1850
   (D) The passage of the Homestead Act
   (E) The establishment of cattle ranching as a dominant industry

7. Supporters of the Gag Resolution of 1836 did so primarily because they felt

   (A) endless debates on slavery were useless and time consuming
   (B) that the issue of slavery should be resolved by the president, not by Congress
   (C) was a matter to be determined by individual states
   (D) not speaking out against slavery in Congress was morally wrong
   (E) that the resolution had little chance of passage because of its many opponents in Congress, but that it remained a worthwhile resolution to support

8. The "corrupt bargain" marked the reemergence of party politics in determining the outcome of which presidential election?

   (A) The election of 1800
   (B) The election of 1824
   (C) The election of 1828
   (D) The election of 1876
   (E) The election of 1884

9. Which of the following individuals was responsible for an invention that shaped the economy of the Antebellum South?

   (A) Eli Whitney
   (B) Nikola Tesla
   (C) Henry Ford
   (D) Edward Ord
   (E) Thomas Edison

10. The line through the parallel 36° 30′, shown in the map above, that was established as the northern latitude beyond which slavery would not be permitted, was overturned due to which of the following events?

    (A) The Supreme Court's Dred Scott decision
    (B) The passage of the Compromise of 1850
    (C) The introduction of the Wilmot Proviso
    (D) The passage of the Kansas-Nebraska Act
    (E) The annexation of Texas

Chapter 7 Summary

Here are the most important concepts to remember from Chapter 7:

o   Slavery became one of the most controversial issues in politics and the social sphere.

o   "Manifest Destiny" and a land acquisition from Mexico spurred America to fully settle the West.

o   The acquisition of new territories continuously spurred debates regarding slavery and the balance of power between North and South.

o   Sectionalism encouraged geographical divides among the major political parties (Whigs vs. Democrats; later, Republicans vs. Democrats).

o   The Whigs were largely ineffective on the national level, paving the way for the emergence of the Republican Party.

o   Northern European immigrants continued to enter the country, motivated by industrial and agricultural opportunity.

Chapter 8
A House Divided: The Civil War and Reconstruction

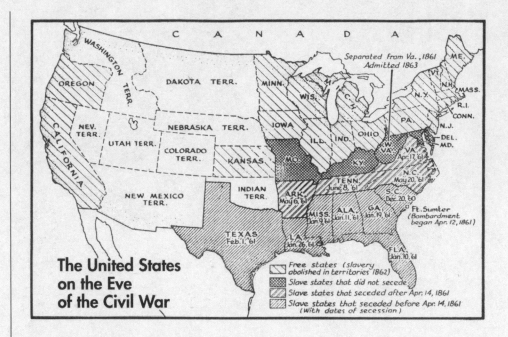

The United States on the Eve of the Civil War

Free states (slavery abolished in territories 1862)
Slave states that did not secede
Slave states that seceded after Apr. 14, 1861
Slave states that seceded before Apr. 14, 1861 (With dates of secession)

ERA: THE CIVIL WAR

1861 to 1865

Secession from the Union

Following Lincoln's election, **South Carolina** proclaimed that its interests could not be represented by the new government and seceded from the Union. Shortly thereafter, six other southern states (Alabama, Florida, Georgia, Louisiana, Mississippi, and Texas) followed suit and withdrew as well. These states formed the **Confederate States of America** and elected **Jefferson Davis** as their new president. The Confederates seized all federal government property in the South, except for two military installations: Fort Pickens, near Pensacola, Florida, and Fort Sumter, which sits strategically at the entrance to Charleston Harbor, South Carolina. Although some abolitionists celebrated the departure of slave-owning Southerners, most Northerners hoped to **preserve the Union**. President James Buchanan (Lincoln had not yet assumed office) disagreed with secession, but took no action to stop it.

As president, Lincoln took an unambiguous stance on secession, declaring it illegal. While Lincoln was careful not to publicly declare Southern states in rebellion, after some debate, he chose to resupply Fort Sumter with munitions and made clear that he would not lose the two remaining U.S. military installations in the South. If the Confederates wanted Fort Sumter, they would have to take it by force. Union leaders did not have to wait long for an answer from their Confederate counterparts. In April 1861, the **Civil War** officially began when Confederate forces attacked Fort Sumter. After a period of resistance, Fort Sumter fell to the Confederates and Lincoln declared an "insurrection" in the Southern states. The bloody war dragged on four savage years and, with the exception of World War II, cost more lives than any conflict in American history.

War Goals and Battles

Lincoln's initial objective in fighting the Civil War was not to free the slaves but to preserve the Union. In order to do this, Lincoln and his military and civilian leadership took a two-pronged approach: defeat Confederate forces while also destroying the South's war-making capacity. Despite an enormous advantage in population, men under arms, and resources, Northern objectives were not easy ones: Success required invading and holding vast swaths of hostile territory, while eliminating the South's military capability and political will to resist. In contrast, Southern leaders, including Davis and his top commander, **General Robert E. Lee**, enjoyed the fervent support of Southern citizens and needed only to resist Union advances into the South. They hoped that a series of key battlefield victories could turn the tide of public opinion in the North against the war, and open the door for a negotiated peace.

Comparison of North and South, 1860		
	North	South
Population	22,700,000 (free) 400,000 (slave)	5,600,000 (free) 3,500,000 (slave)
Soldiers	2,100,000	1,064,000
Miles of Railroad	21,800	8,800
Percentage of National Manufacturing Output	90%	10%
Percentage of National Arms Manufacturing	97%	3%

Despite the expectations of many observers in the North, the first large-scale engagement between Northern and Southern armies, at the **First Battle of Bull Run**, did not result in a Northern rout, but instead ended in a victory for the Confederates. Alarmed by the outcome of the battle, the reality that a long war was at hand sunk in for many Northerners. In the wake of the First Battle of Bull Run, Major General George B. McClellan took command of the Union Army of the Potomac in 1862, and the war began in earnest with its first major series of battles—the **Peninsula Campaign**. While McClellan managed to reach the gates of Richmond in late May 1862, he was turned back, and then forced into retreat following the Union defeat in the **Seven Days Battles**. Following another victory by outnumbered Confederate troops in the Northern Virginia Campaign, including the **Second Battle of Bull Run**, Lee made a bold decision, taking his **Army of Northern Virginia** into Union territory for the first time. Union forces blunted Lee's northward advance at the **Battle of Antietam**, in Maryland, but at great cost—it remains the bloodiest, single-day battle in U.S. history. Lincoln took the opportunity provided by the military victory at Antietam to announce his **Emancipation Proclamation**, drafted months earlier. By issuing the proclamation stating that slaves in the Confederacy were "forever free" (the proclamation had no legal effect on slaves held in Union border states), Lincoln hoped to squelch divided opinions in the North, strengthen the North's moral claim to victory, gain further European support for the Union cause, and to employ the uprising slaves to military advantage. Indeed, upon this national proclamation, a half million slaves fled the plantations to the North, many of whom later joined the ranks of the Union army.

The Union was unable to capitalize militarily on its success at Antietam—defeats at the **Battle of Fredericksburg** and the **Battle of Chancellorsville** followed. **General Thomas "Stonewall" Jackson**, Lee's most celebrated lieutenant, was mortally wounded by one of his own men at Chancellorsville. The Union's fortunes finally turned in July 1863 when Lee's second invasion into the North was repulsed at the **Battle of Gettysburg**. The battle represented a turning point in the strategic outlook of the war; many historians argue that the South's best hope for victory in the war died with Lee's defeat at Gettysburg. Despite this, Gettysburg was no lopsided Union victory, and Lincoln remained frustrated by the leadership of his top commanders. Seeking a change, Lincoln turned to the Western theater, and the commander of the **Army of the Tennessee, General Ulysses S. Grant**. Grant had enjoyed much success, participating in the Union capture of the Confederate **Forts Donnelson** and **Henry**, and had received praise for his command of Union forces during the **Battle of Shiloh** in Tennessee. He rose to national prominence after Union victories at the strategic Confederate stronghold of **Vicksburg**, in Mississippi, and at the **Battle of Chattanooga**, in Tennessee. The fall of Vicksburg gave the Union control of the entire Mississippi and cut the South in two, while the Confederate defeat at Chattanooga opened the heartland of the Confederacy to invasion by Union forces. Following Grant's victory at Chattanooga, Lincoln, seeking a leader with a reputation for aggressive action, appointed Grant commander of all Union armies, a post he would hold for the remainder of the war.

After assuming command of Union forces, Grant, in consultation with Lincoln, devised a plan to bring the war to a close by initiating a series of coordinated assaults on the heart of the Confederacy. While Grant drove toward Richmond, fighting a series of bloody battles of attrition at the **Wilderness, Spotsylvania Courthouse**, and **Cold Harbor** (the casualties of which gained him the moniker of "the Butcher" in the Northern press), **General William T. Sherman**, in what was called **Sherman's March to the Sea**, cut an eight-mile-wide path of destruction from Tennessee to the Atlantic Coast of Savannah. He destroyed civilian property and everything in sight in order to "break the will" of the Confederate population. Such a strategy has come to be known as **Total Warfare**.

After defeat at **Petersburg** and the subsequent fall of **Richmond** to Union forces, Grant finally forced the surrender of the remnants of Lee's tattered Army of Northern Virginia at **Appomattox** in April of 1865.

Pop Quiz

Q: If you had to answer a question about one of the facts on this page, and you didn't know the answer, what would you do?

ERA: RECONSTRUCTION

1861 to 1877: Right After the Civil War

As you have heard and read before, the Civil War was a profoundly devastating event. It grew out of, and deepened, bitter rifts between the North and the South, upsetting the social and economic structure of the entire country and leaving hundreds of thousands of Americans displaced or dead (it resulted in more American casualties than all other American wars combined until World War II).

Lincoln's Plan vs. the Radical Republicans'

Once it seemed certain that the North would win the Civil War, Lincoln devised a plan to deal with the South and its secession from the Union. He wanted to "forgive and forget" as quickly as possible and allow the South to reenter the Union with relative speed and without harsh punishment. His plan was called the **10 Percent Plan**, because it allowed any state to reenter the Union if 10 percent of its voters took a loyalty oath to the Union. But his plan never got very far. A group of congressmen, known as the **Radical Republicans**, favored strong punishment for the South coupled with a long process of reunification.

Lincoln was assassinated before any of the Reconstruction plans got under way. His Vice President, **Andrew Johnson** succeeded him, and although he agreed with Lincoln's moderate polices, he lacked Lincoln's political clout and acumen. In the face of Johnson's disastrously poor advocacy for moderation, Radical Republicans emerged as the most powerful group in the formulation of Reconstruction policy. With its influence in Congress, this bloc of lawmakers passed the **Reconstruction Acts** over the veto of President Johnson. These acts established the laws and strict procedures for the reinstatement of former Confederate states into the Union. The conflict between Johnson and Congress was so intense that Congress impeached Johnson, bringing him to trial in the Senate. Johnson, the first President in U.S. history to be impeached, was acquitted, but by only a single vote.

Civil Rights: Good News/Bad News

For newly emancipated slaves, Reconstruction brought good news and bad. The good news was that the **Thirteenth Amendment**, which prohibited slavery, was passed. The bad news was that Southerners passed the **Black Codes**, rules which restricted African Americans from many rights of citizenship. To nullify the Black Codes, Congress ratified the **Fourteenth** and **Fifteenth Amendments**, which conferred citizenship and ensured equal treatment before the law upon African Americans, and strengthened their right to vote, respectively. In addition, Congress passed—over Johnson's veto—a civil rights act that essentially reiterated equal protection provisions of the Fourteenth Amendment. But the amendments were largely ineffective. White Southerners used other methods to dissuade African Americans from exercising their right to vote, including violence and

Pop Quiz

A: Identify the era that the question refers to; attack the answer choices; eliminate any anti-era answers; and GUESS, GUESS, GUESS!

intimidation from groups such as the **Ku Klux Klan**, a **literacy test** (that many African Americans could not pass because they had been denied an education while enslaved), a **poll tax** (that many African Americans could not afford to pay), prohibitive property requirements, and a **"grandfather clause"** that permitted any man to vote whose grandfather had voted. With the grandfather clause, uneducated or poor whites could vote, whereas uneducated or poor African Americans, whose grandfathers had been slaves, could not.

Economics

Ending slavery was not just a moral issue for the South, but a serious economic one as well. Slavery was the foundation of the plantation system. When slave labor disappeared, economic policies and procedures required radical revision. Large landowners divided up their land and rented it to both white and black **tenant farmers** alike under the **sharecropper system**. The tenant farmer worked the plot of land and then paid a portion of his crop to the landowner as rent. He also usually owed the owner or a merchant some further portion for supplies and seed. As you might imagine, this system wasn't very profitable for the tenant farmer.

The weakening of the agricultural base in the South also opened the possibility for increased industrialization, which had already begun in the North.

Chapter 8 Drill

Turn to Part IV for answers and explanations.

1. The Emancipation Proclamation did not free slaves in states not currently in rebellion during the Civil War. Lincoln most likely drafted the proclamation in this manner in order to

   (A) protect war-time agricultural production in Border States
   (B) avoid a massive northward migration of emancipated Southern slaves
   (C) appease European nations that Lincoln hoped would not enter the war in support of the Confederacy
   (D) avoid secession of Union Border States
   (E) not give the appearance of bowing to the pressure applied by Northern abolitionists

2. Adoption of the Fourteenth Amendment to the Constitution in 1868

   (A) led to increased protections under the law for African Americans only
   (B) prohibited the practice of slavery in the United States
   (C) provided for a guarantee of due process under the law for all American citizens
   (D) established direct election of Senators
   (E) prohibited the federal or state governments from denying any citizen the right to vote based on that citizen's race, color or having previously been a slave

3. Lincoln's principal aim during the Civil War was to

   (A) end slavery, which he viewed as a morally reprehensible institution which could not be permitted to continue
   (B) enlist the direct aid of Great Britain and France in bringing the war to a conclusion
   (C) wage a war of attrition at the end of which a peace treaty could be signed with the Confederacy on terms which were favorable to the Union
   (D) minimize the number of lives lost in the conflict irrespective of the military outcome
   (E) preserve the Union by returning those states in rebellion to it at any cost

4. A historian interested in studying the economic impact of the Civil War on the South would most likely examine which of the following in order to find the most useful information?

   (A) The diary of a Southern plantation owner's wife who suffered through the war
   (B) Reports with data on Southern economic output during the 1850s, 1860s, and 1870s
   (C) Charts showing the population before and after the Civil War of the states that made up the Confederacy
   (D) Estimates of the economic damage that the war would cause to the Confederacy, made in 1861 by the United States War Department
   (E) Newspaper clipping from major Southern newspapers during Reconstruction

5. Andrew Johnson's plan for reconstruction was most strongly opposed in the Senate by

   (A) Liberal Republicans, who considered its treatment of the defeated former Confederate states too lenient
   (B) Southern Democrats, who preferred the prospect of Congressional Reconstruction
   (C) Radical Republicans, who felt Johnson's plan, like Lincoln's ten percent plan, was too lenient
   (D) Southern Democrats, who preferred that a majority of voters in states readmitted to the union first take a loyalty oath
   (E) Radical Republicans, who sought fewer voting right protections for African Americans, fearing that their votes could swing future elections in favor of Southern Democrats

6. Which of the following Civil War battles, considered by many historians to be the turning point in the war, represented Confederate armies' furthest advance northward into Union territory?

   (A) The Battle of Antietam
   (B) The Battle of Cold Harbor
   (C) The Battle of Fredericksburg
   (D) The Second Battle of Bull Run
   (E) The Battle of Gettysburg

7. All of the following methods were used to dissuade African Americans in the South from voting EXCEPT for which of the following?

    (A) poll taxes
    (B) literacy tests
    (C) grandfather clauses
    (D) physical intimidation
    (E) a stipulation that voters meet minimum income requirements

8. The end of slavery in the South brought with it many important economic changes, including

    (A) a sharp decline in the rate of industrialization in the South
    (B) the establishment of the sharecropping system
    (C) the resurgence of the plantation system
    (D) a significant increase in cotton production
    (E) significant profits for most tenant farmers

9. Sherman's March to the Sea was mainly intended by Union war planners to

    (A) break the will of the Confederacy by wreaking havoc in its heartland
    (B) capture and destroy the strategically important city of Atlanta, a hub of Confederate troop movement
    (C) secure Southern railroads to use for the transport of Union troops
    (D) destroy the port of Savannah to isolate the South, cutting it off from external supplies
    (E) outflank and, in combination with Grant's forces, encircle Lee's Army at Vicksburg

10. The passage of Black Codes by Southern state legislatures

    (A) led to Congress passing the Fourteenth and Fifteenth Amendments, conferring the right to citizenships an ensuring equal protection under the law for black citizens
    (B) resulted in Congress, with the support of President Johnson, passing the Civil Rights Act of 1867
    (C) were generally ineffective in limiting the voting rights of American Americans in the South
    (D) never resulted in those laws being implemented, because of the federal troops stationed in the South during reconstruction
    (E) also, unintentionally, limited the voting rights of many poor, non-landowning whites

Chapter 8 Summary

Here are the most important concepts to remember from Chapter 8:

o   Regional tensions over slavery and states' rights led to the Civil War, an event that radically changed American society and the role of the federal government in state affairs.

o   Although black people were liberated from slavery after the Civil War and granted citizenship, white politicians in certain parts of the South sought to restrict their rights to vote. In other areas of the South, black people experienced a smoother transition to freedom.

o   It took many years for the South to fully recover from the economic and social upheaval of the Civil War.

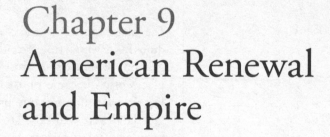

Chapter 9
American Renewal and Empire

ERA: INTO THE WEST

1850 to 1900

People on the Move

Following on the heels of the land purchases of the 1820s and 1840s, pre–Civil War westward expansion was fueled by the ideology of **Manifest Destiny**, which, as you read in the section on regional strife in Chapter 7, held that America had a God-given right to expand from the Atlantic Ocean to the Pacific, regardless of who was already living there (Native Americans included). A sequence of important events provided the impetus for the westward movement en masse that followed. First, the **Gold Rush of 1849** offered a strong economic incentive to get to "California or bust!" Second, the **Compromise of 1850** allowed California to enter the Union as a free state. Shortly after that, the **Homestead Act of 1862** offered cheap land to anyone willing to develop it, and the **Transcontinental Railroad**, built in the 1860s, cut the transit time across America from weeks to days.

The first industry of the West was **mining**, in which settlers tried to get rich quickly by extracting precious minerals (gold was only one of them) from the ground. **Boomtowns** arose wherever mineral deposits were found. But these places often became **ghost towns** when the mines were exhausted. **Cattle raising** and farming became profitable enterprises in the West. Large areas of flat grassland were well suited to both industries. Farmers and ranchers often violently competed for resources, but in the end farmers' homesteads dominated most of the western lands.

Of course, **Native Americans** continued to clash with land- and resource-hungry settlers. In the 1880s, the U.S. government held internally conflicting positions in dealing with the Native American tribes: the Department of the Interior supported some form of Native American independence through a reservation system, while the Department of War actively sought to rid the frontier of the "enemy." About this time, Helen Hunt Jackson wrote a humanitarian report, *A Century of Dishonor,* which exposed the flaws of the inadequate reservation system. This spurred a mild reform movement, which resulted in the **Dawes Act** (1887). The act offered land and citizenship to the heads of Indian families in order to "civilize" them (that is, induce them to adopt white ways), but it also resulted in a loss to Native Americans of millions of additional acres. Its net effect was to open more land for the settlers. **The Burke Act** (1906) tried to rectify the problems of the Dawes Act, but it, too, was relatively ineffective.

ERA: THE INDUSTRIAL REVOLUTION

1865 to the Early Twentieth Century

Following the Civil War, many factors contributed to the rapid rise of industrialization and manufacturing. Remember these important ones: **abundant natural resources**, a **large and available pool of labor** (ex-soldiers, freed slaves, immigrants, women, and children), **improved transportation** (railroads), and other **new technologies** (such as the telegraph).

Big Business

The term **big business** in the context of the SAT Subject Test in U.S. History refers to the large corporations that developed as part of the industrialization of the American economy. While the logic of capitalist thought concludes that free competition in the marketplace produces fair prices for consumers, corporations held a somewhat different interest, that of maximizing their profits (which often meant maintaining fixed, high prices) and minimizing competitive forces. In order to reduce competition with other large businesses, **captains of industry** colluded, setting prices across and within industries, thus forming a market **monopoly** and organizing into legal entities referred known as **trusts**.

As industrialization evolved, two prominent attitudes contributed to the popular support of big business. One was the economic theory of **laissez-faire**, which roughly means "let them do what they want." The idea is that government has no right to interfere with private enterprise and should follow a "hands-off" policy in dealing with businesses and their activities. But despite its official non-interference policy, the government gave businesses considerable economic support through **grants of land, loans**, and **high tariffs**. (A tariff is a surcharge that increases the price of an imported good, thus allowing American producers of a competing good to keep their prices higher than they would if the prices on imports were set at the lower, market rate.)

The second idea that supported business's popular stature was the theory of **social Darwinism**. Like Darwin's theory of biological evolution, this social ideology maintained that life was a struggle in which only the fittest would and should survive. Wealthy businessmen were seen as the embodiment of "the fittest." This rationale was used against social reform, because it maintained that those who lived in poverty deserved their plight (they were "unfit") and that reformers were countering the natural order.

This period of time, which roughly coincided with the final three decades of the nineteenth century, is referred to as the **Gilded Age**. While a very small class of businessmen lived extravagantly, their workers were paid low wages and their consumers were too often fleeced. Wealthy businesses were able to influence, if not buy votes outright, in Congress. The super-rich **robber barons**, so named because of their suspect business practices, included the likes of Rockefeller (oil), Stanford and Vanderbilt (railroads), and J. P. Morgan (banking). Some of the wealthy, like

Business 101
A *trust* is the collective control of an industry by a small group of separate corporations working together. A *monopoly* is the control of an entire industry by a single corporation. (Microsoft is one modern corporation that has dealt with accusations of operating a monopolistic enterprise.)

Andrew Carnegie, believed that they had a responsibility to give large donations to charity. This was known as the **Gospel of Wealth**.

Among the most significant of nineteenth-century industries, **railroads** were the primary long-distance mover of goods and people across the nation. Railroad magnates were more than willing to take advantage of this significance, but their opportunism came at a cost. Owners were often implicated in corruption and political manipulation and their industry was one of the first to be targeted by regulatory reforms.

ERA: INDUSTRIALISM AND POLITICS

1865 to 1900: The Industrial Revolution and Politics

Following the Civil War, with the assassination of Lincoln and the impeachment proceedings against Andrew Johnson, the nation experienced a serious leadership crisis. Many factors contributed to the political and social chaos, including factional disagreements among and within political parties, the movement and resettlement of thousands of people, and the rapid rise of big business and industrialization. Before we explore the major events, let's quickly review the presidents of this time and their actions.

Scandalous Presidents

Ulysses S. Grant led the Union Army to victory in the Civil War, but he was inexperienced as a politician and statesman. His tenure as president—riddled with scandal and corruption—reflected this. Among the worst scandals of the time were under Grant's watch: Black Friday, Credit Mobilier, Whiskey Ring, and Belknap Scandals.

Only four times (so far) has the popular vote in a presidential election failed to match the electoral outcome: in the Hayes-Tilden election of 1876, the Harrison-Cleveland election of 1888, the Bush-Gore election of 2000, and the Trump-Clinton election of 2016.

The election of 1876 produced the first major disputed result in a presidential election. Samuel J. Tilden won the popular vote, meaning that more people actually cast votes for him than his opponent, but he failed to receive a majority of votes in the Electoral College—illustrating a clear pitfall of the Electoral College system set forth by the Constitution. The situation was resolved with the Hayes-Tilden compromise, better known as the **Compromise of 1877**, in which **Rutherford B. Hayes** was made president, and Tilden supporters, many of whom were Southern Democrats, were promised the **removal of Federal troops from the South** in return. This withdrawal marked the end of Reconstruction, and without the protection of a military presence, the white majority in the South freely disenfranchised black citizens.

After Hayes's term in office, and following the abbreviated administration of James Garfield and then of Chester A. Arthur, neither of whom often appear on the SAT Subject Test in U.S. History, the first administration of Democrat **Grover Cleveland** marked a welcome end to many of the scandals that had plagued the era previously. Cleveland supported measures to improve the function of government, by minimizing the role of nepotism in hiring practices. During his re-election campaign, he argued strongly that protective tariffs, which artificially raised prices on imported goods to protect domestic producers, should be lowered to cut costs for consumers. Cleveland lost the next election in a close race to **Benjamin Harrison**.

The most interesting person in government during Harrison's tenure was **William McKinley**, a powerful, pro-business, Republican congressman. He sponsored the legislation that created the eponymous **McKinley Tariff**, which raised taxes on many goods by about 50 percent. Voters were outraged by the policy, and voted accordingly in the history-making election of 1892, in which Cleveland was re-elected to a non-consecutive second term over the Republican Harrison. Cleveland's second term would prove a rocky one. Harrison had dropped an economic depression in his lap, and the ensuing **Panic of 1893** lasted for most of Cleveland's second term.

McKinley and Imperialism

The election of 1896 was notable for several reasons; Cleveland was blamed for the Panic of 1893 and was not re-nominated by the Democrats. Instead, the farmers of the South and the West forged an alliance with the laborers of the East in support of a young, dynamic candidate, **William Jennings Bryan**. McKinley ran with strong Republican support despite the tariff fiasco. In the end, McKinley and the pro-business interests of the Republicans won the presidency. Under McKinley, the United States continued its **expansionist policies** and became more deeply involved in international affairs.

Panic Attack!
A panic is what economists call a "sudden loss of public confidence in the financial markets." (Sounds familiar, doesn't it?) Panics, fittingly, are marked by runs on banks and widespread fear of bank and business failures. Listed below are some of the most siginificant panics in U.S. history. Most of these panics were accompanied by high unemployment rates and bank closures, and they all resulted from major economic changes in American history.

Panic of 1819 Caused by heavy borrowing for the War of 1812; first major financial crisis in U.S. history

Panic of 1837 Caused by over-speculation (over-estimating the value of investments) and the failure of Andrew Jackson's economic policies; sparked a massive five-year depression

Panic of 1873 Caused by railroad bankruptcies and Ulysses Grant's "tight" monetary policies

Panic of 1893 Caused by more railroad bankruptcies and the collapse of the money system; the worst economic depression up to that point in U.S. history

Panic of 1907 Caused by a run on the failing Knickerbocker Trust Company. One of the results was the creation of the Federal Reserve System ("the Fed").

Panic of 1929 Caused by, among other things, rampant unchecked speculation by investors and corporations. Beginning of the Great Depression.

Black Monday (1987) A brief worldwide stock market crash caused by changes in interest rates, inflation, and oil prices. Although Black Monday remains the largest one-day percentage decline in the Dow Jones Industrial Average, it did not result in long-term damage to the United States economy.

The **Spanish-American War** of 1898 was a hallmark product of McKinley's expansionist policies. The war's genesis stemmed from a Cuban insurrection against Spain. At first, most Americans wanted to stay out of the conflict (although they supported Cuban independence). But tabloid newspaper accounts of the war, known as **yellow journalism**, blatantly falsified stories and photographs of Spanish "atrocities" in Cuba. Such reporting helped turn popular opinion toward intervention. The press's manipulation of public opinion reached a zenith with the sinking of the *U.S.S. Maine*, a U.S. battleship, anchored in Havana Harbor. An explosion onboard left 260 Americans dead, but the cause or responsible agent was never definitely determined. Despite a distinct lack of evidence implicating Spain, the press "tried and convicted" Spain of bombing the Maine.

McKinley issued a warning and strict conditions to Spain soon after the event. Spain accepted McKinley's terms but Congress had already moved to mobilize for war, and thus, war began. The war itself was relatively brief. The United States was well-armed and won the war with comparatively few casualties. The modern American Navy, led by Commodore Dewey, and the **Rough Riders**, a cavalry unit, led by **Theodore Roosevelt** in the **Battle of San Juan Hill**, distinguished themselves. In the end, Spain surrendered all claims to Cuba, which emerged as an independent nation, and the United States acquired Puerto Rico, Guam, and the Philippines.

Two other events concerning this period may be tested, both concerning our **trade relationship with China**. At this time, foreign powers (Germany, Japan, Great Britain, France, and Italy) sought to maintain **spheres of influence** in China, or geographical areas over which they had special influence. To crack Europe's monopoly, John Hay, the U.S. secretary of state, orchestrated the **Open Door Policy**, which established the joint right of these nations to trade with and within China. This arrangement was threatened by the **Boxer Rebellion** of 1899–1901. The Boxers were a Chinese nationalist group that wanted to expel all foreigners from China. Led by the United States, an armed force of several European nations suppressed the Boxer uprising, restored the rule of the Qing dynasty, and ensured that China would be open to American and European trade. Hay was influential in restoring "order" in China and in derailing the designs of some foreign powers on partitioning the country into colonies in accordance with existing European spheres of influences.

1895 to 1920: Forces for Change

After decades of political scandals, big-business corruption, and a period of imperialistic leanings in the United States' foreign policy, many Americans felt dissatisfied with the economic, social, and political conditions of the day, and decided to make changes. The reform movements of the early twentieth century came to be known as the **Progressive Era**. Presidents **Theodore Roosevelt, William Howard Taft**, and **Woodrow Wilson** were powerful agents in directing the reform movement, but social factors also greatly influenced this time period. Reformers advocated for the rights of workers, women, and African Americans and protested against trusts and large businesses that pursued profits at the expense of worker and consumer well-being.

Literary Muckrakers

A group of writers called **muckrakers** dedicated themselves to exposing political and corporate corruption, and focusing attention on social ills such as poverty. By championing the cause of the disaffected and shining light on the questionable practices of business behemoths, these writers garnered support for reform platforms. Muckraking magazines like *McClure's* attracted many young, unknown authors, who were able to gain notoriety through their scandalous stories. Among those important muckraking authors were **Ida M. Tarbell**, whose 1904 *History of the Standard Oil Company* condemned the monopolistic tactics of that corporation. The book helped lead to Standard Oil's breakup by the **Supreme Court**, after a landmark ruling that it had violated the terms of the **Sherman Antitrust Act**. Another pioneering author was **Upton Sinclair**, whose 1906 novel, *The Jungle*, which exposed unsafe conditions in Chicago's meatpacking plants, spurred Congressional action leading to the passage of federal legislation involving food and consumer safety. **Jacob Riis** was a journalist and a photographer who attempted to alleviate urban poverty by exposing the condition of slums to the middle and upper classes. His book, *How the Other Half Lives*, helped lead to improvements in urban neighborhoods ranging from indoor plumbing to expanded public education.

Regulation and Antitrust Legislation

By the 1880s, voters—suffering under an unbridled laissez-faire policy—began to call on the government for help. Small producers complained that big businesses were pushing them out of the market; farmers complained about increased transportation prices; and consumers demanded protection from high prices and the restoration of free, or at least non-monopolistic, trade. Antitrust laws were passed at first by state legislatures, and later by the federal government. But political corruption often made it very difficult to enforce any of these new legislative restrictions on business interests.

To regulate the railroads, some states set **maximum rate laws**, establishing the highest price a railroad could charge. The courts initially declared those laws unconstitutional. About a decade later, in response to an increasingly loud public outcry, the federal government passed its first legislation to regulate the actions of business, the **Interstate Commerce Act of 1887**, which forbade railroads from forming monopolistic price agreements and outlawed some of their discriminatory pricing practices. This act proved hard to enforce.

> ### Supply and Demand
> The concept of supply and demand is one of the most fundamental tenets of economics. Basically, the price of a good is determined by the *supply* of the good (how much there is of it) and the *demand* in the market for that good. The higher the price, the higher the quantity supplied, because obviously a producer wants to sell a lot of high-priced items. But if the price gets *too* high, demand for the item will fall. The market aims for equilibrium: the price at which there is exactly enough supply of an item to meet consumers' demand for it.

The **Sherman Antitrust Act** (1890), the most commonly tested piece of antitrust regulation with which you should be familiar for the SAT Subject Test in U.S. History, made it illegal for any business to restrain trade by formation of a trust or by conspiracy. But, for nearly a decade of the law's existence, the government did not, or could not (the act was vaguely worded), aggressively enforce its provisions. None of the U.S. presidents of the time were willing to strongly oppose business interests. Ironically, the Sherman Antitrust Act was sometimes used instead to disrupt unions.

Labor

As previously mentioned, the Industrial Revolution could never have taken place without the large supply of labor available to business for a relatively low price. The term **organized labor** refers to the groups or unions that tried to represent the collective interests of workers as they bargained for higher wages and better working conditions. As business and industry grew, so too did these **labor unions**. Some influential unions were the **Knights of Labor**, the **American Federation of Labor** (AFL), led by Samuel Gompers, and the **Industrial Workers of the World** (IWW), referred to as "Wobblies," a militant anti-capitalist group. Often the conflicts between labor and management resulted in **strikes** and **boycotts**, as disaffected workers walked off the job. Most people sympathized with the individual grievances of workers but were scared by the sometimes violent outcomes of organized labor's strikes and protests.

The **Haymarket Square Riot** (1886) in Chicago is one historic protest that ended in violence. At a mass meeting organized to protest police treatment of striking workers (officers had killed two striking workers the day before), someone threw a bomb, killing several police officers and injuring many more. The police charged the crowd, killing many protesters. In the end, labor leaders were blamed, and some who weren't even there were convicted of inciting the riot. Public sympathy for the plight of workers suffered and skepticism toward union groups grew. Public dislike for immigrants, who made up a notable percentage of the membership of unions, didn't help matters, a fact used by the police to whip up anti-union sentiment.

It was not until the twentieth century that labor reformers began to utilize state legislatures and the court system to create more lasting changes in labor. Middle-class and working-class people formed **coalitions** to protect public health and safety, and by 1916 almost two-thirds of the states had enacted laws requiring compensation for victims of accidents at work (also known as **Workmen's Compensation**). The **National Child Labor Committee** pushed states to set minimum ages for employment (ranging from 12 to 16) and proposed laws that prohibited children from working more than 8 or 10 hours per day. Many states also enacted hourly limits for women.

Prohibition

As Progressive reformers strove to improve the work lives of the middle and lower classes, they also began to push for improvement in the personal lives of these people. Followers of the **Temperance Movement** criticized excessive drinking and felt that alcohol was responsible for many of society's ills, including, poverty, disease, abuse, and decreased worker productivity. Groups like the **Anti-Saloon League** allied themselves with the **Women's Christian Temperance Union**, and shifted attention from individual responsibility to the responsibility of the government to regulate alcohol sale and consumption. **Prohibitionists** felt that the Temperance movement did not go far enough toward ridding society of alcohol's evils, and wanted the federal government to completely ban alcohol. The Prohibition movement was supported by many women, religious leaders, prominent political leaders such as President Taft, and more radical members like **Carrie Nation**, who often vandalized saloons with a hatchet. The Prohibitionists' efforts came to fruition when the **Eighteenth Amendment** went into effect in 1920. This amendment outlawed the manufacture, sale, and transportation of "intoxicating liquors." While the amendment was later repealed due to its role in the rise of **organized crime** and lack of success in eliminating the use of alcohol, it did reflect the Progressive goal of protecting the family and the workplace through legislation.

Women

After the Civil War, the Industrial Revolution, and rise of organized labor, women began to feel that it was now time for their needs to be heard. In order to do this, women lobbied for **suffrage**, or the right to vote. **Elizabeth Cady Stanton, Susan B. Anthony**, and **Carrie Chapman Catt**, who led the **National American Woman Suffrage Association**, all felt that the right to vote was essential in order for women to pursue political and economic equality with men. Supporters of suffrage felt that women deserved the right to vote on issues that would affect them both in the home and the workplace, while others argued that enfranchising women would have a humanizing effect on the political world. Women sought suffrage through letter writing campaigns, marches, and public demonstrations; however, the passage of the **Nineteenth Amendment** in 1920, which granted the right to vote to women, probably had more to do with their contributions during **World War I** than anything else. By working in factories, as medical volunteers, and caring for families while men were away at war, women showed that they could handle public responsibilities and therefore deserved the right to be involved in public affairs.

In addition to suffrage, women at the turn of the twentieth century in America advocated for reform in the field of medicine, specifically in reproductive health. **Margaret Sanger**, a trained nurse and founder of the **American Birth Control League**, later the **Planned Parenthood Federation of America**, believed that women should have the right to determine when to have a child. Sanger helped reverse state and federal laws that had prohibited the publication and distribution of information about sexual reproduction and contraception.

The Slow March of Progress
Although a constitutional amendment extending voting rights to women was sent to Congress in the 1880s, the Nineteenth Amendment wasn't ratified until 1920.

Women and the Vote
Suffrage   The right to vote in public elections

Elizabeth Cady Stanton (1815–1902)   As an early feminist, Stanton sought to stand up for the rights of all disenfranchised people. She therefore was very influential in the temperance and abolitionist movements.

Susan B. Anthony (1820–1906)   A highly influential early feminist (and friend of Elizabeth Cady Stanton), who advocated suffrage and temperance.

Seneca Falls Convention (1848)   A meeting organized in support of women's rights by Elizabeth Cady Stanton and Lucretia Mott. The convention produced *The Declaration of Sentiments*, a document asserting women's suffrage and other rights.

Nineteenth Amendment (1920)   A landmark victory for suffragists, the Nineteenth Amendment promised all women in the United States the right to vote.

Early Civil Rights Movement

Although the **Thirteenth, Fourteenth**, and **Fifteenth Amendments** abolished slavery, extended citizenship to former slaves, and gave African American men the right to vote, respectively, the second half of the nineteenth century was far from idyllic for African Americans. As **Reconstruction** came to an end, many parts of the United States, especially the south, returned to governing systems based on white supremacy. **Racial segregation** (division on the basis of race) was legalized under **Jim Crow Laws**, which restricted African Americans to the rear of streetcars and buses, to separate public drinking fountains and toilets, to separate schools and hospitals, and even to separate cemeteries. The Supreme Court upheld these laws in the famous case *Plessy v. Ferguson*. In its decision, the Supreme Court held that laws requiring **"separate but equal"** facilities were constitutional.

Despite the lack of support from the Supreme Court, many strong African American leaders emerged during the Progressive Era. The **National Association for the Advancement of Colored People (NAACP)** and the **National Urban League** were multiracial groups founded to combat racial discrimination and pursue political, educational, social, and economic equality for all people. While most African Americans were in favor of racial equality, they were split as to how this could best be achieved. **Booker T. Washington**, an educator who founded the **Tuskegee Institute**, an all-black vocational school, advocated that rather than fight for political rights, African Americans should strive for economic equality through job training and hard work. Washington presented these views at the **Atlanta Exposition** in 1895 in a speech known as the **Atlanta Compromise**. Whites welcomed Washington's views as they advised African Americans to work quietly rather than to agitate openly for equality. In sharp contrast to Booker T. Washington, **W. E. B. Du Bois**, who helped found the NAACP, argued that African Americans should aggressively pursue political, social, and economic rights. Du Bois believed that a **"Talented Tenth"** of the African American population should assume roles of academic and community leadership, advancing the race through intellect and skill. **Marcus Garvey**, a Jamaican immigrant and founder of the **UNIA (Universal Negro Improvement Association)**, believed that blacks should separate from corrupt white society. Garvey promoted black owned businesses and founded the **Black Star** Line to help blacks emigrate to Africa through his **"Back to Africa"** movement. Although he was the most extreme of the three African American leaders, Garvey still attracted a large following among African Americans.

Immigrants

Between 1900 and 1915, America experienced its largest ever influx of immigrants. More than 15 million people, mostly from southern and eastern Europe, moved to the United States. This number was almost equal to the number of immigrants who had come to the United States in the previous 40 years. These people came for many reasons including political unrest in their home countries, the search for religious freedom, or economic opportunity and a chance at the **"American Dream."** These new immigrants settled mostly in cities and dramatically changed the social, cultural, and economic landscape of the areas in which they lived. Many of these new citizens came from non-English-speaking countries and struggled to **assimilate** to American culture. The United States also had difficulty absorbing these new immigrants. Cities became over crowded as growing numbers of job-seekers moved in, looking for work in factories and other industries. City services were often unable to keep up with the demands of a growing population; reformers from the middle and upper class hoped to help improve the situation. One such reformer, **Jane Addams**, was part of the **Settlement House** movement, which created houses in poor urban areas where middle and upper class volunteers would live and provide services to the local community such as daycare, education, healthcare, and food.

Roosevelt and the Square Deal

President **Theodore Roosevelt**, also known as Teddy, campaigned on his signature **Square Deal** platform. The Square Deal emphasized equal treatment for all Americans, a notion that Roosevelt championed. Roosevelt, an active outdoorsman and celebrated veteran of the Spanish-American war, harbored a deep suspicion of big business and rarely missed an opportunity to proclaim his particular brand of populism. His reputation as **"The Trustbuster"** stemmed from his invoking of the **Sherman Antitrust Act** and the **Interstate Commerce Act** to pursue many of the most prominent trusts of the time. Roosevelt instructed the Justice Department to use antitrust laws to prosecute trusts that were harmful to the consumer; this instruction resulted in the **Northern Securities Case**, which broke up the railroad monopoly controlled by J. P. Morgan. Teddy Roosevelt was also an environmentalist. He was instrumental in the establishment of the **National Park** system and he advocated for federal management of natural resources through the **National Conservation Commission**. Upton Sinclair's muckraker writing, and Roosevelt's memories of the Spanish-American War (in which he described the canned meat costing more lives than Spanish bullets), led to wide support for the **Meat Inspection Act** and the **Pure Food and Drug Act**, both of 1906. The Meat Inspection Act required that government agents monitor the quality of processed meat, and resulted in increased confidence in American food products among American and foreign consumers. The Pure Food and Drug Act prohibited dangerously altered foods and required that labels list the ingredients in products in order to help consumers make educated decisions.

Taft—Moving to the Right

Roosevelt handpicked **William Howard Taft** as his chosen successor. While Taft was not as exciting or dynamic as Roosevelt, he did share Roosevelt's reforming spirit, especially in regard to railroad regulation. As president, Taft tried to bring together the liberal and conservative factions of the Republican Party; however, in practice, Taft often showed himself to be more conservative than liberal. Another crucial distinction between Taft and Roosevelt was Taft's lack of appetite for a legislative fight; absent much political courage, Taft often abandoned controversial elements of reform legislative. His compromise on key acts like the **Payne-Aldrich Tariff** disappointed Progressives. The high tariff of about 57 percent, in place since President McKinley, had been targeted for repeal or modification by Roosevelt, and later Taft. Progressives and conservatives in Congress fought bitterly over the reform bill and when it was passed, it included only a slight reduction of the tariff. Taft signed the bill, however, fearing that larger cuts would be impossible to get through Congress, and proving once again to an increasingly dissatisfied public that he was no Teddy Roosevelt. Taft was successful, though, in expanding national forest reserves, and supported labor reforms such as the eight-hour workday and mine safety legislation. Taft also championed the reform of governmental organization itself. Two important amendments were ratified during Taft's presidency. The **Sixteenth Amendment** allowed the government to collect income taxes. This was implemented alongside a graduated tax (sometimes called a progressive tax; higher tax rates for higher incomes), and made the American tax system fairer to the poor and middle classes. The **Seventeenth Amendment** allowed for the direct election of senators. Previously, Senators had been chosen by state legislatures. Taft also created the department of Labor and Commerce.

Aggressive Foreign Policy (Roosevelt and Taft)

At the turn of the twentieth century, the United States was a burgeoning world power. American foreign policy during the time was as tough as President Roosevelt's advice on diplomacy, "Speak softly, but carry a big stick." Roosevelt practiced his own advice, which has come to be known as **Big Stick Diplomacy**.

Following the success of the **Spanish-American War**, the United States began to broaden its territorial ambitions. With the acquisition of Guam and the Philippines and expanded trade with Asia, the United States. sought to provide its east coast with free access to the Pacific Ocean. The United States government encouraged an insurrection in part of Columbia, and then used its connections with the government of the new nation that emerged, Panama, to begin building a passage between the Atlantic and Pacific Oceans through the **Panama Canal**. Theodore Roosevelt, who visited the canal while it was being built, reinterpreted the **Monroe Doctrine** to justify such American intervention in the domestic and foreign affairs of the Caribbean and Latin America as part of his **Roosevelt Corollary**. The doctrine contributed to the evolution of the United States' involvement in the internal affairs of foreign nations, while also providing a frequent target for those critical of America's interventionist and imperialistic behavior. Roosevelt's foreign policy portfolio was not limited to the Americas. He also involved himself in matters concerning Europe and its colonies, and assisted in negotiations to end the Russo-Japanese War—work for which he was awarded the Nobel Peace Prize.

While Roosevelt's dominating presence served him well in diplomatic negotiations, Taft used economic incentives to influence decisions in Latin America and elsewhere. This technique, known as **Dollar Diplomacy**, used private funds to serve American diplomatic goals while simultaneously earning profits for American investors. Taft used this policy to increase trade with these regions, install leaders friendly to the United States, and maintain the balance of power among U.S. interests and the interests of other foreign nations there.

After Roosevelt returned from a year-long safari (hunting of course) in Africa, he found that Taft's policies had become increasingly more conservative. In response, Roosevelt chose to run as the head of his own, newly formed **Progressive** party,

Double Duty

William Howard Taft is the only former President to also serve on the Supreme Court of the United States. He was the tenth Chief Justice, from 1921 to 1930.

the **"Bull Moose"** Party. Unfortunately for Roosevelt (and Republicans) his bid for a third term in the White House did not meet with electoral success, as the Bull Moose ticket split the Republican vote and Woodrow Wilson, a Democrat, easily won the election.

Woodrow Wilson

Although Roosevelt and Taft considered themselves to be reformers, Wilson outdid them both. While the earlier presidents used the legislative and judicial systems to regulate trusts and big business, Wilson wanted to abolish trusts altogether, and wholly eliminate corruption and corrupting influences in business and politics. He also opposed protective tariffs, instead helping to pass the **Underwood Act**, which was the first tariff meant to generate revenue rather than shelter domestic producers from foreign competition. The effects of this bill, however, are hard to measure because **World War I** began soon after, greatly disrupting international trade.

In addition to the Underwood Act, Wilson's first term saw the passage of two other pieces of legislation to regulate business. First, The **Federal Trade Commission** was established to prevent businesses from misrepresenting their products (i.e. selling products like chicken pot pie with no chicken in it) and unfairly stifling competition. Second, the **Clayton Antitrust Act** was designed to fill gaps in the Sherman Antitrust Act and further empower courts to regulate monopolies. Although these measures did encourage economic fairness, business interests retained significant influence throughout Wilson's presidency.

Outside of regulating business, Wilson also supported the rights of labor, increased aid to farmers, and initiated banking reform. The **Federal Reserve Act**, Wilson's principal piece of banking reform legislation, created the nation's first central banking system since the **Bank of the United States'** charter lapsed in 1836. The establishment of a central bank expanded consumer and commercial credit and eased the transfer of funds throughout the country. It also made currency more elastic so that the money supply was better able to meet the borrowing needs of banks. Many banks had lent **speculatively** and few dollars remained to be lent in the face of resulting underperforming loans. The injection of additional credit by the Federal Reserve Board loosened the grip on credit and alleviated the credit squeeze from which the nation was suffering. Furthermore, the establishment of the central bank had longer term implications, as the nation's finances no longer depended on the gold supply and as interest rates became tied to the market's demand for credit.

Chapter 9 Drill

Turn to Part IV for answers and explanations.

1. All of the following were scandals during the Grant administration EXCEPT

   (A) Black Friday
   (B) Credit Mobilier
   (C) Teapot Dome
   (D) Whiskey Ring
   (E) Belknap Scandals

2. Maximum rate laws were part of a larger attempt to

   (A) place restrictions on potentially abusive business practices by railroads
   (B) provide federal subsidies to struggling railroads
   (C) break up railroad monopolies
   (D) undercut the newly enacted, but widely unpopular, Interstate Commerce Act of 1887
   (E) institute a laissez-faire approach to federal oversight of business

3. Which of the following agencies was established to ensure that businesses did not misrepresent their products to consumers?

   (A) Federal Communications Commission (FCC)
   (B) Federal Trade Commission (FTC)
   (C) Securities and Exchange Commission (SEC)
   (D) Tennessee Valley Authority (TVA)
   (E) National Recovery Administration (NRA)

4. Which of the following Congressional actions came about partly in response to the publication of Helen Hunt Jackson's report on the inadequacy of the reservation system in *A Century of Dishonor*?

   (A) Underwood Act
   (B) Interstate Commerce Act
   (C) Civil Rights Act of 1967
   (D) Dawes Act
   (E) Knox-Porter Resolution

5. The main effect of the Haymarket Square Riot in Chicago in 1886 was

   (A) the nonviolent resolution of the rioting laborers' grievances
   (B) that the police were widely regarded by the public as the aggressors in inciting violence during the riot
   (C) that union leaders were held in a generally higher regard after the incident, than before it
   (D) public perception of immigrants, who bore a disproportionately greater share of police violence, improved
   (E) that public sympathy for the labor movement was eroded

6. The faction of Republicans, led by Senator Roscoe Conkling of New York, that toward the end of the 19th century strongly supported the patronage system, were referred to by what name?

   (A) Stalwarts
   (B) Carpetbaggers
   (C) Half-Breeds
   (D) Mugwumps
   (E) Loyalists

9. The case brought by the Justice Department against Standard Oil Company of New Jersey which led to its break-up in 1911, was done so under what legislation?

   (A) Sherman Antitrust Act
   (B) Wagner Act
   (C) Fair Labor Standards Act
   (D) Clayton Antitrust Act
   (E) Dingley Act

10. By the end of the 19th century, most new immigrants to the United States settled in

   (A) cities, where an increasing number of manufacturing jobs offered work
   (B) cities, where government programs provided food and housing
   (C) suburban areas, where living conditions were more comfortable than in crowded urban areas
   (D) rural areas, where growing agricultural opportunities attracted many immigrants who were farmers in the countries from which they emigrated
   (E) rural areas, where labor unions encouraged new immigrants to settle in order to avoid new immigrants competing with union members for existing jobs

7. The political cartoon is a satirical depiction of what presidential candidate's vocal support for the use of silver currency?

   (A) William Jennings Bryan
   (B) William McKinley
   (C) William Howard Taft
   (D) Samuel Tilden
   (E) Grover Cleveland

8. All of the following contributed to the development of the Industrial Revolution in the United States EXCEPT

   (A) the invention of the steam engine
   (B) an influx of immigrants from Europe
   (C) the availability of natural resources
   (D) the introduction of interchangeable parts
   (E) a large pool of slave labor

Chapter 9 Summary

Here are the most important concepts to remember from Chapter 9:

o The Industrial Revolution changed not only industry, but also virtually every aspect of American daily life, ushering in urbanization and manufacturing, stimulating immigration and migration North.

o Large businesses stimulated economic growth and largely thrived on little to no governmental regulation.

o Work opportunities opened up for women and minorities—but also led to widespread child labor.

o Corruption in government and corporate abuses of power led to social reformers calling for change.

o America transitioned from a largely rural and agricultural society to an urban industrialized society.

Chapter 10
The World at War

Pop Quiz

Q: What was America's foreign policy at the onset of both World War I and World War II?

ERA: WORLD WAR I

1914 to 1920

For the SAT Subject Test in U.S. History, the events that led to the First World War and the peace plans that followed it are more important than what happened as the war itself was waged.

Most historians assign blame for the outbreak of war in Europe in 1914 on the tangled web of secret alliances entered into by European nations in the years preceding the war. Most all of the belligerents were drawn into the fight within a few months of hostilities commencing. Britain, France, and Russia led the **Allies**; Germany, Austria-Hungary, and the Ottoman Empire anchored the **Central Powers**. Wilson and many Americans desperately wanted to stay out of the war and maintain **U.S. neutrality**. Circumstances, however, made this increasingly difficult to do.

Although Wilson tried to mediate between the Allies and the Central Powers with calls of **"peace without victory,"** no one in Europe was willing to listen. American popular sentiment rested more with the Allies, a tendency further exaggerated by Germany's aggressive use of submarine warfare. Germany claimed that it was justified to fire upon any ship within the war zones surrounding Great Britain and Ireland, whereas the United States felt that under international law, neutral merchant ships should not be attacked. The 1915 **sinking of the *Lusitania***, a luxury passenger liner, was an example of German submarine tactics—it was sunk without a warning or search of the ship. The incident killed 1,198 people, 128 of them American, and turned public opinion sharply against Germany. A similar, though less severe incident, involving a French passenger ship, the *Sussex*, further worried those who hoped for continued American neutrality. When the United States issued an ultimatum to Germany, it responded with the Sussex pledge, in which Germany pledged to not sink commercial vessels absent appropriate warning or without attempting to save human lives. The German gesture allayed fears of immediate entry into the war in Europe, but concerns over America's preparedness for war, if necessary, reached new heights.

In the election of 1916, Wilson ran on the slogan "He kept us out of war," and won despite a deep national rift over whether or not the United States should enter the conflict.

In early 1917, Germany announced that it would resume its unrestricted campaign of submarine warfare in the Atlantic and, soon after, torpedoed five American merchant ships, killing all hands. Making matters worse, the **Zimmermann Telegram** (1917), an intercepted diplomatic message from Germany to Mexico, surfaced. The telegram suggested that if an alliance between the two countries were made, and if the United States entered the war, Germany would help Mexico "reconquer [its] lost territory in New Mexico, Texas, and Arizona." Wilson asked Congress to declare war on Germany shortly thereafter.

Despite outrage over the contents of the Zimmermann Telegram, Wilson did not want to portray America as an aggressor, and his war message to Congress was colored with moralizing rhetoric. He described the war as an effort to make the world "safe for democracy" and to forge "a peace founded upon honor and justice."

Peace Negotiations

Although Wilson had an outspoken advocate for the equitable treatment of defeated Central Powers, it was very hard for the victorious Allied Powers to hide the thinly veiled nationalism of their postwar objectives. Indeed, many of the Allied nations entered the war under the assumption that victory would entitle them to specific land gains. Wilson put forward a plan that he proclaimed as "the only possible program" for maintaining peace after the war. It was entitled the Fourteen Points Plan. Many of the points dealt with arms reduction, freedom of the seas, and other aspects of international relations. The fourteenth point was the most dramatic, calling for a "general association of nations"—a **League of Nations**—that would work to assure the political independence of all nations.

The **Fourteen Points** did not fare well at the negotiations in Paris. The Allies ignored Wilson's pleas against vengefulness, and the resulting **Treaty of Versailles**, which set the terms of the peace, levied harsh punishment on the Central Powers, especially Germany—from the Allied perspective, the greatest villain of the war. The treaty did establish a League of Nations, excluding the Central Powers and Communist Russia, and it was hoped by some that this body offset the more punitive terms of the treaty. After Wilson's diplomatic struggles in Paris, he came home to even more trouble— the U.S. Senate refused to ratify the treaty. Republicans in Congress, led by Senator **Henry Cabot Lodge** vehemently opposed the fundamental notion of a League of Nations. They feared that membership in the League would obligate the United States to enter another world war to, ironically, "defend the peace." Wilson refused to compromise or accept any of the Senate's proposed amendments aimed at allaying such fears. The Senate, in turn, refused to ratify the treaty. Wilson hoped to rally public support for his plan, but fell seriously ill during the process, dooming the treaty to its eventual defeat in the Senate, despite the fact that the Senate's proposed changes were eventually included in an amended treaty. Warren G. Harding, Wilson's successor as president, was opposed to U.S. involvement in the League of Nations as well. The United States never participated in the League, and its absence is frequently cited as one of the reasons for the League's failure. In 1921, Congress passed the **Knox-Porter Resolution**, bringing a separate,

Treaties in American History

Landmark treaties have defined the closure of American wars. Below are the treaties most likely to appear on the SAT Subject Test in U.S. History.

Treaty of Paris (1763) Ended the French and Indian War and marked the beginning of British dominance in North America

Treaty of Paris (1783) Ended the American Revolution by guaranteeing American independence

Treaty of Ghent (1814) Ended the War of 1812, essentially declaring it a stalemate

Treaty of Guadalupe-Hidalgo (1848) Ended the Mexican-American War; United States gained California, Utah, Nevada, and parts of other states

Treaty of Versailles (1919) Ended World War I and required that Germany pay extensive war reparations (fines) to certain Allies

Paris Peace Accords (1973) Ended U.S. participation in the Vietnam War; the United States declared neither victory nor defeat

formal end to hostilities between the United States and the Central Powers. The harsh terms of the Treaty of Versailles bred resentment in war-crippled Germany. This, coupled with the failure of the League of Nations and U.S. isolationism in the 1920s, is often considered to be one of the causes of Hitler's rise to power and, ultimately, World War II.

ERA: THE ROARING TWENTIES

1920 to 1929

Conservatives in Office

After the war and its aftermath, Warren G. Harding and Republican politicians called for a **"return to normalcy"** and won landslide victories in the process. By "normalcy," Harding's supporters meant peacetime life in the United States, as it was before the war. Unfortunately, this also included the continued, sometimes corrupt, influence of business interests, a rollback of many Progressive reforms, and an increasing American isolationism in foreign affairs.

Harding was happy to let the members of his cabinet and the Republican Congress hold the reins of government, a decision that left his administration marred by a series of scandals involving senior members of government. One of the most testable scandals of the Harding administration was the **Teapot Dome scandal**, which involved the Secretary of the Interior receiving bribes in exchange for extending oil-drilling rights on Navy petroleum reserves to oil companies without bidding. Harding died of a stroke in 1923, just as these and other allegations were coming to light.

Calvin Coolidge, Harding's Vice President and Republican successor, actively cooperated with investigations of government corruption, a decision that reflected his personal integrity and helped build his administration's reputation for transparency. His deft political skill at a time of general economic prosperity was a recipe for easy victory in the following presidential election. The Coolidge administration enjoyed a strong relationship with American industrial and commercial interests. When, in 1928, Coolidge chose not to run for reelection, the architect of that relationship, Herbert Hoover, his secretary of commerce, was nominated as his replacement on the Republican ticket. Again, the Republicans won easily. Hoover, an engineer by training, was seen as an efficient and skillful administrator who was expected to continue business-friendly policies and run the government like a well-oiled machine.

Roaring Restrictions

The 1920s were largely a reaction to the reform-minded spirit of the Progressive era and domestic sacrifices that accompanied World War I. Liberal reformism from the previous decade was dismissed as radical, and the ideals of Wilson and his peace plan were cast as invasions of personal freedom. Interests shifted toward personal gratification, and more Americans preferred to kick up their heels and have fun. Also, this was the decade of **Prohibition**, the outlawing of alcohol, which did nothing so much as to create a vast market in illegal liquor. At least among the urban middle and upper class, many people treated the government's moralism with irreverence and disdain, evident by the prevalence of bootlegging and speakeasies. The prevailing attitude was that businesses and private citizens alike should be able to do what they wished without government interference.

The loosened social strictures led to many new freedoms for women, who had recently gained the right to vote with the ratification of the **Nineteenth Amendment** to the Constitution. Black Americans soldiers returned from World War I to a country that had considered them worthy to wear a uniform and die on the battlefields of Europe but not deserving of equal participation and protections in American society. Nevertheless, some black Americans benefitted from the higher-paying jobs now available in the factories of the North, having migrated there from the South, seeking these higher paying jobs. Historians call this phenomenon the **First Great Migration**.

The postwar period was also an era of many new restrictions on immigration and political activism. With American isolation, also came an increasingly narrow definition of what was American and what was counter to that Americanism. The Russian Revolution occurred in 1917, and anti-labor and anticommunist activists in the United States often painted labor unions and other progressive groups as communist subversives, fanning the flames of an intense antiradical and anticommunist sentiment that took hold across the country. Even before the Russian Revolution, as early as the late 1890s, some politicians attempted to link anti–eastern European and anticommunist feelings to reinforce both prejudices and stigmatize labor unions, which were especially popular among urban eastern European immigrants. Remember two terms that exemplify this mania: the **Red Scare**, the paranoid panic that dangerous communists might be lurking in every shadowy corner, and the **Palmer Raids**, in which Attorney General A. Mitchell Palmer conducted raids—often violating the constitutional rights of those arrested—against suspected communists. The revitalized **Ku Klux Klan's** membership swelled during the 1920s and expanded outside of the South to the cities of the Northeast and Midwest in response to the growing opportunities for blacks as well as the xenophobia of the time, which directed hatred at Catholics, Jews, and foreigners, as well as blacks. During the 1920s, **Sacco and Vanzetti**, two Italian immigrants, were tried for and convicted of robbery and murder in Boston, Massachusetts. The trial is now widely regarded as critically biased against the Southern European immigrant pair because of their ethnicity and anarchist politics. Despite the attention that their potentially wrongful conviction drew, the two were eventually executed. That xenophobia also led to **nativist** fears of an impending human flood washing over the United States caused by destruction in Europe during the war. In response, Congress instituted immigration quotas, and then made them permanent with the passage of the **Immigration Act of 1924**, allowing only a small fraction of people to enter the United States, especially from central, southern, and Eastern Europe, as well as Jews. Most immigration from the Asia-Pacific region was prohibited altogether. These quotas remained intact until the 1960s, and would have a tragic effect on those trying to escape persecution in Europe in the mid-1930s during the rise of increasingly oppressive regimes there.

Another famous example of the cultural clashes of the 1920s is the John T. Scopes trial, or the **Scopes Monkey Trial**. The case revolved around the issue of teaching Darwin's theory of evolution in public schools. It tested the divide between fundamentalist Christian beliefs and current scientific theories. William Jennings Bryan, the former Populist presidential candidate, argued the fundamentalist case, while **Clarence Darrow** defended Scopes, the teacher who was arrested for teaching evolution in his Tennessee high school science class. Despite Darrow's energetic defense, Scopes lost the case; the judge had excluded all defense evidence, making the jury's decision to convict an easy one. The case was eventually overturned on appeal, but the Scopes Trial eventually succeeded in changing public opinion regarding the merits of teaching evolution in public schools.

ERA: THE GREAT DEPRESSION AND THE NEW DEAL

The 1930s to World War II

The Crash

The decade from 1919 to 1929 was one of stunning growth and continued prosperity. The three Republican administrations, led by Andrew Mellon in the Treasury Department, pursued business-friendly policies, providing businesses tax breaks and supporting high protective tariffs. Businesses boomed, consumer and corporate debt ballooned, and a great number of speculative investments were common. All seemed well until **Black Tuesday**, October 29, 1929, when the stock market crashed and about $30 billion worth of equity value evaporated. Thus began the period known as the **Great Depression**. Its immediate results were widespread unemployment, numerous business failures, and a drastic drop in the **gross national product (GNP)** and in the personal income of almost every American. Hoover genuinely believed that market mechanisms and individual initiative (entrepreneurship) would pull the nation from its financial death spiral, and failed to take measures to intervene in the economy.

After several years of economic misery, Hoover could no longer resist calls for action and did pass a bill to establish the **Reconstruction Finance Corporation (RFC)**, which was designed to lend government money to banks and other private business enterprises. Later that year, the **Relief and Construction Act** was passed to provide communities emergency relief and to actually fund the RFC. These actions were too little, too late, however. **Hoovervilles**, shantytowns in which thousands of homeless squatted, became a stark symbol of the Hoover administration's failures to stem the deepening Great Depression.

To be fair to Hoover, the market crash was an event unlike any other in the nation's history up until that point and economists were divided regarding the best course of action, and many agreed with Hoover's incorrect belief that "prosperity [was] right around the corner."

Franklin D. Roosevelt and the New Deal

If prosperity contributed to the carefree, laissez-faire attitude of the 1920s, the Great Depression, by contrast, caused many people to rethink government's purpose. They were quite ready for the government to take some responsibility for the economic well-being of the nation and its people. This dramatic shift in public opinion was punctuated by the election of 1932, as the new Democratic **President Franklin D. Roosevelt** (FDR) ushered in an unprecedented era of reform as part of his **New Deal** program. (He easily won reelection to a second term, so you can think of 1932 to 1940 as all one era under the New Deal.)

Relief, Recovery, Reform

The three R's: relief, recovery, reform. That's the key to thinking about the New Deal.

During his first **Hundred Days** in office, a time frame he set for himself, FDR promised quick work to improve the state of the nation. He wanted to provide relief in the form of money, jobs, or loans to all Americans; he hoped to spur recovery by passing legislation to assist business and agriculture; and he wanted to reform banks and other economic institutions to make them more stable. While these programs were not an unmitigated success, it is certain that FDR projected a reassuringly strong sense of leadership and instilled in the country a new confidence. His oratorical skills and charisma may have helped the country as much as any of his specific programs, as Americans took heed of the famous words that he spoke at his inauguration: "The only thing we have to fear is fear itself."

The New Deal marked the first time that the government seriously introduced elements of a modified **planned economy**, a system in which the government helps to influence economic developments, rather than leaving the market system to operate freely. Many of FDR's policies were undergirded by the work of economist **John Maynard Keynes**. Keynes argued that the nation could "spend its way back to prosperity," with the government doing the spending, in contrast to the laissez-faire economics that had proven so destructive during the Depression. Needless to say, Keynesian policies weren't terribly popular with economic conservatives, who opposed government interference in the economy.

During the 1930s and 1940s, FDR established a litany of economic programs; some failed while others succeeded. A few important ones are contained in the following chart, but rather than commit the entire alphabet soup of New Deal programs and their acronyms to memory, you just need to remember that any legislation during this period dealt with trying to end the Depression and provide assistance to affected Americans.

Program		Function
CCC	Civilian Conservation Corps	Provided work for unemployed young men
NIRA/ NRA	National Industrial Recovery Act (National Recovery Administration)	Established rules for fair competition; the idea was to keep prices down and employment up
WPA PWA	Works Project Administration Public Works Administration	Both programs gave people jobs; some went to writers and artists, some for building roads and hospitals
AAA	Agricultural Adjustment Act	Paid farmers to reduce their production, hoping this would bring higher prices for farm goods
TVA	Tennessee Valley Authority	A government-owned business that helped produce and distribute electrical power services to a large number of people

FDR's banking reforms included the creation of the **Federal Deposit Insurance Corporation (FDIC)** to insure personal bank deposits and the **Securities and Exchange Commission (SEC)** to regulate the trading of stocks and bonds. The administration also passed the first laws guaranteeing minimum wage, unemployment insurance, and creating **Social Security** to provide payments and economic security to the elderly.

ERA: WORLD WAR II

1939 to 1945

The political situation in Europe began to worsen beginning in the mid-1930s. Adolf Hitler had risen to power in Nazi Germany, Italy was under the fascist rule of Benito Mussolini, and the Allied Powers and the United States watched nervously. No one, with the possible exception of Hitler, was anxious to repeat the carnage of World War I, so negotiating and compromise took place even in the face of ongoing German and Italian aggression (two-thirds of what would later comprise the Axis powers of World War II) that trampled one small European nation after another beneath the boots of their invading armies. However, despite the best efforts of European diplomats and leaders, the policy of **appeasement** failed. Germany violated the terms of the Munich Conference of 1938 by invading Poland in 1939. This prompted Great Britain and France to finally abandon diplomatic efforts and to declare war on Germany. Although the United States provided financial and material support to the Allies, it at first remained officially neutral.

During the war, Hitler also carried out a policy of genocide (which the Nazis referred to as the **"Final Solution"**) intended to eliminate Jews and other supposed enemies of the Third Reich. Referred to collectively as the **Holocaust**, the monstrous result was the murder of millions of Jews and many others, including Gypsies and homosexuals.

Neutrality, at First

A philosophy of isolationism continued to hold sway in the United States during the run up to World War II. In hopes of avoiding the problems that had led to the country's entry into World War I, Congress passed a series of measures, beginning with the first **Neutrality Acts** (1935–1937). The acts forbade selling weapons or giving loans to the warring nations and prohibited U.S. citizens from traveling on the ships of said countries. Later, in 1939, the act was revised to allow weapon sales on a **"cash and carry"** basis to belligerent nations, meaning that friendly nations could come to the United States and buy supplies, so long as they shipped the weapons themselves, thereby avoiding placing American merchant ships at risk of being sunk. Public opinion, it should be noted, turned progressively toward the Allied cause, but continued to stop short of a desire to commit American troops to the fighting. **The Lend-Lease Act of 1941** expanded the power of the president to lend, lease, sell, exchange, or otherwise do what he saw fit in order to provide arms and supplies to nations that served the United States' best interests, namely the Allies. This action was taken largely at the behest of Roosevelt, who especially hoped to help the beleaguered British weather the continued onslaught by German forces in the **Battle of Britain** and forestall German invasion of the country.

Near this time, in 1940, Roosevelt ran for an unprecedented third term, making the case to voters that it would be dangerous to switch leaders during a worldwide conflict of such monumental scale. He won, but not by the landslide margins that he had previously enjoyed.

In 1941, Roosevelt met with **Winston Churchill**, the British Prime Minister, to discuss the Allied war aims. He also gave armed U.S. merchant ships approval to fire upon German submarines on sight—hardly typical of a nation at peace. Isolationists in the United States were outraged, but the debate soon became moot.

During the late 1930s, Japan began to aggressively attack on its territorial goals in the Pacific, invading China. After joining the Axis Powers in 1940, its aggression worsened. On December 7, 1941, the "date which will live in infamy" as FDR noted before Congress, the armed forces of the Japanese launched a surprise attack on **Pearl Harbor**, Hawaii. The shocked nation ended its long period of isolation and declared war on Imperial Japan. A few days later, Germany and Italy declared war on the United States, and the United States reciprocated in kind. The United States had fully committed itself to the Second World War.

"Yesterday, December 7, 1941—a date which will live in infamy—the United States of America was suddenly and deliberately attacked by naval and air forces of the Empire of Japan."
—President Franklin Delano Roosevelt, 1941

The Home Front

The United States had been preparing to some extent for the possibility of war throughout the late 1930s and into the early 1940s, but the mobilization of forces, including weapons, soldiers, and other war materials, after Japan attacked Pearl Harbor was on a scale never before seen in modern warfare. The sheer magnitude of the American war machine's output proved to be the ultimate key to Allied success. Once the U.S. government declared war, the war effort came to include almost every American. The country's entire economic and social structure adapted to the task of producing what was required for victory. A few test-worthy events: **rationing** and price-fixing were accepted for consumption of meat, sugar, gasoline, and other staples; women went to work at war factories by the thousands (**"Rosie the Riveter"** became a popular cultural icon), doing jobs that had previously been considered the domain of men exclusively; and the sale of war bonds and a large-scale revision of tax laws were instituted to finance the war. In the midst of the war came the election of 1944, when Roosevelt was elected to a record fourth and final term. Harry S. Truman became his vice president. A few months later, Roosevelt died in office, and Truman assumed office, where he saw the war to and through its conclusion.

War Ends, Peace Talks Begin

As with the other wars on the SAT Subject Test in U.S. History, it isn't necessary to remember the different battles that were fought, but you should know how the war ended and the outcome of peace negotiations.

The war in Europe ended in May 1945, as **Allied troops entered Berlin** from both sides, the United States and Great Britain from the west and the Soviet Union from the east. Upon realizing his imminent defeat, Hitler is believed to have committed suicide along with his wife in a bunker underneath Berlin. Following Germany's defeat, the United States shifted its focus solely to the defeat of Japan in the Pacific. After issuing an ultimatum calling for Japan's unconditional surrender (an offer which was refused), the United States dropped an **atomic bomb** on **Hiroshima**, and then dropped another bomb, three days later, on **Nagasaki**. Following the enormous devastation wrought in Hiroshima and Nagasaki, the Japanese government, upon the direction of the **Emperor Hirohito**, accepted Allied terms of surrender.

Well before the war was over, the Allied Powers set about forging an agreement concerning the soon-to-be defeated powers of Germany and Japan. The three main issues to be settled were **occupation**, the **prosecution of war criminals**, and the negotiation of **peace treaties**. Still, the consultations between the Allied Powers dragged on for several years, complicated by the tensions between the Western Allies and the Communist Soviet Union. This tension was shown most dramatically as the occupation of Germany was negotiated. A **divided East and West Germany** emerged from the talks, with the Federal Republic of Germany as the Western-influenced sphere and the German Democratic Republic as part of the Eastern bloc. The **Nuremberg Tribunal** was held to prosecute Nazis—high-and low-level alike—for their war crimes, which included international aggressions and their systematic attempts to exterminate the Jewish people. In Japan, General Douglas MacArthur ruled the occupied nation and its territories until a U.S.–Japan peace treaty was signed in the early 1950s, bringing the arrangement to a close. On a more positive note, through these many postwar conferences and negotiations, the United Nations was established in 1946 with representatives from 51 countries in attendance.

Chapter 10 Drill

Turn to Part IV for answers and explanations.

1. Most historians regard the Washington Naval Conference of 1921 as consistent with which aspect of American foreign policy during the period?

   (A) An unwillingness to engage in international diplomacy
   (B) A policy of containing Japanese expansion in the Pacific, by force, if necessary
   (C) A desire to avoid involvement in foreign wars
   (D) A reluctance to participate in arms reduction agreements
   (E) Directly challenging British naval supremacy in the Atlantic

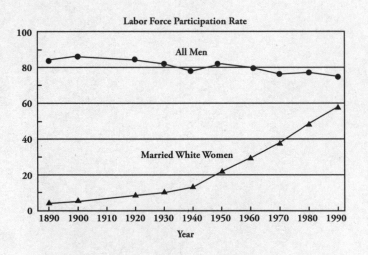

Labor Force Participation Rate

2. The doubling of the number of married white women employed outside the home between 1940 and 1950, as shown in the graph, is most likely a result of which of the following?

   (A) The unavailability of male labor due to World War II
   (B) An increase in male unemployment as a result of the Great Depression
   (C) New legislation banning discrimination on the basis of sex in hiring practices
   (D) A growing awareness on the part of employers regarding the value of women in the workplace
   (E) An increase in the number of skilled female workers in the workforce

3. The theories of economist John Maynard Keynes theories are reflected in which of the following economic policy actions undertaken by Franklin Roosevelt during the Great Depression?

   (A) A general tightening of the money supply to correct for the overextension of credit by lenders during the 1920s
   (B) Elimination of farm subsidies to help trim deficit spending and balance the federal budget
   (C) Allowing certain large public banks that were unsound and a risk to the economy to fail
   (D) Establishing a national program of medical insurance for the poor and elderly in order to ensure their access
   (E) Increasing federal spending on public works and other stimulatory programs

4. The foreign policies of Warren G. Harding, Calvin Coolidge, and Herbert Hoover may be best characterized by

   (A) imperialism
   (B) interventionism
   (C) isolationism
   (D) engagement
   (E) internationalism

5. The Atlantic Charter was an agreement between which two powers?

   (A) The United States and France
   (B) The United States and Canada
   (C) Great Britain and Canada
   (D) Great Britain and France
   (E) Great Britain and the United States

6. Which of the following German actions during World War I most influenced the United States' entry into the war on the side of the allies?

   (A) The unrestricted use of submarine warfare
   (B) The German invasion of the Soviet Union
   (C) The use of chemical weapons against British and French forces
   (D) An intercepted diplomatic message proposing the return of formerly Canadian lands annexed by the United States to Canada in exchange for Canadian support
   (E) The significant number of civilian deaths attributed to German offensives

7. Both congressional opposition to American participation in the League of Nations and Washington's Farewell Address shared what similarity in their outlook on foreign affairs?

(A) That the United States should expand its territorial holdings, providing new markets for American goods and a buffer against foreign invasion of the Continental United States

(B) That the United States should build a strong system of international military alliances in order to provide mutual protection against attack

(C) That all settlements of foreign wars must include provisions for punishing defeated aggressors, as a deterrent against future attacks of aggression

(D) That permanent alliances are potentially dangerous, and the United States should avoid them or risk being drawn into foreign conflicts

(E) That the United States should play a central role in foreign affairs, leading by example and promoting democratic principles internationally

8. "He kept us out of war" was the slogan of which successful presidential re-election campaign?

(A) James Buchannan
(B) Ulysses S. Grant
(C) William McKinley
(D) Woodrow Wilson
(E) John F. Kennedy

9. All of the following are generally considered causes for the Great Depression EXCEPT for

(A) the sharp decline in international trade after 1930
(B) the expansion of the money supply by the Federal Reserve
(C) an increase in speculative lending
(D) runs on banks and those banks' subsequent failure
(E) the significant cost of World War I

10. The "Red Scare" following World War I and the Russian Revolution was the most immediate cause of which of the following?

(A) Laws restricting immigration
(B) The revelation that Attorney General A. Mitchell Palmer had been in secret communication with Communist sympathizers
(C) The public Congressional hearings of Senator Joseph McCarthy
(D) The concern that without American intervention, post–World War I Europe was vulnerable to communist revolution
(E) The significant number of legitimate arrests and successful prosecutions of communist revolutionaries that resulted from the Palmer Raids

Chapter 10 Summary

Here are the most important concepts to remember from Chapter 10:

o   Land in the West was largely settled and the boundaries of the continental United States became fixed.

o   America became embroiled in foreign conflicts.

o   Isolationism and anti-immigrant sentiment collided with globalism and social reform.

o   The Great Depression became the longest protracted economic challenge in American history.

o   American Indians settled on reservations as sovereign nations under the oversight of the Bureau of Indian Affairs.

o   Communications and transportation technologies revolutionized daily American life.

Chapter 11
An American Century

ERA: POSTWAR—COLD WAR

After World War II

Truman and the Fair Deal

Truman had the unenviable task of succeeding the immensely popular Roosevelt in the Oval Office. Not only would it have been hard to match FDR in terms of personal magnetism and political stature, but many people, Republicans especially, felt that the Democrats had had an unnaturally long stay in the White House and were eager to see him depart. So, even though Truman pursued a continuance of many of Roosevelt's policies, he found new resistance to those policies from Republicans in Congress. Truman's first term was so paralyzed by partisan gridlock that few observers gave him any chance for a successful re-election campaign. They were wrong. Truman won the Presidential election of 1948 by the slimmest of margins. In his victory, Truman felt vindicated and sensed an electoral mandate to continue his reformist agenda. Unfortunately for Truman, Republicans were able to continue to block any action on his agenda during his second term. In the next election, Truman chose not to run, and Republican moderate and World War II hero **Dwight D. Eisenhower** won the White House.

Let's Make a Deal

Both Teddy and Franklin D. Roosevelt, as well as FDR's successor Harry S. Truman, offered "deals" to the American public. We've listed them here, so that you can keep them straight in your head.

	President	What's the Deal with This?
Square Deal	Teddy Roosevelt	Government promised to regulate business and restore competition
First New Deal	Franklin D. Roosevelt	Focused on immediate relief and the recovery of banks
Second New Deal	Franklin D. Roosevelt	Addressed the shortcomings of the First New Deal and responded to a changing political climate
Fair Deal	Harry S. Truman	Extension of New Deal vision and provisions for reintegrating World War II veterans in society (i.e., GI Bill)

The Cold War

Immediately following the world war (and the dropping of two atomic bombs), tensions between the Western Allies and the Soviet Union deepened. The term **Cold War** means that despite the fact that there was no direct combat between the two blocks, a sustained period of military and political tension existed. In Europe, the Soviet Union maintained de facto control of Eastern Europe, which Winston Churchill referred to as being **"behind the iron curtain"** of authoritarian rule. The United States and Western European nations were closely aligned in opposition to the Soviet Union and its Communist **puppet states**. The possible consequences of the Cold War between the nuclear-armed rivals becoming a hot one were enormous, with annihilation, or **Mutual Assured Destruction (MAD)**, as a frightening potential outcome of—and deterrent to—nuclear war.

Pop Quiz

Q: In what other era was the fear of Communism in America as great as the period of McCarthyism during the 1950s?

Cold War tensions were largely fueled by deep mutual suspicion. The United States (and its allies) and the Soviet Union (and its allies) each viewed the other as bent on world domination. In fact, both nations did become actively involved in the internal affairs of other nations the world over, inciting, supporting, or opposing revolutions and waging proxy wars through funding, arming and training rebels, counter-revolutionaries, and allies, and by establishing "puppet governments." Ironically, both the United States and the Soviet Union did so in order to combat the supposed designs of the other.

After World War II, Truman—the first Cold War president—responded to the Soviet threat with a policy of **"containment"** that became known as the **Truman Doctrine**. According to this policy, the United States committed itself to stop the spread of communism in Europe and around the globe. This policy set the tone for the remaining decades of the Cold War and pledged U.S. economic and military aid to help "free peoples," wherever they may be, resist Soviet "aggression." Soon after, Truman's secretary of state, **George C. Marshall**, argued that the best way to "protect" nations from communism was to help them become prosperous and politically stable. The **Marshall Plan** provided grants and loans to war-torn European nations. It was targeted against "hunger, poverty, desperation, and chaos," and aimed to eliminate conditions that Marshall and others in the State department feared could become ripe for Communist revolution. Soon, this economic support helped bring about a strong postwar recovery in Western Europe and cemented a partnership between those nations and the United States that would endure throughout the Cold War.

This alliance was formalized by the formation of **NATO (North Atlantic Treaty Organization)** in 1949. In the treaty establishing the organization, the ten signatory nations of Western Europe and the United States and Canada pledged to stand together, and that by mutual obligation of that treaty, an attack on any one member state would be considered an attack on all member states. The communist Eastern European nations countered with the formation of their coalition, known as the **Warsaw Pact**, in 1955.

It was during the Truman administration that the United States scored its first major Cold War victory, in what has become known as the **Berlin Airlift**, during which time the allies organized a massive relief effort to supply Western-controlled sectors of Berlin, being blockaded by the Soviets, by air.

The **Korean War**, which occurred under Truman, became a stage on which Cold War hostilities were played out. After World War II, Korea had been divided into North Korea, under Soviet control, and South Korea, under American occupation. Following the withdrawal of both Soviet and U.S. troops at the end of World War II, North Korea, led by Soviet-trained military leaders and equipped with Soviet arms, attacked South Korea without provocation, with the declared intention of unifying the Korean peninsula. The initial North Korean invasion across the **38th parallel** into South Korea pushed overwhelmed South Korean defenders back to the so-called Pusan Perimeter. Led by America, the United Nations Security Council, in the absence of the boycotting Soviet representative, declared North Korea an aggressor and sent a force led by General MacArthur to

Pop Quiz

A: After World War I and the Russian Revolution, there was great fear that radical communists were trying to take over the U.S. government. The fear of communism was partially due to a distrust of foreigners in general, and it was also spurred on by Attorney General A. Mitchell Palmer, who was in many ways as bad as McCarthy.

The Domino Theory
"You have broader considerations that might follow what you might call the 'falling domino principle.' You have a row of dominoes set up. You knock over the first one, and what will happen to the last one is that it will go over very quickly."
—President Harry S. Truman, 1954

the region under orders to defend South Korea. MacArthur launched a bold counter-offensive, spearheaded by an amphibious landing behind North Korean lines at **Inchon**, outflanking and encircling much of the North Korean army. Taking advantage of the breakout, U.N. forces pursued remaining North Korean forces north of the 38th parallel, pushing them as far as the Yalu River on the North Korean-Chinese border. In response to events, China chose to intervene. The (Chinese) People's Liberation Army crossed over the Yalu in support of North Korea. The Chinese counter-attack pushed the combined U.N.–South Korean force back to and behind the 38th parallel. It was during this period that the already strained relationship between Truman and McArthur reached a boiling point, with Truman relieving McArthur of command after McArthur publically criticized him. An extended period of brutal, stalemated, trench warfare ensued around the parallel, until, in July 1953, an armistice agreement was reached that set the border between the two Koreas at the 38th Parallel and established the **Korean Demilitarized Zone (DMZ)**.

Eisenhower was elected shortly before the end of the Korean War, and his administration was firmly entrenched in the Cold War ideology. During his presidency, the Middle East erupted in the area around the **Suez Canal** in **Egypt**. It began when **Israel**, which was formally established as a nation only a few years earlier, attacked Egypt in the hope of destroying bases from which Arab militants launched attacks on Israeli settlements. Meanwhile, England and France, angered by Egypt's recognition of Communist China, withdrew plans to build a dam on the Suez Canal. In response, Egypt's President **Gamal Abdel Nasser**, an outspoken Arab nationalist, seized the assets of the European company that owned and operated the canal. In retaliation, Britain and France chose to join the Israeli attack on Egypt in what many international observers decried as a restoration of prewar imperialism.

Thus, the atmosphere of the Cold War, coupled with a new dimension of a Middle East power struggle, contributed to small "hot" wars within the larger context of the Cold War. Following the withdrawal of England, France, and Israel (under U.S. pressure), Eisenhower asked Congress to commit economic and military resources to the region in an effort to undermine growing communist influence there. This policy became known as the **Eisenhower Doctrine**.

Also under Eisenhower, the **space race** began when the Soviets launched the first space satellite, *Sputnik*, in 1957. Initially fueled by U.S. fears over the apparent Soviet technological superiority, as Cold War tensions continued, the race become a show of scientific bravado and one-upmanship between the two nations.

The Cold War Hits Home

The period following World War II was colored with fear and sometimes exaggerated perceptions of the Soviet Union and the communist threat. Many people, public officials and private citizens alike, suspected **communist infiltration** of the government and other important positions by spies and double-agents was behind the theft of state secrets and the manipulation of public opinion. Many government employees were forced to resign following invasive probes of their lives. In several highly publicized cases, once-respected figures were jailed for treason on the thinnest of grounds. Two people, **Julius and Ethel Rosenberg**, were executed for spying.

In the vanguard of the deep anticommunist sentiment in the country was **Senator Joseph R. McCarthy**, who led a crusade to rid the government of supposed communists, and their "fellow travelers," or "sympathizers"—labels the senator affixed to virtually anyone who disagreed with him. Joseph McCarthy's tactics, which became known derisively as **McCarthyism**, were ruthless, and his claims were often unsubstantiated. McCarthy's downfall came quickly when his bullying tactics were displayed during a televised Senate committee investigation of alleged spies in the army. When popular opinion turned against him, the Senate voted to censure his actions as unbecoming of his office, but not until far too many lives were shattered by demagoguery.

After World War II, Congress demonstrated a marked anti-labor and anti-union sentiment. Throughout the war, labor had forgone wage increases in order to support the nation's war effort. When it was over, inflation rose dramatically and workers—whose salaries now lacked much of the purchasing power they once had—demanded compensation for their sacrifice. But the Republican Congress sided with management and passed tough legislation restricting organized labor tactics. One such bill, the **Taft-Hartley Act**, enjoyed public support, despite its obvious anti-labor leanings, as labor unions were tainted in the popular imagination by an air of communist ideology. The law passed despite Truman's veto. In response, and to strengthen their bargaining position through growth in numbers, the two most powerful labor union coalitions joined to form the **AFL-CIO (American Federation of Labor–Congress of Industrial Organizations)**.

Postwar Affluence

The decade following World War II brought general affluence and an improved standard of living for most Americans. Also, when soldiers returned from World War II, they and their spouses again began making babies, lots of babies. The explosive increase in the birthrate in the postwar period was known as the **"baby boom,"** the demographic implications of which are still felt today in the United States.

Nonetheless, many groups of Americans remained economically disenfranchised and failed to enjoy the same improved standard of living enjoyed by other Americans. This was especially true of black Americans. These differences worsened with the growth of suburbs, as white Americans left the cities for less congested, greener areas. As they left in what came to be known as "white flight," they took their buying power (and tax payments)

Important Civil Rights Legislation

The key pieces of civil rights legislation in the twentieth century:

- *Brown v. Board of Education* (1954)
  Declared the previous policy of segregation of schools and other public institutions unconstitutional
- **Civil Rights Act of 1964**
  Strengthened voting legislation and outlawed discrimination based on a person's race, color, religion, or gender
- **Twenty-fourth Amendment** (1964)
  Prohibited the use of poll taxes to deny people the right to vote
- **Voting Rights Act of 1965**
  Specifically prohibited the use of discriminatory practices such as literacy tests that had been used to deny blacks the right to vote in some states

with them. Blacks and other minority groups that remained came to make up increasingly larger proportions of the cities' populations. This physical separation of the racial groups, accompanied by relatively stagnant income levels for African Americans, contributed to some of the tensions that would erupt in the 1960s.

Civil Rights

Indeed, in the South, these physical separations had been enshrined in law for decades. But during this period, these laws came into serious question. ***Brown v. Board of Education of Topeka*** (1954) was a landmark Supreme Court decision that helped open the door for civil rights progress. Under the 1896 Supreme Court ruling ***Plessy v. Ferguson***, public schools and other institutions were legally segregated under the "separate but equal" doctrine. In reality, the white schools and facilities far surpassed the quality of those for African Americans. In the 1954 decision, the Supreme Court unanimously reversed this decision and declared this policy unconstitutional. **Chief Justice Earl Warren** wrote in the majority opinion that "separate educational facilities are inherently unequal" and ordered that all public schools desegregate. This ruling helped to unify the black community, which began to organize openly against the segregation that was so tightly woven into the fabric of southern society.

The **Montgomery Bus Boycott** of 1955 was sparked when **Rosa Parks**, a black woman, refused to give up her seat on a bus to a white man. Her subsequent arrest was the last straw for many residents of Montgomery, who were upset by the city's unfair public transportation policies. The black community united under the leadership of a young preacher and civil rights leader named **Martin Luther King Jr. (MLK)**, and refused to ride the buses. The boycott continued for over a year until the Supreme Court handed down its decision that segregated seating was, in fact, unconstitutional.

Many white Southerners were angered by this upsetting of their racially stratified society. A widely publicized incident illustrating the discord that resulted, took place in **Little Rock, Arkansas**, in 1957, as the city's board of education selected nine black students to enroll at the previously all-white Central High School. The governor of the state ordered the Arkansas National Guard to bar the students from the building. President Eisenhower declared the governor's action to be in violation of federal law. When the governor withdrew the National Guard, an angry white mob sought to block the students from entering the school. In order to end the stand-off, Eisenhower federalized the Arkansas National Guard and sent additional **federal troops** to protect the black students; the soldiers remained through the entire school year. Outside of his actions in Little Rock, Eisenhower also supported the **Civil Rights Acts of 1957 and 1960**, which sought to remove the voting barriers that many Southern states had put into place and also to help minimize the **violence** that had been directed toward African Americans (e.g., the bombing of black churches and schools) in many places across the South.

MLK and Malcolm X

The Reverend Dr. Martin Luther King Jr. and **Malcolm X** were both influential civil rights leaders, but their views on how to improve social, economic, and political conditions for African Americans were diametrically opposed. Martin Luther King Jr. believed in **nonviolent protest**, styling many of his demonstrations on the successful initiatives of Mohandas Gandhi in India. King envisioned integration of the races and equality of living conditions across different cultures and ethnicities. Malcolm X, on the other hand, felt that nonviolence was too passive and bound by an attitude of subservience. In general, he held more radical views than King and the mainstream civil rights movement. He believed that **violent means** might be necessary to protect civil rights and that African Americans should form a separate society from mainstream white America to achieve true equality. Tragically, both men were felled by assassins' bullets; Malcolm X was shot in New York City in 1965 and Martin Luther King Jr. was shot in Memphis, Tennessee, in 1968.

ERA: THE 1960s

Kennedy/Johnson and the Great Society

In 1960, **John F. Kennedy**, elected in a close contest against Richard M. Nixon, brought a sense of optimism to the nation with his youthful idealism and promotion of individual responsibility. His charms failed to extend to Congress, however. He advanced several progressive pieces of legislation that received minimal support there, but he did succeed in establishing the **Peace Corps**, a volunteer organization that sends teachers and provides technical assistance to developing countries.

President Kennedy was assassinated while riding in a Dallas motorcade in 1963. When **Lyndon B. Johnson**, who had been vice president, assumed the presidency, he outlined ambitious goals for the nation, arguing that government should play a greater role in people's lives. He called his vision the **Great Society**, promising a country in which poverty, disease, lack of education, and racial discrimination could and should be eliminated. This was no doubt a tall order to fill, but Johnson did make progress toward correcting inequity in housing, public schools, and civil rights. His most important legislation was the **Economic Opportunity Act (1964)**, which was billed as "The War on Poverty." Unfortunately, Johnson was challenged to fund his war on poverty, as at the same time, he was paying for an even more expensive war, the **Vietnam War**, which was technically not a war at all—at least not in the constitutional sense. Although the conflict lasted more than 12 years and cost the lives of more than 50,000 American soldiers, Congress never officially issued a declaration of war.

A Sign of Progress

In 2008, 40 years after the assassination of Martin Luther King Jr., Barack Obama, a senator from Illinois, was elected the first African American President of the United States.

Cuba and Vietnam—Hot Cold War

The Cold War relationship between the United States and the Soviet Union was pushed to the breaking point during the Kennedy administration when Cuba became the close-to-home stage for a potentially catastrophic standoff between the two. By most accounts, the **Cuban Missile Crisis (1962)** was the nearest the world ever came to the Cold War becoming hot. Leftist Cuban revolutionaries, led by Fidel Castro, had recently overthrown the U.S.-supported dictator **Fulgencio Batista**, and repelled an American-financed and CIA-coordinated invasion at the **Bay of Pigs**. Fearing additional American efforts to undermine his rule, Castro sought and received Soviet military and economic aid. The crisis began after a U.S. spy plane discovered that the Soviets and the Cubans were readying offensive **missiles** in Cuba. Kennedy ordered a blockade of all Soviet ships coming into the area and demanded that the bases be dismantled. The Soviets refused. As the Soviet Union and the United States engaged in a dangerous game of nuclear **brinksmanship** (the practice of pushing a dangerous situation to its limit in hopes of gaining an advantage), war seemed increasingly likely, until **Nikita Khrushchev**, the Soviet premier, in the words of then Secretary of State Dean Rusk, "blinked," agreeing in secret negotiations to dismantle the missile sites if the United States pledged not to invade Cuba and remove ballistic missiles from Turkey at a later date.

The nation's approach to Vietnam was the ultimate Cold War policy gone awry. Although the Vietnam War is at its core a story of anticommunists versus communists—not an especially unique one in the annals of Cold War geopolitics—the full narrative is much more complicated. The war was waged between the communist **North Vietnamese**, with support from their Chinese, Soviet, and **Viet Cong** (a South Vietnamese communist guerilla group) allies, and the government of **South Vietnam**, supported by its primary ally, the United States. Throughout the 1950s, the Vietnamese, led by future American-antagonist and North Vietnamese president **Ho Chi Minh**, waged a war of liberation against French colonial rule. It was during this period that American military advisors first arrived. Following the military defeat and subsequent withdrawal of the French from Indochina, Vietnam was partitioned into Northern and Southern states. The government of North Vietnam and their Viet Cong allies in the South sought to reunify Vietnam under a single, communist government. The United States justified its involvement in Vietnam as part of a larger **containment strategy**, the crux of which was to stop the expansion of communism on a state-by-state basis, wherever revolutionary elements pursued the establishment of communist rule. This containment doctrine had at its intellectual heart the **domino theory**, which held that if one country in a region fell to communism, all of the nations in that region were then put at risk of falling. The South Vietnamese did not fare well in the early stages of the war, as poor training and rampant corruption limited the effectiveness of the South Vietnamese Army against the guerrilla tactics of the Viet Cong. The United States blamed South Vietnamese President **Ngo Dinh Diem** for much of the failure, and supported a coup that removed him from power, only further destabilizing the political situation in the country. After an initially modest commitment of American forces to the country, troop levels began to increase sharply in the early 1960s. The U.S. military presence in Vietnam increased dramatically following the 1964 **Gulf of Tonkin incident**, in which a U.S. destroyer conducting intelligence-gathering operations engaged North Vietnamese fast attack craft after reportedly coming under fire. President Johnson seized upon the incident to request that Congress authorize an increase in the scope and pace of military action against North Vietnam. The **Gulf of Tonkin Resolution** provided the President with just such an authorization. Conventional ground forces began deployment to Vietnam in large numbers thereafter. The American military strategy involved bringing to bear overwhelming firepower in search and destroy operations, and against the cities of the North, including a massive, sustained bombing campaign. As the war dragged on, the scale and cost—both in terms of dollars spent and lives lost—of America's military involvement continued to balloon. Nonetheless, American forces did enjoy a margin of continued success tactically—sufficiently enough to convince many Americans that the war in Vietnam was a winnable one. This changed in 1968, when the Communists launched the **Tet Offensive**, a coordinated offensive aimed at overthrowing the government of South Vietnam. The Tet Offensive failed in its goal of overthrowing the South Vietnamese government, but it turned the tide of the war nonetheless, as it persuaded many American voters that despite extraordinary effort and enormous sacrifice, the United States was no closer to victory than when the war began. A significant **anti-war movement** grew throughout the 1960s, which was both a reflection of and a stimulus for the larger counter-cultural movement of the decade. A growing sense that the United States was mired in a quagmire in Southeast Asia, along with increasingly vocal public opposition to the war, led to a slow, but steady reduction in American force levels as part of a program referred to as **Vietnamization**. Initiated under President **Richard Nixon**, who succeeded Johnson, Vietnamization aimed to transfer an increasingly large share of ground combat responsibilities to the Vietnamese, allowing for a drawdown of American forces in the region. In keeping with Nixon's campaign promise to bring the war in Vietnam to an "honorable conclusion," the United States signed the **Paris Peace Accord** in 1973. Direct U.S. military involvement in the conflict ended that same year with the passages of the Case-Church Amendment in Congress. However, American withdrawal from Vietnam did not put an end to the fighting. The war itself ended with the **fall of Saigon** and the reunification of Vietnam in 1975.

A Different War at Home

At home, unrest continued to grow throughout the 1960s: The civil rights movement reached a fever pitch, as African Americans demanded equal treatment, many young people vehemently opposed the Vietnam War and U.S. military policy, and the word **hippie**, a term used to describe Americans who were part of the "counterculture" of the 1960s, entered the American lexicon. **Women's rights** re-emerged as an issue of significance in the public debate, as part of the broader **women's liberation movement** that began toward the end of the decade. In addition, an infant **environmental movement** first emerged, in no small part due to the work of Rachel Carson. Carson's book, *Silent Spring*, published in 1962, brought to light the detrimental environmental effects of the widespread use of pesticides, helping to bring about a ban on the use of the pesticide DDT, and the establishment by executive order in 1970 of the **Environmental Protection Agency (EPA)**.

Silent Spring (1962)
Why was it a "silent spring"? Because all the chirping birds had been killed by pesticides. Rachel Carson's landmark book explained the harmful effects of pesticides and helped raise awareness about the importance of protecting the environment. This is a favorite of the SAT Subject Test in U.S. History.

As mentioned previously, the Vietnam War became a deeply unpopular one, perhaps the most unpopular war in America's history, in fact. Few Americans understood the aims of the war and many found it increasingly difficult to reconcile the importance of fighting Communism in a far-flung corner of Southeast Asia with the cost of Johnson's escalation of the war and the often personal immediacy of his reinstatement of the draft, all played out in every American home as part of the first war to be **nationally televised**. Striking images of the human costs of war, both American and Vietnamese, contradicted any lingering sense of war's romanticism, and undermined the government's public assertions that the United States was succeeding in a fight that would soon conclude with victory. Public protest and acts of resistance increased after revelations contained in the ***Pentagon Papers*** made public that the United States had secretly engaged in, among other things, bombing campaigns of **Laos** and **Cambodia**. At **Kent State University**, during an antiwar protest in 1970, national guardsmen fired on the demonstrators, killing four students. A shocked nation became even angrier about the war and demanded loudly that it come to an end.

In the 1950s, progress had been made in confirming and strengthening some civil rights for African Americans, but starting in the early 1960s, the pace of progress quickened. African Americans became more forceful in claiming their rights and denouncing their "second-class citizen" status. Under the leadership of Martin Luther King Jr., protesters embraced the tactic of nonviolent resistance to achieve their goals. They engaged in several types of demonstrations. **Sit-ins** involved blacks going into "whites only" restaurants and other establishments, sitting down, and refusing to leave, even as service was denied them. On **Freedom Rides**, African Americans and their white supporters rode interstate buses to test the interstate desegregation legislation passed in the 1950s. Freedom riders encountered hostility and violence as the buses rode into "whites only" bus terminals. Eventually, the government explicitly ordered that interstate buses be desegregated, and airplanes and trains voluntarily followed suit. Another form of demonstration was the mass demonstration or **march**; the most famous example of this was the **March on Washington, D.C.** to make clear the scale of support for civil rights legislation that had been advanced by Kennedy. The assembled group was the largest ever in the nation's capital, and it held that record for more than 20 years. During this protest, Martin Luther King Jr. gave his historic **"I Have a Dream"** speech from the steps of the Lincoln memorial.

After an extended delay due to the actions of Southern Congressmen, the **Civil Rights Act of 1964** was passed and signed into law by President Johnson. It mandated new, stronger voting protections for African Americans and prohibited discrimination in public accommodations, housing, and employment based on a person's race, color, religion, or gender. The strength of the law was tested the next year in **Selma, Alabama**, a city that had a large population of African Americans, of whom only a few were registered to vote. The local police violently suppressed groups demonstrating for their voting rights and prevented them from registering.

Martin Luther King, Jr., and other members of his **Southern Christian Leadership Council (SCLC)**, became involved and organized a march from Selma to the state capitol in Montgomery. Although King and his supporters advocated nonviolence, many of those who opposed them, including the local police forces, were openly and frequently violent. The first attempt to march on Montgomery was aborted because of brutal retaliation on the marchers by police and an angry mob. The incident came to be known as **Bloody Sunday**. In another infamous incident in **Birmingham, Alabama**, police used fire hoses, nightsticks, cattle prods, and dogs to disband nonviolent protesters. The incidents were televised, offering the opportunity for many Americans to see for the first time the face of violent racial hatred. It helped generate much sympathy and support for the civil rights movement among white Americans, and was a turning point in the legislative effort to pass new civil rights measures in Congress.

The onslaught of violence endured by African American protesters spurred division within the ranks of the civil rights movement about how best to respond to it. The NAACP and Martin Luther King Jr. continued to advocate nonviolent protest, but more militant African American groups felt those who insisted on nonviolence were sending young marchers into harm's way unduly. **Malcolm X**, who acted as the chief spokesman for the **Nation of Islam** (sometimes referred to as the Black Muslims), favored total separation of the races, although he eventually broke with the Nation of Islam and rethought his separatist views toward the end of his short life. **CORE (Congress on Racial Equality)** and **SNCC (Student Nonviolent Coordinating Committee)** represented those who had come to advocate more forceful self-protection, as did the **Black Panthers**, one of the best-known groups of the period. Across this militant front, the term **Black Power** was often used, not only in reference to the idea that African Americans should arm themselves for an "imminent" revolution against the white power structure, but in reference to the empowerment that they believed came from self-pride.

ERA: THE 1970s AND 1980s

"Tricky Dick"

Richard Nixon came into office at the end of the 1960s promising to end U.S. involvement in Vietnam. Lyndon Johnson had chosen not to run for reelection because of the enormous unpopularity of the war with which he was so closely associated. Once in office, Nixon slowly went about fulfilling the commitment he made to the electorate, and the United States slowly drew down forces in Vietnam between 1969 and 1973. Elsewhere in the foreign policy sphere, Nixon pursued a policy of **détente**, or that of eased tension, between the United States and the Soviet Union, with whom he negotiated a series of arms reduction agreements. At a summit in Moscow in 1972, Nixon and his Soviet counterpart, **Leonid Brezhnev**, signed the **Anti-Ballistic Missile (ABM) Treaty** and the **Strategic Arms Limitation Treaty (SALT 1)**. The ABM Treaty placed limits on the development and deployment of anti-ballistic missile technology by the treaty signatories, while SALT I froze the number of ballistic missiles deployed by both nations. Nixon also historically **visited Communist China**, the first American president to do so. Nixon's trip was an important step forward in establishing diplomatic relations with the Asian power.

Civil Disobedience (1849)
American transcendentalist Henry David Thoreau pioneered the practice of civil disobedience—that is, nonviolent resistance of authorities who enforce unjust laws. This philosophy inspired activists like MLK and formed the basis for many of the tactics of the Civil Rights Movement.

At home, Nixon built his political support upon what he called the **"Silent Majority,"** a supposed majority of Americans who were tired of big government, cultural and social unrest, and racial strife. In domestic affairs, advocated for **New Federalism**, which would devolve power away from the federal government and back to the states. Nixon also resorted to price controls in an effort to stabilize the economy. Notably, he also signed into law key environmental bills such as the **Clean Air Act (1970)** and, as mentioned earlier, created the Environmental Protection Agency.

Nixon enjoyed fairly wide popularity and easily won reelection in 1972. But, his fall from the pinnacle of political power came swiftly, as the **Watergate** scandal unfolded during his second term. Men tied to the president and his reelection campaign were caught breaking into the Democratic National Headquarters at the **Watergate Hotel** in Washington, D.C. The subsequent scandal and cover-up became national news. In 1974, Nixon resigned his office (the only president in American history to do so) rather than face almost certain impeachment.

Ford/Carter/Reagan

Only about 5% of the questions on the SAT Subject Test in U.S. History will pertain to historical events after Richard Nixon. Nevertheless, you should still study these facts, especially if your history teacher neglected to teach this more recent time period in class.

Gerald Ford, Nixon's vice president, assumed office after Nixon's resignation, but lost in 1976 to a Democrat, **Jimmy Carter**. The presidencies of Ford and Carter were plagued by a troubled economy and by an **energy crisis** triggered by unrest in the Middle East. Neither Ford's nor Carter's presidencies helped the ailing economy recover, and under Carter, the nation faced **stagflation**, a troubling combination of double-digit inflation (higher prices, especially for gasoline) and steep, persistent unemployment. Because of an oil shortage manipulated by the **Organization of Petroleum Exporting Countries (OPEC)**, a cartel of mostly Middle Eastern producers that controlled much of the world's production of crude oil, the Middle East became an even more important focus of American foreign policy. Although Carter had some foreign policy success (he helped broker the **Camp David Accords,** an Egyptian-Israeli peace treaty signed after nearly two weeks of secret negotiations at the presidential retreat at Camp David, Maryland), it was overshadowed by events in Iran. Following the overthrow of the American-backed **Shah of Iran's** government in 1979, fifty-two Americans were taken hostage at the United States Embassy in Tehran, Iran, by Iranian revolutionaries. Following a series of negotiations that failed to secure the hostages' release, an aborted rescue mission, **Operation Eagle Claw**, was launched, that resulted in the death of eight service members. The **Iranian hostage crisis** stretched on for more than a year, and along with the debacle that

Energy Crisis

During the 1970s, the Arab nations that controlled most of the world's oil supply refused to ship oil to any Western countries, including the United States. This boycott created an energy crisis that hit America hard. As a result of the oil embargo, gasoline prices skyrocketed and people waited in long lines to fill up their cars.

followed the attempted rescue attempt, severely damaged American credibility and cost Carter's 1980 re-election bid. The hostages' ordeal came to an end when they were released shortly after **Ronald Reagan** was inaugurated.

Reagan, who has become an icon of American conservatism, set about to accomplish a series of conservative economic and foreign policies goals during his two terms in office. His **supply-side economic plan**, which included sweeping reductions in marginal tax rates, presupposed the idea that reducing tax rates on the rich would lead to productive investment of those tax savings by the rich that would **trickle down** to the less affluent of society. This policy, coupled with massive spending on the military and curtailment of funding for social programs, created a financial boom in the 1980s. Much of Reagan's second term centered on a congressional investigation of the **Iran-Contra affair**. Iran-Contra concerned two ill-advised foreign policies: the sale of arms to Iran (in hopes of improving relations with the nation, then, as now, considered an enemy to the United States), and the use of revenues from those sales to buy weapons for the **Contra** (anticommunist) rebels of **Nicaragua**. Both policies violated U.S. law; the subsequent investigation, however, resulted in few convictions and never directly implicated Reagan.

ERA: 1990s AND BEYOND

Bush/Clinton/Bush/Obama/Trump

George H. W. Bush (Reagan's vice president) won the 1988 election, benefiting from Reagan's popularity and a particularly negative presidential campaign season. His greatest successes were in foreign affairs. He led an international coalition in the **Persian Gulf War** that easily expelled **Iraq**, led by Iraqi dictator Saddam Hussein, from its tiny, oil-rich neighbor and American ally, **Kuwait**. He was also president during the disintegration of the Soviet Union. Bush established friendly relations with the new Russian government, led by Boris Yeltsin, that succeeded the Soviet regime. On domestic issues, Bush's results were more mixed. Complicating his troubles was the perception that he cared little about domestic policies, preferring to focus on the international matters in which he was so well versed. When the economy took an unexpected downturn in 1992, challenger **Bill Clinton** saw an opening and seized it. His campaign focused relentlessly on the economy, but the successful third-party candidacy of **H. Ross Perot** siphoned crucial votes from Bush, sealing his electoral defeat.

You should at least know the following major events regarding the Clinton administration. The early years were marked by bitter partisan struggles, especially after conservative Republicans took control of Congress in 1994. The conflict led to a **1995 government shutdown** that lasted nearly a month. As a result of the conflict, Clinton's popularity soared and Congress's plummeted, and when the government resumed operating, Clinton enjoyed greater legislative successes than he had previously. He **reformed the welfare system**, secured the rights of workers to maintain health care provisions after changing jobs, **increased the minimum wage**, and signed the North American Free Trade Agreement (NAFTA), into law. NAFTA, a trade agreement that dramatically lowered trade barriers between the United States, Canada and Mexico, was ratified after a heated battle in Congress. Critics of the pact claim that it cost manufacturing jobs lost to Mexico, while its supporters point to the dramatic uptick in North American trade that it precipitated.

Clinton's image, if not ultimately his popularity (buoyed by a strong economy) was damaged when a federal investigation into his financial dealings, unearthed evidence of an **extramarital affair** with a White House intern. Congress determined that Clinton had lied about the affair under oath (in a hearing concerning a separate sexual harassment suit), and subsequently **impeached** him on charges of perjury. It was only the second impeachment in U.S. history (Andrew Johnson's was the other). The Senate, while censuring Clinton for his actions, acquitted him of the charges. Nonetheless, Clinton left office as a remarkably popular president, especially in light of the humiliation of the impeachment scandal, due in no small part to the historic **economic expansion** that he presided over in the late 1990s. Huge growth in the stock market, low unemployment, and the creation of new industries and jobs, namely the Internet and computer-related technologies, all contributed to the boom years of the Clinton administration.

Republican **George W. Bush**, son of former President George H. W. Bush, became president in 2001 after one of the most controversial presidential elections in history, in which he won a narrow and contested victory over Democratic candidate and former vice president, **Al Gore**. The 2000 election was the first time since 1888 that the winner of the popular vote did not also earn a majority of votes in the **Electoral College**. On election night, the popular vote between the two candidates was so close that the Electoral College votes in several states could not be accurately determined. In addition, **Ralph Nader's** candidacy for the Green party succeeded in siphoning off at least some votes from the relatively liberal Gore campaign. It was highly unusual that the outcome of a national election would remain in dispute even after weeks of debates following election day. There were charges of voting irregularities and court challenges regarding which absentee ballots would be counted. The election results in Florida were particularly controversial because the governor of Florida, Jeb Bush, was not only a Republican, but he was the Republican presidential candidate's brother. Election officials who "called" Florida for Bush were, in some cases, affiliated with the winning party and candidate. The Supreme Court ultimately validated the election in their *Bush v. Gore* decision. Bush emerged as the winner, although the election was so close that subsequent counts have not produced clear results. Following his inauguration, Bush faced a challenging first two years in office. He had early political success in enacting his tax reduction package, known as the **Bush tax cuts**, but the economy slowed due to a variety of factors including the burst of the **Internet bubble**, in which many new Internet-related companies failed, and the discovery of accounting irregularities and securities fraud leading to the collapse of several major public companies **(Enron, WorldCom)**.

On **September 11, 2001**, four commercial airliners were hijacked and used as weapons of destruction. Two planes were flown into the **World Trade Center** in New York City, exploding and causing the towers' collapse; another plane was flown into the **Pentagon** in Washington, D.C., causing extensive damage; and a fourth plane crashed in a field near **Shanksville, Pennsylvania**, the hijacking thwarted by crew and passengers who perhaps prevented its striking some other terrorist target. More than 2,800 people were killed in the tragedy. The attacks, attributed to Saudi-born **Osama bin Laden** and a radical Muslim terrorist group named **al Qaeda**, shocked the United States and the world. President Bush responded by launching a **"War on Terror"** which included, but was not limited to, a war in Afghanistan against the **Taliban**, a group that supported and harbored anti-American terrorists, including Osama bin Laden and other members of al Qaeda. Following the attacks, there was increased security nationwide in an effort to protect citizens against terrorism, prompting concerns over potential violations to **civil liberties** as well as **racial and ethnic profiling**. Also during Bush's first term, the United States **invaded Iraq**. The invasion of Iraq, which removed Saddam Hussein from power, was publically justified prior to the war on the basis of Iraq possessing an arsenal of weapons of mass destruction that threatened both Saddam's neighbors and, through his connections to terrorism, the United States. The invasion and subsequent **occupation of Iraq** became mired in controversy, as Saddam's weapons of mass destruction were never found, and as an increasingly violent sectarian feud destabilized the fledging postwar Iraqi democracy and cost the lives of American service members and Iraqi civilians caught in the cross-fire.

The **economic crisis of late 2008**, fueled by a collapse in the housing and housing credit market, has caused many people to reevaluate the economic and social reforms and policies enacted not just during George W. Bush's and Bill Clinton's presidencies, but during the first President Bush and Reagan years, as well. The economic crisis, along with America's War on Terror, became major campaign issues in 2008, when the United States elected its first African-American president, **Barack Obama**. During his first term in office, Obama signed into a law a bill rolling back the Bush tax cuts, the **Tax Relief, Unemployment Insurance Reauthorization, and Job Creation Act** of 2010, and ended the military's **Don't Ask, Don't Tell** policy, which banned homosexuals from serving openly in the armed forces. He also enacted a sweeping healthcare reform bill, the **Patient Protection and Affordable Care Act,** or **Affordable Care Act**, often referred to as **"Obamacare."** The controversial legislation is one of the most hotly debated issues in American politics in decades. In foreign policy matters, Obama ordered the final withdrawal of American troops from Iraq and the military action that led to the death of Osama Bin Laden in Abbottabad, Pakistan.

We can't say how historians will evaluate the late twentieth and early twenty-first centuries in light of terrorism, globalization, and the worldwide financial crisis and its aftermath, but it's probably safe to say that the United States will still play a significant—but possibly significantly different—role in the increasingly interconnected and interdependent global community.

2016 was host to a combative presidential election between former Secretary of State and First Lady Hillary Clinton and real estate tycoon Donald Trump. Much to the surprise of political pundits, Trump won the election. The SAT Subject Test in U.S. History will not test you on such a recent event.

Chapter 11 Drill

Turn to Part IV for answers and explanations.

1. "Supply-side" economics is most closely associated with which American president?

   (A) Ronald Reagan
   (B) Richard Nixon
   (C) Bill Clinton
   (D) Jimmy Carter
   (E) Gerald Ford

2. The failed Bay of Pigs Invasion occurred during the administration of which U.S. President?

   (A) Theodore Roosevelt
   (B) Franklin Roosevelt
   (C) John F. Kennedy
   (D) Dwight D. Eisenhower
   (E) James Monroe

3. Two policies that aimed to increase government's role in improving social and economic conditions faced by the poor and working class were the

   (A) New Freedom and New Deal programs
   (B) New Frontier and New Freedom programs
   (C) Square Deal and New Deal programs
   (D) Square Deal and Great Society Programs
   (E) New Nationalism and Great Society programs

4. Which of the following was NOT a serious economic issue faced during Jimmy Carter's presidency?

   (A) Persistently high unemployment
   (B) A stock market bubble
   (C) Slow economic growth
   (D) High crude oil prices
   (E) High interest rates

5. "I have here in my hand a list of 205 that were made known to the Secretary of State as being members of the Communist Party and who nevertheless are still working and shaping policy in the State Department."

   The Senator who made this statement during a speech on the Senate floor would go on to chair the House Un-American Activities Committee. In what year did he make these remarks?

   (A) 1854
   (B) 1892
   (C) 1933
   (D) 1950
   (E) 1974

6. During the 1940s and 1950s, the population of American suburbs

   (A) increased greatly, as the birth rate and population increased and as Americans migrated from urban areas to the suburbs
   (B) increased slightly, as the birth rate and population remained fairly constant, but as Americans migrated from urban areas to the suburbs
   (C) remained at the same level that it had been prior to World War II
   (D) decreased slightly, as the birth rate and population increased as Americans migrated from suburbs to urban areas
   (E) decreased greatly, as the birth rate and population remained fairly constant, but as Americans migrated from urban areas to the suburbs

7. The Eisenhower Doctrine was formulated to provide economic and military aid in response to which of the following concerns?

(A) The perceived growing influence of the Soviet Union in the Middle East
(B) The destabilizing influence of the Korean War in Asia
(C) The decisive military defeat of Israel, Great Britain, and France during the Suez Crisis
(D) The threat of invasion of Western Europe by the Warsaw Pact nations
(E) The danger posed by Communist political infiltration of war-torn Europe

8. "I think it will be a safer world and a better world if we have a strong, healthy United States, Europe, Soviet Union, China, Japan, each balancing the other, not playing one against the other, an even balance."

The quote above is by what president in regard to his policy of détente?

(A) Ronald Reagan
(B) Harry Truman
(C) Richard Nixon
(D) Dwight Eisenhower
(E) Lyndon Johnson

9. Which of the following DOES NOT correctly pair a president with a foreign policy crisis that occurred during his administration?

(A) Eisenhower, Suez Crisis
(B) Lyndon Johnson, Gulf of Tonkin Incident
(C) John Adams, XYZ Affair
(D) William McKinley, the sinking of the U.S.S. Maine
(E) Bill Clinton, the Iraqi invasion of Kuwait

10. Based upon the methods Martin Luther King, Jr. encouraged civil rights activists to adopt, with which of the following statements would he most likely agree?

(A) Complete separation of the races is the only possible solution to the question of racial conflict.
(B) Slow, consistent progress toward economic and educational equality will prepare the civil rights movement to demand greater political equality at a later time.
(C) Nonviolent pursuit of the immediate end of segregation represents the best course for achieving lasting racial equality.
(D) Political activism can never achieve the aims of the civil rights movement without the use of force.
(E) In the face of violent opposition to nonviolent protest, the most reasonable course of action is to accept segregation.

Chapter 11 Summary

Here are the most important concepts to remember from Chapter 11:

o   After World War II, American life was economically prosperous—while fears of Communism dictated foreign policy.

o   Left-wing liberalism promoted both a larger role for government in society and changing social norms.

o   As industry and population grew, environmental concerns became more pressing.

o   In response to a growing liberalization of government, conservatives gained a new voice in public discourse.

o   After the collapse of the Soviet Union and the fall of the Berlin Wall, American fears shifted to the threat of Middle Eastern terrorism.

o   Immigration, both legal and illegal, grew exponentially, prompting internal debate.

o   Computer technology and the Internet become widely available, revolutionizing industry, education, and the social sphere.

Chapter 12
The American
Legacy

On the SAT Subject Test in U.S. History, questions pertaining to American literature, art, music, and important Supreme Court cases often appear. We'll review them as a group in this chapter.

AMERICAN LITERATURE

Early American Writing

American writing prior to 1700 primarily originated from the Northern colonies and focused on religious issues. **Edward Winslow** recorded the history of the first years of the Massachusetts Bay Colony in his diary; historian and theologian Cotton Mather wrote a history centered on God's shaping of historical events in the colony and equating leaders of the colony with biblical heroes. **John Winthrop** discussed the religious underpinnings of the colony and of Puritan life; **William Bradford**, the first governor of the Massachusetts Bay Colony, wrote histories focused on religious themes. More controversially at the time, **Roger Williams**, who later founded Rhode Island, wrote in favor of separation of church and state, while **Thomas Morton**, in a deeply satirical voice, derided settlers for their religious hypocrisy. Puritan poets were equally concerned by religious themes in their writing, the most notable of whom, **Anne Bradstreet**, wrote poems that prominently featured the Puritan family.

The Great Awakening, a religious revival that swept across New England in the early 1700s, brought with it the recorded sermons of Calvinist ministers, including **Jonathan Edwards** and **George Whitfield**.

Native American and African American literature, the latter of which included the poetry of **Phillis Wheatley** and the slave narrative of **Olaudah Equiano**, appeared for the first time in the eighteenth century.

Literature of the Revolutionary War

Not surprisingly, most of the prominent writers of the Revolutionary War era were interested in political matters. Two of the most important figures of the period were **Thomas Paine** and **Benjamin Franklin**. Franklin's wit—and the developing American identity his writing reflected—shone through in *Poor Richard's Almanac*, one of the colony's most popular publications. Paine, a noted pamphleteer, was sharply critical of the English. The critiques of English-colonial relationships that he put forth in *Common Sense* and *The American Crisis* played an important role in shaping colonial thought. During the course of the war proper, the satire of **John Trumbull** helped lighten the national mood.

In the post-revolutionary period, raging political debates still dominated the minds of American writers. Jefferson's notes and letters, as well as the Federalist essays of Madison, Hamilton and Jay, all reflected on questions of government and its role in society.

Nineteenth-Century Literature

American writing found a unique voice in the nineteenth century, beginning in the wake of the War of 1812. It was during this period that the first American novels were written. Many of the first novels were written and published in hopes of spurring book sales. **Susana Rowson** wrote America's first bestseller—*Charlotte Temple*—a tale of a British school girl's seduction by a soldier, that remained America's best-selling novel until the publication of *Uncle Tom's Cabin* (1852), by Harriet Beecher Stowe. **Washington Irving**, renowned for his short stories and novels, helped legitimize fiction writing as a profession, and set his stories exclusively in the United States. **James Fenimore Cooper's** romantic histories of frontier life, including the *Leatherstocking Tales* and *The Last of the Mohicans*, were immensely popular not only in the United States, but in Europe as well. **Edgar Allen Poe** was among the most famous, and most unique, authors of the period. His suspenseful short stories, including *The Pit and the Pendulum* and *The Fall of the House of Usher*, as well as his poems, including "The Raven," explored the macabre and were credited with expanding the nascent mystery genre. In the 1830s, **Ralph Waldo Emerson** published a groundbreaking series of nonfiction pieces, in which he pushed back against prevailing social pressures and championed his belief in the value of individualism and oneness with nature. His influential work and his public lectures on the subject were the intellectual inspiration for the **Transcendentalist** movement of the mid-nineteenth century. Henry David Thoreau proved himself to be every bit Emerson's equal as a nonconformist thinker. After living in relative isolation in a cabin bordering a wooded pond near Concord, Massachusetts, Thoreau wrote *Walden*, a reflective memoir that urges self-reliance and personal independence from more cumbersome aspects of society.

Two of America's great poets flourished during the nineteenth century—**Walt Whitman** and **Emily Dickinson**. Whitman embraced the optimism of a youthful, expanding nation, and matched it with a willingness to experiment stylistically in both meter and verse. His most recognized work, *Leaves of Grass*, exemplified this approach. In many ways Emily Dickinson was the antithesis of Whitman—her poetry was subtle, insightful, and meticulously structured, reflecting the mores of the more staid elements of society.

Mark Twain, the pen name of Samuel Clemens, wrote with great humor and a sensitivity to the changing use of American language. His characters in such books as *The Adventures of Tom Sawyer* and *The Adventures of Huckleberry Finn* told stories of life on the Mississippi and spoke plainly in the vernacular of the day, but also served as a vehicle to point out the hypocrisies of society. **Henry James's** thick, often daunting prose, explores the complex interface between the Old World and the New, in stories of Americans living in Europe.

Twentieth-Century Literature

By the dawn of the twentieth century, American writers expanded the scope of their stories, poetry and novels to include the experiences of Americans from all walks of life. **Theodore Dreiser** wrote *Sister Carrie* about a girl with rural roots ascending to the heights of Chicago society. **Stephen Crane**, well known for writing the Civil War novel *The Red Badge of Courage*, portrayed the struggles of prostitutes in *Maggie: A Girl of the Streets*. **Edith Wharton** dissected the lives of the Northeastern elite with whom she had become so familiar, in many of her books, including her best-known book, *The Age of Innocence*.

Political writers with a strongly Progressive streak helped shape the reformism dialogue of the period. Upton Sinclair's *The Jungle*, and Ida M. Tarbell's muckraking articles drew wide attention to the problems of food safety and the previously unquestioned powers of trusts. **William Faulkner**, regarded as the greatest Southern writer and author of works such as *As I Lay Dying, Absalom, Absalom!*, and *The Sound and the Fury*, created complicated novels that introduced the "stream of consciousness" in writing, wherein characters' jumbled internal monologues concealed subtly multi-faceted meaning.

The generation of writers that came of age during World War I imbued their writing with a perceptible undercurrent of disillusionment. **Gertrude Stein** and other members of the self-described **"Lost Generation"** of expatriate intellectuals in Paris were noted for their novel fiction, influenced by the modern artistic and philosophical communities with which they interacted. **F. Scott Fitzgerald** prototypically seized upon the pleasure-seeking, listless indulgence of the **Jazz age**. **Ernest Hemingway** shuttled the dead, dying, and injured as an ambulance driver in World War I. Shaped by the harsh realities of war, Hemingway's many later writings are characterized by their direct, uncluttered prose and strong, unaffected male characters.

John Steinbeck's works are a masterpiece of Depression-era literature. *The Grapes of Wrath*, follows the Joads, a poor Oklahoma family that flees the Dust Bowl in hopes of finding a better life in California. Other Steinbeck novels—*Tortilla Flat, Cannery Row, East of Eden*, and *Of Mice and Men*, all included a similarly sympathetic social message.

Some of the finest examples of American poetry were produced during the early part of the twentieth century. **Robert Frost, T. S. Eliot, Ezra Pound**, and **Langston Hughes** all produced major works. Frost was known for his use of pastoral (nature-driven) themes and colloquialisms. Eliot's Nobel-prizing winning poetry is characterized by its complexity and density. Ezra Pound's literary scope was especially expansive, as he culled references made in his work widely from sometimes obscure or esoteric sources while also packing his poetry with complex symbolism and experimental structures. Hughes was a prolific poet and leader of the Harlem Renaissance, who chronicled the experiences and emotional landscape of American blacks in works such as "A Dream Deferred."

Dramatic playwrights including **Eugene O'Neill** rose to prominence beginning in the 1920s, setting the stage for later successful playwrights such as **Arthur Miller** and **Tennessee Williams**.

After World War II

The romantic imaginings of the **Beatniks** dominated the postwar literary enterprise. The "Beat Generation" navigated the liberalizing tendencies of a generation responding to the pressures and deprivations of World War II, exploring drugs, Eastern religion, and music with a new spirit of freedom. Works such as **Jack Kerouac's** *On the Road*, **Allen Ginsburg's** poetry, and **William S. Burroughs'** *Naked Lunch* reflected the thoughts of a generation in search of itself.

As the Cold War deepened, works such as **J.D. Salinger's** iconic *Catcher in the Rye* and **Sylvia Plath's** *The Bell Jar*, continued to challenge the perceived irrationality that surrounded America's place in the world, and the life of Americans at home. The war novel itself took on a new, more subversive form as well. **Norman Mailer's** *The Naked and the Dead*, *Catch-22* by **Joseph Heller**, and **Kurt Vonnegut Jr.'s** *Slaughterhouse-Five* each offered a fresh, but often troubling, literary perspective on the war. John Updike's series of four award-winning novels chronicling the successes and failures of Harry "Rabbit" Angstrom elevated the discussion of the oft-literarily overlooked American middle class.

Some of the most powerful literature written by **African American** authors were also crafted in the postwar years. **Ralph Ellison's** *Invisible Man,* chronicling the experiences of a black man in the North, laid bare the still-raw racial tensions plaguing America. **Richard Wright's** controversial polemics, made no less so by his Communist political ties, included *Native Son* and *Black Boy*, and reflected on life in the segregated South. More recently, **Toni Morrison** has explored race, beauty and self-image in such books as *The Bluest Eye, Song of Solomon* and *Beloved*, while **Maya Angelou's** books, essays and poetry touch on topics such as identity, family ties, and race. Her most famous work remains the semi-autobiographical *I Know Why the Caged Bird Sings*.

AMERICAN ART MOVEMENTS

The history of American art is a common source of questions on the SAT Subject Test in U.S. History. We'll briefly review some of the topics that you can expect to see.

Early American Art

Most American Art of the late eighteenth and early nineteenth century either depicted historical sciences or were portraits. **Charles Wilson Peale**, a self-taught artist (a trait shared by many painters of the period), painted many of the most important figures of the Revolutionary period. **Gilbert Stuart's** iconic, unfinished portrait of George

Washington, is one of the most well-recognized and celebrated works of the time. Another portrait painter, **John Singleton Copley,** took as his subjects many members of the merchant elite, including Paul Revere. **Benjamin West** became well known for his paintings depicting scenes of the French and Indian War; **John Trumbull** for his works showing pitched battles of the Revolutionary War.

Art in the Nineteenth Century

The **Hudson River School**, America's first "homegrown" artistic movement, began in the 1820s and 1830s and captured the simple beauty of the area in and around the Hudson River Valley of New York. **Thomas Doughty, Frederic Edwin Church**, and **Albert Bierstadt** were all prominent members of the school. **Robert S. Duncanson**, another member of the school, was one of America's first significant African American painters. At about the same time that the members of the Hudson River School were busy capturing the transcendent elements of nature, **John James Audubon** was painting and cataloguing birds for later publication in his seminal work on the subject, *The Birds of America*.

Winslow Homer captured scenes of the rural American landscape in his works in the latter half of the nineteenth century, at the same time that painters of the **American Great West** were active. Captivated by the staggering scale and diversity of cultures in the American West, as well as by the character of the American westward movement, painters such as **Frederick Remington, George C. Bingham**, and **Charles M. Russell** brought forth a genre that sought to convey the history and emotion of the westward migration and of the cowboy culture that followed. While paintings of historical scenes were less popular in the nineteenth century than they had been in the preceding century, **Emanuel Leutze's** painting of **George Washington Crossing the Delaware** is among the most widely recognized American paintings of all time. Many of the artistic products of the nineteenth century still retained a strong sense of romanticism. One exception is the work of **Thomas Eakins**, whose paintings centered on the lives of the city-dwelling, middle class.

The era also featured a noteworthy class of American expatriate artists living and working in Europe, among them the **impressionists James Whistler, John Singer Sargent**, and **Mary Cassat.**

The European influence in America contributed to the popularity of the **Art Nouveau** style around the close of the nineteenth century. French for "New Art," this style was in many ways a reaction to more academic forms of art and was defined by dynamic curving lines and references to the natural world, taking cues from philosophy and extending into architecture and applied art. Historically, its greatest significance lies in its place as a connector between the revival styles of nineteenth century art and architecture and the modernism of twentieth-century art.

Twentieth-Century Art

Twentieth-century art is often described as either a reaction to, or in some cases a rejection of, previous artistic conventions. Much of the art of the period was also sensitive to and informed by the cultural, social, and economic upheavals surrounding its creators. **Ashcan painters**, among them **George Bellows, John Sloan, George Benjamin Luks, Everett Shinn,** and **Robert Henri**, created art that faithfully portrayed the struggles of the urban working class. Ashcan painters were part of the group of painters sometimes referred to as **"The Eight"** that exhibited their work at the **Macbeth Galleries** in New York, in protest against the limited selection of styles of work displayed by the conservative, but enormously influential, **National Academy of Design**.

The next movement to take hold of American art in the twentieth century was Modernism—a style imported from Europe and practiced by cubist and abstract painters. Important early American modernists include **Morgan Russell, Alfred Henry Maurer, Stanton MacDonald-Wright, Patrick Henry Bruce**, and **Georgia O'Keeffe**.

Among the most important events in the history of modern art in the United States was the exhibition known as the **Armory Show**. The exhibition took its name from the National Guard Armory in New York where it was held in 1913. It introduced American art viewers to the modernist styles of avant-garde European artists, opening the door for further acceptance of the works of American modernists in artistic circles. Because of its enormous popularity, the exhibition took to the road, showing in Chicago and Boston.

Not all American artists embraced European modernism. **Reginald Marsh, Guy Pène du Bois, Charles Sheeler**, and **Grant Wood** all were post–World War I artists who painted in a modified realist style, while **Edward Hopper** avoided painting social scenes and focused on shape and light.

Also after World War I, a group of artists, following the newly completed Santa Fe Railroad, migrated westward, eventually settling in artists colonies, and painting works that prominently included elements of the **American Southwest**. Some of those works eventually found their way into advertising materials produced by the Santa Fe Railroad. **Georgia O'Keefe**, an artist who visited the Southwest and eventually settled in New Mexico, became especially famous for her paintings of bones, flowers, and Southwestern landscapes.

In architecture, the enormously popular **Art Deco** style's elegant geometric forms came to symbolize 1920s America. One of the most famous examples is New York City's **Chrysler Building**.

Beginning in the 1920s and continuing into the 1930s, a new wave of well-educated and politically minded African American artists spearheaded a new movement in art and literature with its roots in and around Harlem, New York. The work of the photographer **James Van DerZee** and the artists **Charles Alston,**

Augusta Savage, Palmer Hayden, Archibald Motley, Sargent Johnson, and **Lois Mailou Jones** all typified the movement, known as the **Harlem Renaissance**.

The first contemporary American art form that gained worldwide recognition and influence was that of **abstract expressionism**. While abstract expressionists represented a litany of specific techniques and styles, they were broadly unified by their use of large canvases, experimentation with different brushstrokes, and techniques of applying brightly colored paints to canvas. **Jackson Pollock**, probably the most important American abstract expressionist, pioneered **Action Painting**: a method by which paint was poured from a can or dripped from a can onto canvas.

Later abstract artists preferred works of mixed media as well as satirical renderings of ordinary objects and elements of American popular culture. These so-called **Pop Artists**, including **Andy Warhol** and **Roy Lichtenstein**, painted a variety of images—from comic characters to soup cans.

The impact of realism was reflected through **Andrew Wyeth's** rural landscapes, **Norman Rockwell's** illustrations of everyday American life—widely recognized from their placement on the covers of *Saturday Evening Post* magazines—and the cityscapes of **Edward Hopper**.

AMERICAN MUSICAL MOVEMENTS

You should also be familiar with some of America's music, musical influence, and musical movements that appear on the exam.

Other than the mostly ceremonial music of Native Americans, the earliest American music was imported, brought to the colonies as the folk music of the English, French, and Spanish settlers and West African slaves. The music of early European settlers often took the form of religious compositions and **ballads**, while the music of African slaves featured **polyrhythms** and followed the **call-and-response** style, including **work songs**, sung by slaves in the field, and spirituals that blended African styles with traditional European hymns. During the Great Awakening of the nineteenth century, spirituals spread across the country, influencing later musical styles.

With the expansion of the United States also came the inclusion of new ethnic and cultural groups and their distinct musical traditions, including **Cajun** and **Creole** music in Louisiana, new Spanish and Mexican styles in the American southwest, Chinese and Japanese music—especially along the Pacific coast—and Eastern Europe music, including the **polka**, brought to the United States by Czech and Polish settlers. Around the turn of the twentieth century, **ragtime**, with its syncopated rhythms, grew from its roots in New Orleans and St. Louis to become a nationwide sensation. Scott Joplin's "The Entertainer" is the most famous (and most frequently tested) composition in the style. Ragtime contained elements of African polyrhythms, and perhaps surprisingly also, of the **march**, popularized by the legendary composer of patriotic marches, **John Philips Sousa**.

During the twentieth century, American popular music came into its own right. Jazz and the blues, with roots in urban and rural black communities, respectively, changed the face of American popular music. Originally performed in cities such as Chicago, New Orleans, and Memphis, the simple, narrative ballads of the blues grew out of spirituals and work sounds of the previous centuries, while jazz fused European and African music in a syncopated, often improvised style. Many of the greatest hits of late nineteenth and early twentieth century popular music were produced as sheet music by the publishers and songwriters of **Tin Pan Alley** in New York. Tin Pan Alley's dominance of American popular music came to an end with the advent of the phonograph and the radio. The ability to record and sell or broadcast albums meant that for the first time musical stars such as **Louis Armstrong**, one of the most famous musicians of the Jazz age, and female blues performer **Mamie Smith**, emerged. Jazz came also to include big band swing, a widely recognized dance genre of the 1930s featuring large ensemble orchestras in often glamorous settings. At the same time, the American musical theater grew in popularity, initially through **vaudeville** variety shows, and later in a more mature form through the acclaimed works of composers such as **George Gershwin and Richard Rodgers**, and lyricists **Ira Gershwin** (George's brother), **Lorenz Hart**, and **Oscar Hammerstein**.

During the 1940s, folk singers such as Pete Seeger became popular, influenced by earlier folk singer-songwriters such as Woody Guthrie, whose music is synonymous with that of the Great Depression. Post–World War II American saw several booms—an economic boom, a baby boom—and a boom in the popularity of a unique new form of music, **rock and roll**, which followed on the heels of rockabilly music in the 1950s. Also during the 1950s, **soul music** evolved from its gospel origins, and **country music** began to grow in popularity. **Teen stars** such as **Frank Sinatra** expanded the reach of music beyond adult-only audiences—a trend that would continue in the 1960s, when the **Beatles** (a British group that was part of the so-called "British invasion" of the decade) captured the attention of millions of American teens. It was also during the 1960s that music—especially rock and roll—became closely linked to the **counterculture** and **youth movement** of the decade, as the iconic musicians of the era became associated with the social and political tumult of the era, and events such as **Woodstock** became symbols of a generation. During the same decade, female soul singers **Diana Ross** and **Aretha Franklin** gained fame, and **James Brown** invented an entirely new type of soul, referred to as **funk**. Together, soul and funk were strong musical influences on the Black Power and civil rights movements that weighed heavily on the decade's political discourse.

IMPORTANT SUPREME COURT DECISIONS

Over the years, the Supreme Court has rendered a number of landmark decisions that appear as part of questions on the SAT Subject Test in U.S. History. These cases have either settled an existing question of law or established an important new legal precedent that guided later decisions. The cases and their significance are described as follows:

Chisholm v. Georgia, 419 (1793). States may be sued in federal court by citizens of other states. This decision was invalidated by the Eleventh Amendment.

Marbury v. Madison (1803). Congress cannot pass laws that contravene the Constitution; the first example of judicial review.

McCulloch v. Maryland (1819). State laws cannot restrict the valid exercise of the implied powers granted to the federal government under the Necessary and Proper Clause of the Constitution.

Gibbons v. Ogden (1824). The Commerce Clause of the Constitution grants Congress the authority to regulate interstate commerce.

Dred Scott v. Sandford (1857). Enslaved and formerly enslaved persons of African descent cannot be United States citizens and, as a consequence, lack the standing to bring suit in federal court.

Reynolds v. United States (1879). Religious belief is not a legitimate defense against indictment for criminal acts.

Plessy v. Ferguson (1896). Segregation is constitutional so long as separate facilities remain equal in quality, the so-called "separate but equal" doctrine. This case was overturned by *Brown v. Board of Education* (1954).

Muller v. Oregon (1908). Oregon's progressive-era reforms restricting the working hours of women are constitutional, because of the state's compelling interest in their health.

Schenck v. United States (1919). Speech that is intended to result in a crime and that poses a "clear and present" danger in its expression is not protected speech under the First Amendment.

Korematsu v. United States (1944). President Franklin Roosevelt's Executive Order interning Japanese-American citizens during World War II was constitutional.

Morgan v. Virginia (1946). Virginia's state law segregating interstate buses is unconstitutional.

Brown v. Board of Education (1954). The Court overturned the separate but equal doctrine, ruling that segregation in public education is illegal.

Mapp v. Ohio (1961). Evidence obtained via an illegal search or seizure is inadmissible as evidence in a state court.

Baker v. Carr (1962). The federal courts have the authority to review redistricting of state legislative districts.

Engel v. Vitale (**1962**). School-led prayer in public schools violates the Establishment Clause of the Constitution.

Gideon v. Wainwright (**1963**). All defendants have the right to counsel, and if they cannot afford an attorney, they must be provided one by the state.

New York Times Co. v. Sullivan (**1964**). In pursuing libel cases, government officials must show not just that published reports are false, but that they were published with malicious intent whether true or false.

Wesberry v. Sanders (**1964**). Districts from which members of the House of Representatives are selected must be, as nearly as is possible, equal in population.

Griswold v. Connecticut (**1965**). This ruling explicitly defined a right to privacy in striking down a Connecticut law banning the use of contraceptives by married couples.

Miranda v. Arizona (**1966**). Law enforcement must advise suspects of their rights to remain silent, consult with counsel, and have such counsel appointed if they are unable to afford an attorney.

Loving v. Virginia (**1967**). Laws prohibiting interracial marriage are illegal.

Roe v. Wade (**1973**). Most laws prohibiting a woman's ability to receive an abortion prior to the third trimester of pregnancy were struck down by the ruling, which held that such laws unduly violated a woman's right to privacy under the Fourteenth Amendment's due process clause.

United States v. Nixon (**1974**). The President cannot invoke executive privilege for purposes of withholding evidence in criminal proceeding.

Bush v. Gore (**2000**). The ballot recount in Florida during the 2000 presidential election violated the Equal Protection Clause of the Constitution. This ruling ended the recount and resolved the disputed outcome of the election in Florida.

Chapter 12 Drill

Turn to Part IV for answers and explanations.

1. Which of the following art movements, especially popular during and associated with the 1920s, can be seen in such iconic architecture as that of Chrysler Building in New York City?

   (A) Impressionism
   (B) Art Nouveau
   (C) Hudson River School
   (D) Neo-classicalism
   (E) Art Deco

2. Freedom Riders rode interstate buses to test interstate desegregation legislation passed in the 1950s. The Supreme Court previously struck down a state law segregating buses in which of the following cases?

   (A) *Loving v. Virginia*
   (B) *Morgan v. Virginia*
   (C) *Mapp v. Ohio*
   (D) *Miranda v. Arizona*
   (E) *Muller v. Oregon*

3. The Supreme Court under John Marshall handed down decisions that

   (A) often clashed with Thomas Jefferson, and other Democrats' view on the Constitution
   (B) were careful to limit the scope of the federal government to those specific powers that were granted it under the Constitution
   (C) nearly always favored states on questions pertaining to the federal government's power over them
   (D) that included a rejection of the constitutionality of judicial review
   (E) generally favored a broad interpretation of the federal government's powers as provided for by the Constitution

4. Martha Graham was best known for which of the following?

   (A) The popularity of the films in which she starred
   (B) Her novels that focused on poverty and issues of social injustice
   (C) Her crusading articles against abusive business practices
   (D) Emotional, minimalistic dance performances
   (E) Short stories that captured the spirit of the 1920s

5. Civil disobedience, a practice that later inspired many who advocated for nonviolent resistance during the civil rights movement, is most closely associated with which of the following philosophies or movements?

   (A) Manifest Destiny
   (B) Transcendentalism
   (C) Black power
   (D) Post-modernism
   (E) Nativism

6. The so-called "lost generation" of American writers are most closely associated with which of the following decades?

   (A) 1870s
   (B) 1920s
   (C) 1940s
   (D) 1950s
   (E) 1970s

7. The Supreme Court's decisions in *Dred Scott v. Sandford*, *Plessy v. Ferguson*, and *Brown v. Board of Education* are all examples of

(A) the court's unwillingness to offer rulings at odds with existing state or federal policies
(B) the court's consistent rejection of racially discriminatory actions
(C) cases dealing with the legality of slavery
(D) rulings specifically affirming or denying the constitutionality of segregation in the South
(E) cases in which the courts dealt with questions relating to matters of race

8. Which of the following writers was associated with the Harlem Renaissance?

(A) Langston Hughes
(B) T.S. Eliot
(C) John Steinbeck
(D) Mark Twain
(E) Alex de Tocqueville

9. The improvisational character of which musical style is closely associated with the loosening of social restrictions and the rejection of cultural tradition during the 1920s?

(A) Spirituals
(B) Blues
(C) Jazz
(D) Rock 'n' Roll
(E) Ragtime

10. Which of the following painters is well known for painting scenes that featured iconic elements of the American West?

(A) Frederic Remington
(B) Normal Rockwell
(C) John James Audubon
(D) Andy Warhol
(E) Jackson Pollock

Part IV
Drill Answers and Explanations

CHAPTER 6 DRILL ANSWERS AND EXPLANATIONS

1. **D** The English colonial system during the seventeenth and eighteenth centuries was largely based on the principles of mercantilism. Mercantilism argued that the purpose of colonies was to enrich the mother country by providing natural resources and then purchasing the manufactured goods produced by the mother country, usually at an inflated price.

2. **C** The Columbian Exchange was the exchange of animals, plants, culture, human populations, diseases, technology, and ideas between the Americas, Europe, and Asia following Christopher Columbus's voyage to the New World and the subsequent exploration and settlement there by European nations.

3. **A** European nations explored the New World for raw materials, land to be settled, a shorter trade route to Asia, and for precious metals such as gold. They did not, however, search for trading partners among the previously existing inhabitants of North and South America. Most European nations saw Native Americans as obstacles to colonialism, and at best, as people to take advantage of in terms of trade.

4. **E** The Proclamation of 1763 prohibited colonists from settling beyond the Appalachian Mountains in order to limit the amount of land the British had to defend and the number of clashes between French Settlers, Native Americans, and colonists. Although the British had won the right to this territory in the French and Indian War, it did not have the capability to defend or control all of it.

5. **C** The First Continental Congress met to create a list of grievances to send to the King of England and Parliament. Its other main purpose was to organize a boycott of British goods. The delegates did not yet plan military action as they hoped to reach some sort of agreement with Great Britain, so III is incorrect.

6. **C** While the colonists disagreed with many of the King and Parliament's policies, anti-monarchist sentiment was not one of the major reasons that the colonists wanted to separate from Great Britain.

7. **B** Thomas Paine's *Common Sense* argued that the Americans should split from England and form a republic, with no king or nobility. Paine felt it went against nature for an island to rule over a whole continent. *Poor Richard's Almanac* was an almanac written by Benjamin Franklin, which had advice and data about weather, farming, and household tasks. The Olive Branch Petition was the letter sent from the colonists to the King of England, asking him to prevent further conflict. *Civil Disobedience* was Henry David Thoreau's essay in which he argued against allowing governments to overrule one's own conscience.

8. **D** The American alliance with France provided money, weapons, and a navy, all of which were invaluable to the cause of independence. The Continental Army's familiarity with the territory did give them an advantage over the British, as was the fact that the Americans were fighting for a cause that was extremely personal to them. The Continental Army did employ nontraditional military practices like shooting from behind trees or rocks rather than in the open; however, the British military was much better trained and equipped as it was one of the most powerful militaries in the world at the time.

9. **A** British colonial policies, such as the Stamp Act, Tea Act, etc., which were passed without the colonists being represented in Parliament, created conflicts between the colonies and England. As these conflicts became more frequent and more severe, the movement towards independence grew as well. Choice (B) is not true because the colonies were a source of income for Great Britain. Choice (C) is not true because the split between Patriots and Loyalists was not only territorial. Choice (D) is not true because the French Revolution happened after the American Revolution. Choice (E) is not true because colonists came to America for economic and religious freedom but did not want to break completely with England.

CHAPTER 7 DRILL ANSWERS AND EXPLANATIONS

1. **B** The primary purpose of the Tariff of 1828, which angered many in the primarily agrarian South, was to protect manufacturing from foreign competition by increasing the cost of imported manufactured goods.

2. **A** Personal liberty laws were passed in the North for the first time in response to the Fugitive Slave Act of 1793. The laws took a number of forms, but did such things as provide for jury trials for escaped slaves or barred escaped slaves from being housed in local jails. The Fugitive Slave Act of 1850 included several provisions intended to void the protections of these personal liberty laws.

3. **E** The passage of both the Tariff of 1828 and the Tariff of 1832 imposed steep taxes on the importation of British goods and angered many politically influential Southerners who depended on trade with Britain. In response, proponents of nullification suggested that when a federal law grossly contravenes the interests of a state, that state has the right to nullify the law in question.

4. **C** While the Kentucky and Virginia Resolutions, drafted by Jefferson and Madison in response to the Alien and Sedition Acts, and the South Carolina Ordinance of Nullification were written in response to different specific issues, both shared a common, underlying theory—that federal laws could be overridden by the states in instances when the interests of the two were in conflict.

5. D Net population growth would be determined by four factors: birth rate, death rate, immigration rate (the rate at which new immigrants enter a country), and emigration rate (the rate at which those resident in a country depart it). Any source providing specific data on one of those four factors in the United States during the period indicated in the question would be useful in isolating the contribution of immigration to total population growth relative to those other factors. The source in (D) does this, while the others do not.

6. A One of the first significant events promoting mass migration westward was the California Gold Rush of 1849. This preceded the completion of the first transcontinental railroad (in 1869, a major event in western immigration after the Civil War), the passage of the Compromise of 1850 and the Homestead Act of 1862, and the establishment of cattle ranching as a dominant industry. The latter occurred only after mining activity, the first major industry that gave birth to a number of Western boomtowns, waned.

7. A Many in Congress felt that endless debates on slavery were counterproductive and that the divisive issue distracted from other important matters. The resolution passed over the objection of a few members who objected on moral grounds, and was rescinded eight years later.

8. B When no candidate received a majority of votes in the presidential election of 1824, the election was sent to the House of Representatives for resolution. While Andrew Jackson received the plurality of the popular vote, the House elected John Quincy Adams. Many of Jackson's supporters believed that Henry Clay, the influential speaker of the House, had thrown his weight in the House behind Adams in exchange for being appointed Secretary of State by Adams. This fueled a four-year "revenge" campaign by Jackson's supporters, and signaled a split in the previously unified Democratic-Republicans and the emergence of a new group of Jacksonian Democrats.

9. A Eli Whitney invented the cotton gin, a device that made the large-scale production of cotton profitable in the Antebellum South and greatly solidified the economic foundation on which the southern plantation system was built.

10. D While the Kansas-Nebraska Act was intended by its primary sponsor, Illinois Senator Stephen Douglas, to allow for the construction of a transcontinental railroad by organizing the Kansas and Nebraska territories, its outcome was disastrous. By admitting Kansas and Nebraska under popular sovereignty—allowing the citizens of each territory to vote on whether or not slavery would be permitted in the territories—the Missouri Compromise, which had prohibited slavery in lands obtained as part of the Louisiana purchase, was effectively repealed. This set the stage for the enormous bloodshed that followed the influx of pro- and anti-slavery groups into the territories ahead of voting on the slavery issue.

CHAPTER 8 DRILL ANSWERS AND EXPLANATIONS

1. **D** By issuing the Emancipation Proclamation, Lincoln explicitly extended Union war goals to include ending slavery. However, public opinion on immediate emancipation in the North was mixed, and Lincoln was concerned that emancipating slaves in states not currently in rebellion would be received poorly in slave-holding Border States.

2. **C** The Fourteenth Amendment to the Constitution is one of the Reconstruction Amendments. Its Due Process Clause prevents states from depriving citizens of due process and its Equal Protection Clause requires that states protect all citizens—regardless of race—equally under the law.

3. **E** From the Civil War's outset, Lincoln made plain his war aims—to fulfill the obligation he felt to the office of the Presidency and, accordingly, to preserve the Union.

4. **B** A historian interested in the impact of the Civil War on the economy of the South would be interested in data that indicated Southern economic output in the decades immediately preceding, and after, the Civil War. Choice B would provide this information.

5. **C** Radical Congressional Republicans were concerned that Johnson's plan for Reconstruction, like Lincoln's Ten Percent Plan, was too lenient in its treatment of defeated Southern states. Johnson's plan for Presidential Reconstruction circumvented Congress, directing readmission of states via Presidential decree. When Southern states elected former rebel leaders to positions in newly formed civil governments and instituted Black Codes, Congress took action to countermand such laws over Johnson's vetoes. Following a conflict over the Fourteenth Amendment and the Tenure of Office Act, which Johnson violated, Johnson was impeached by the House of Representatives, narrowly avoiding conviction during a trial in the Senate.

6. **E** During the summer of 1863, Lee began his second invasion of the North, hoping that a successful Confederate advance into Pennsylvania could change the tenor of the political debate and perhaps open the door for a negotiated peace. Lee's Army of Northern Virginia and George Meade's Army of the Potomac met and fought a pitched battle over three days at Gettysburg. Lee's defeat and subsequent retreat back into Virginia represented the Confederacy's farthest advance into Northern territory and a turning point in the Civil War.

7. **E** Southern laws passed during Reconstruction to prevent blacks from voting (including poll taxes, literacy tests, grandfather clauses—these were laws that typically exempted whites and that stipulated that those whose grandfathers were not eligible to vote were not themselves eligible to vote) and physical intimidation were all used to effectively disenfranchise blacks. Income tests for voters, however, were not commonly instituted in the South.

8. **B** The Southern economy was thrown into upheaval in the wake of slavery's end in the South. The sharecropping system evolved to partially replace the plantation system in Southern agriculture. In the sharecropping system, sharecropping farmers, many of whom were former slaves, received a loan for food and supplies from a merchant and were provided land, seeds, equipment and other necessities for farming from landholders. After selling his harvest and paying off his debt to the merchant and the landowners, sharecroppers were often left with very little—if any—profit.

9. **A** During Sherman's campaign in Georgia, Union troops marched from the captured city of Atlanta to the port city of Savannah, levelling infrastructure, industry, military targets and in many cases civilian property, along the way. This "March to the Sea" was one of the first examples of the concept of "total warfare" in modern military history. Its main purpose being to disrupt the Southern war effort and to discourage further resistance by Southerners.

10. **A** In response to the passage of Black Codes by recalcitrant Southern legislators, Republicans in Congress passed both the Fourteenth and Fifteenth Amendments. These amendments granted citizenship to freed slaves, ensured due process and equal protection under the law for all, and prohibitied disenfranchisement on the basis of race, color, or having previously been a slave.

CHAPTER 9 DRILL ANSWERS AND EXPLANATIONS

1. **C** The Black Friday, Credit Mobilier, Whiskey Ring, and the Belknap Scandals all occurred during the scandal-prone administration of Ulysses S. Grant. The Teapot Dome Scandal, which involved the improper leasing of federal oil reserves in Wyoming and California, occurred during the equally scandal-prone Harding administration.

2. **A** Maximum rate laws were part of a larger Progressive effort to regulate the potentially abusive practices of large business interests. In particular, maximum rate laws set caps on rates charged by railroad carriers and in doing so, limited their capacity to act collusively.

3. **B** The Federal Trade Commission (FTC) was established by the Federal Trade Commission Act during the Wilson Administration. Its mandate was to protect consumer interests and to police anticompetitive, monopolistic practices by businesses—both important areas of concern for Progressive reformers and Democrats, including Woodrow Wilson.

4. **D**   The Dawes Act of 1887 was passed in response to a growing public perception that the reservation system was failing—a perception in part fueled by *A Century of Dishonor*. The Dawes Act itself permitted the President to divide tribal lands and award Indians who lived separately from the tribe United States citizenship. The authors and supporters of the legislation hoped that individual land ownership by Indians would aid in their assimilation into American culture.

5. **E**   The Haymarket Square Riot began as a peaceful protest, but after a demonstrator threw a bomb into a crowd of police, the police acted violently to suppress the protest. A number of police officers and rioters died in the ensuing melee, during which the police opened fire on the crowd. Several anarchists, with alleged ties to organized labor, were tried and convicted in connection with the riot. Public sentiment toward labor soured dramatically as a result of the riot and its apparent ties to anarchists.

6. **A**   During the late 1800s, U.S. Senator Roscoe Conkling, and other conservatives who opposed Rutherford B. Hayes' civil service reforms, were referred to as "Stalwarts." More moderate, reform-minded Republicans who were opposed to the patronage system and supported the passage of the Pendleton Civil Service Reform Act were referred to as Half-Breeds.

7. **A**   William Jennings Bryan was a three-time Democratic nominee for President and a leading voice in the Populist movement of the late nineteenth century. Bryan, a so-called "Silverite," strongly opposed the gold standard and the moneyed interests which he felt it favored, and instead advocated for an inflationary policy via free coinage of silver. In his legendary "Cross of Gold" speech given at the 1896 Democratic National Convention and referred to in the cartoon, he blasted banking and industrial interests for advocating for the continuation of the gold standard at the expense of the working class.

8. **E**   Industrialization in the United States was driven by the advent of new technologies, available immigrant labor, and abundant natural resources. Industrialization occurred much more rapidly in the Northeast, where slave labor was unavailable, than in the Antebellum South, where it remained tied to the plantation. After the Civil War, industrialization continued at an even more rapid pace, especially in the Northeast.

9. **A**   The Sherman Antitrust Act was a landmark piece of reformist legislation that allowed the federal government to protect consumers by pursuing powerful, and often monopolistic, business trusts that acted anticompetitively. This legislation provided the legal instrument by which the Justice Department brought suit against John D. Rockefeller's powerful Standard Oil trusts.

10. **A**   During the latter half of the nineteenth century, waves of immigrants landed on American shores. Many of them settled in growing urban areas, contributing significantly to that population growth. These new immigrants found work in the factories of the burgeoning industrial centers of the Northeast and Midwest.

CHAPTER 10 DRILL ANSWERS AND EXPLANATIONS

1. **C**   The United States' strong aversion to foreign military engagement during the interwar years led to bilateral and multilateral arms reduction and limitation agreements in foreign policy decisions. This was intended to contain threats through diplomacy. The Washington Naval Conference of 1921 sought to limit the number and type of warships built by the United States and eight other signatory nations. While the treaty did help preserve the peace during the 1920s, it likely also enabled the Japanese to emerge as a significant naval threat in the Pacific in the years prior to World War II.

2. **A**   The male workforce available for employment in war industries declined as many of the men that otherwise would be employed in factories volunteered for or were drafted into the armed services. To meet the surge in labor demands caused by the war effort, many women entered the labor force, some of whom entered areas of employment (such as factories) where women were previously considered unfit to work.

3. **E**   Keynesianism, a school of economic thought built on the work of British economist John Maynard Keynes, argues that during times of economic crisis and deep dislocation, the intervention of central banks and fiscal policy makers is required to increase the money supply and stimulate the economy via public spending. Keynes' views contrasted sharply with those of many of the classical economists of the time, and informed many of Franklin Roosevelt's New Deal-era economic policies.

4. **C**   Throughout the 1920s, a strong isolationist streak pervaded American foreign policy. This was largely a reaction to the public consensus, driven by the nation's shared experience during World War I, that the United States should avoid military involvement overseas. This time period corresponds to the Presidencies of Warren G. Harding, Calvin Coolidge, and Herbert Hoover. The nation was not finally, fully stirred from its isolationist tendencies until the Japanese attack on Pearl Harbor in 1941.

5. **E**   The Atlantic Charter was a pivotal policy statement initially agreed to between the United States and Great Britain that set a number of broad principles for the Allies' war aims and their vision of a post-war world. These principles outlined in the Atlantic Charter would inspire many of the provisions of the numerous international charters drafted after World War II.

6. **A**   President Wilson resisted calls to enter World War I after the loss of 139 American citizens aboard the *RMS Lusitania*, a British passenger ship torpedoed and sunk by a German U-boat in 1915. A German apology and promise to not engage in neutral shipping was sufficient to satisfy an outraged American public that was, nonetheless, still somewhat reluctant to enter the war in Europe. However, following the disclosure of the Zimmermann Letter and the resumption of unrestricted German submarine warfare in 1917, the United States chose to enter the war on the side of the Allied Powers.

7. **D**   George Washington warned against the dangers of entangling permanent alliances in his Farewell Address. This was the same issue that caused significant concern for Republican opponents of American membership in the League of Nations. Led by Senator Henry Cabot Lodge, Wilson's chief antagonist in the Senate, these Senators were worried by the potential consequence of the Treaty of Versailles and of American involvement in the League of Nations for a nation that had just emerged from a costly war in Europe.

8. **D**   Of the Presidents listed, only Woodrow Wilson served a first term during a period when the significant possibility of war existed and was forestalled, and who also mounted a successful re-election campaign.

9. **B**   Most economists agree that the Federal Reserve's failure to expand the money supply to meet the needs of banks facing huge redemptions by depositors—at a time when many banks faced potential failure—precipitated a number of bank failures and constrained the availability of credit, exacerbating an already serious economic problem.

10. **A**   Following World War I and the Russian Revolution, social and political upheaval seemed none too uncommon in Europe. Many Americans feared that the same thing could occur in the United States. The xenophobia present in American society after World War I, and the significant number of foreign-born immigrants in the labor movement—already closely associated with socialism and left-leaning politics—led to a deep suspicion of foreigners and their presumed socialist and subversive tendencies.

CHAPTER 11 DRILL ANSWERS AND EXPLANATIONS

1. **A**   Ronald Reagan was a strong proponent of supply-side economics, which rests on the premise that reducing tax rates on the largest taxpayers—the wealthy—will lead to an investable surplus that will trickle down to the less affluent through job creation and economic growth. Reagan acted on this theory during his term by pushing legislation through Congress decreasing the top marginal tax rates significantly.

2. **C**   The failure of the Bay of Pigs invasion, an effort to overthrow the Communist Cuban regime of Fidel Castro in 1961 by CIA-supported Cuban exiles, was an enormous embarrassment for the new Kennedy administration, and served to heighten tensions between Castro and the United States—tensions that would come to a head during the Cuban Missile Crisis the following year.

3. **D**   Theodore Roosevelt's Square Deal programs centered on conservation of natural resources, placing restrictions on the power of large business interests and providing protection to consumers—thereby helping working- and middle-class Americans. Johnson's Great Society program aimed to eliminate poverty and curb racial injustice, sharing the common aim of improving the day-to-day lives of, among others, working-class and poor Americans.

4. **B**   While the Carter administration was plagued by a number of problems, including slow economic growth, an Arab oil embargo, and persistently high interest rates, it not surprisingly did not face a stock market bubble, as there was little economic optimism to fuel the development of such a bubble.

5. **D**   During the 1950s, Senator Joseph McCarthy was the public face of the widespread American fear of Communist subversion. McCarthy fueled those fears by famously claiming in public hearings that he possessed specific information implicating a significant number of important government and military figures as Communist sympathizers and spies. While McCarthy was unable to substantiate his claims, leading to his censure by the Senate, his demagoguery inspired the term "McCarthyism," which has become associated with the era.

6. **A**   After World War II, the population of areas surrounding American cities ballooned with America's growing, Baby-Boom era population, as many—especially white Americans, as part of the phenomenon known as "white flight"—fled cities to suburbs.

7. **A**   During the mid-1950s, many in the Eisenhower administration were deeply concerned by growing Soviet influence in the Middle East. Nationalist Egyptian President Nasser accepted economic aid from the Soviet Union; Britain, France and Israel, withdrew from Egypt at the end of the Suez Crisis. President Eisenhower, fearing a power vacuum that would increasingly be occupied by the U.S.S.R., indicated to Congress via the Eisenhower Doctrine that any Middle Eastern nation being threatened by an aggressor nation could request economic and military aid from the United States. Eisenhower specifically singled out the Soviet Union in this speech, linking the Middle East to the international fight against Communism.

8. **C**   Richard Nixon's historic visit to the People's Republic of China in 1972 was an important diplomatic overture that set the stage for the normalization of relations between the United States and China. Nixon, whose anti-Communist credentials were well established by the time of his visit, was relatively immune to charges of being "soft on communism," and hoped that by forging a relationship between the United States and China, he would strengthen the American hand in the Cold War power struggle with the U.S.S.R, while also enjoying a boost in political popularity at home.

9. **E**   All of the crises presented in the question are correctly paired with the President who was in office when they occurred, with the exception of Bill Clinton and the Persian Gulf War. Following Iraq's 1990 invasion of its neighbor to the south, Kuwait, Bill Clinton's predecessor, George H. W. Bush, successfully led a coalition of nations to expel Saddam Hussein's Iraqi force from Kuwait during the Persian Gulf War.

10.   **C**   During the Civil Rights Movement, Martin Luther King, Jr., was a strong, moderating voice, urging nonviolent means of advocating for an immediate end to segregation in the United States.

CHAPTER 12 DRILL ANSWERS AND EXPLANATIONS

1.   **E**   The Chrysler Building is a prominent example of Art Deco architecture. The movement, which was inspired by and succeeded the Art Nouveau style, became significant during the period between the First and Second World Wars and was characterized by bold colors and geometric shapes that reflected the rapid technological advancements of the era.

2.   **B**   In 1946, the Supreme Court ruled in the case of *Morgan v. Virginia* that a Virginia law segregating interstate buses was unconstitutional, holding that the buses represented a form of interstate commerce and were, accordingly, covered by the Constitution's Interstate Commerce Clause.

3.   **E**   Throughout John Marshall's long tenure as Chief Justice of the Supreme Court, the Court routinely handed down rulings that emphasized the flexibility and broad scope of the powers that the federal government could exercise under the Constitution, helping to build a strong Federalist system of government in the process. By striking down an act of Congress in *Marbury v. Madison* and establishing the principle of judicial review in doing so, the Marshall Court helped elevate itself to an equal place of importance alongside the other two branches of government.

4.   **D**   Martha Graham is widely held as the most important figure of twentieth-century dance and was renowned for the emotion and expression she brought to her performances of modern dance.

5.   **B**   Transcendentalism, the literary and philosophical movement that was advanced by writers such as Henry David Thoreau and Ralph Waldo Emerson—a century before the Civil Rights Movement—emphasized spiritual sensitivity, self-reflection and self-reliance. Thoreau's doctrine of passive resistance, expressed in *Civil Disobedience*, was an important intellectual influence of anti-war and Civil Rights leaders in the 1960s.

6.   **B**   The group of expatriate American writers that came of age during World War I including F. Scott Fitzgerald, T. S. Eliot, and Gertrude Stein, are known as The Lost Generation.

7.   **E**   In all three cases mentioned in the question—*Dred Scott v. Sandford*, *Plessy v. Ferguson*, and *Brown v. Board of Education*—the Supreme Court dealt with a question of race. The Supreme Court hoped to finally resolve the question of slavery by ruling in the Dred Scott Decision that Dred Scott was not a United States citizen and did not have status to sue in Federal Court and that his emancipation would unconstitutionally deprive his owner of property. Rather than resolve the issue of slavery, however, the ruling only further enflamed the already heated public debate over slavery. Nearly 40 years later, in *Plessy v. Ferguson*, the Court held that the separate but equal doctrine was constitutional, giving Constitutional validation to the legal principle upon which segregation rested. The court's ruling would stand until it was overturned by the *Brown v. Board of Education* in 1954.

8.   **A**   Langston Hughes was an African-American poet, playwright, novelist and social activist who pioneered the art form known as Jazz Poetry and was a key leader of the Harlem Renaissance—the cultural and intellectual movement that sprang up in the Harlem neighborhood of New York City in the 1920s.

9.   **C**   Termed the "Jazz Age" by a great author who wrote of the period, F. Scott Fitzgerald, jazz music is closely associated with the 1920s. The syncopated rhythm and improvisation of Jazz corresponded to the era's dynamism, in many ways a reaction to the deprivation of World War I, which incorporated a new sense of modernity and a rejection of certain, more restrictive social mores. This is especially clear in the popularity of jazz dance music during the decade.

10.   **A**   Frederic Remington became famous for his romantic paintings of cowboys, American Indians, and other depictions of the Old American West.

Part V
Additional Practice Tests

Chapter 13
Practice Test 2

U.S. HISTORY
SUBJECT TEST 2

Your responses to the U.S. History Subject Test questions must be filled in on Test 2 of your answer sheet (the answer sheet at the back of the book). Marks on any other section will not be counted toward your U.S. History Subject Test score.

When your supervisor gives the signal, turn the page and begin the U.S. History Subject Test.

U.S. HISTORY SUBJECT TEST 2

Directions: Each of the questions or incomplete statements below is followed by five suggested answers or completions. Select one that is best in each case and then fill in the corresponding oval on the answer sheet.

1. One direct result of the Tea Act of 1773 was

   (A) a sharp decline in tea exports from British East India
   (B) an increase in the price of coffee beans
   (C) a drop in profits among American colonial tea merchants
   (D) an armed revolt from the American colonists in Massachusetts, New York, and Maryland
   (E) a disruption of British trade in tobacco and sugar

2. All of the following played a role in encouraging American colonists to rebel against the British government EXCEPT

   (A) Henry David Thoreau
   (B) Samuel Adams
   (C) Patrick Henry
   (D) Thomas Paine
   (E) Thomas Jefferson

3. Which of the following is the best definition for the economic term *overspeculation*?

   (A) Overanalyzing the pros and cons of a decision before making it
   (B) Making investments based on the theoretical value of a company rather than its actual value
   (C) Buying more stock than there is available for a company
   (D) Valuing the dollar based on inflated gold prices
   (E) Buying stocks from different companies in the same field in order to increase profits

4. The government body most responsible for deciding how to raise federal revenue is the

   (A) Internal Revenue Service
   (B) House of Representatives
   (C) Executive
   (D) General Accounting Office
   (E) Supreme Court

5. Which of the following best describes the difference in economy between the Northern states and the Southern states before the outbreak of the Civil War?

   (A) The North relied upon manual labor while the South did not.
   (B) Northern factories had better working conditions than southern factories.
   (C) The South was primarily agricultural while the North relied upon industry.
   (D) The standard of living in the South was higher than that in the North.
   (E) The North offered more employment opportunities to blacks than did the South.

6. The completion of the Erie Canal led to the most economic growth in which of the following cities?

   (A) Boston
   (B) Baltimore
   (C) Richmond
   (D) Philadelphia
   (E) New York

7. Which of the following states were settled by Quakers?

   I. Pennsylvania
   II. Virginia
   III. Utah

   (A) I only
   (B) II only
   (C) I and II only
   (D) I and III only
   (E) I, II, and III

8. Laissez-faire capitalism was most strongly endorsed by

   (A) moderate socialists
   (B) mercantilists
   (C) free-market industrialists
   (D) abolitionists
   (E) labor unions

9. Which of the following would be most useful in determining the political views of American women in the 1870s?

   (A) Voting returns from the presidential elections of 1876
   (B) Membership rolls of the major political parties
   (C) Diaries and published works by women indicating political viewpoints
   (D) Comparable viewpoints of French women of the same period
   (E) Voting returns of American men of the same period

10. All of the following contributed to the growth of manufacturing during the middle of the nineteenth century EXCEPT

    (A) the completion of the transcontinental railroad
    (B) the development of labor-saving machines
    (C) the perfection of the assembly line
    (D) an increase in the discovery and use of natural resources
    (E) increased production made possible by the economies of scale available to large companies

IMMIGRATION 1881–1920

Year	Total in Thousands	Rate[1]
1881–1890	5,247	9.2
1891–1900	3,688	5.3
1901–1910	8,795	10.4
1911–1920	5,736	5.7

[1] Annual rate per 1,000 U.S. population. Rates computed by dividing the sum of annual immigration totals by the sum of annual United States population totals for the same number of years.

11. Which of the following can be inferred from the above table?

    (A) More immigrants arrived in the United States between 1911 and 1920 than during any other period from 1881 to 1920.
    (B) The period between 1891 and 1900 marked the lowest rate of immigration between 1881 and 1920.
    (C) Political persecution in Europe led to a rise in immigration to the United States between 1881 and 1920.
    (D) World economic factors led to a rise in immigration from East to West.
    (E) During the years between 1881 and 1920, the U.S. government provided incentives to draw immigrants to the United States.

12. Literary scholars would categorize the fiction writers Ernest Hemingway and Sinclair Lewis as

    (A) naturalists
    (B) futurists
    (C) transcendentalists
    (D) romantics
    (E) evolutionists

GO ON TO THE NEXT PAGE

13. The efforts of the United States government to rectify the problems of the Great Depression led to increases in all of the following EXCEPT

    (A) the role of government in managing the economy
    (B) the role of government in supporting the arts
    (C) the regulation of the banking industry
    (D) the use of presidential power in creating government agencies
    (E) the abolition of the sale or manufacture of alcohol

14. The Economic Opportunity Act and the Civil Rights Act were signed into law by President

    (A) Harry S. Truman
    (B) Franklin D. Roosevelt
    (C) Lyndon B. Johnson
    (D) Herbert Hoover
    (E) Theodore Roosevelt

15. The Cuban Missile Crisis and the Berlin Airlift share which of the following characteristics?

    (A) They were both Cold War confrontations between the United States and the Soviet Union.
    (B) They were both precursors to multinational military engagements.
    (C) They were both examples of the policy known as détente, demonstrating a willingness of the United States to negotiate with communist countries.
    (D) They were both unsuccessful military campaigns that embarrassed President Jimmy Carter.
    (E) They were both examples of the superiority of U.S weapons technology.

16. Native American tribes living prior to the arrival of Columbus could best be described as

    (A) uniform in language and religious beliefs
    (B) isolated from one another
    (C) diverse in customs and culture
    (D) nomadic herders of livestock
    (E) eager to assist European settlers

17. Colonies were established in the New World for the purpose of gaining each of the following EXCEPT

    (A) religious freedom
    (B) commercial interests
    (C) better trade routes
    (D) military advantage
    (E) manufacturing sites

18. The taxes imposed upon the American colonies in the late 1700s were a direct result of

    (A) expenses incurred by the British during the French and Indian War
    (B) efforts of the colonists to exert influence over British politics
    (C) a loss of control over British colonial holdings
    (D) a desire on the part of France to turn the colonists against the British government
    (E) war reparations that Britain owed to the French government

19. All of the following were arguments that women used when seeking suffrage EXCEPT:

    (A) The right to vote was essential to women's quest for equality with men.
    (B) Women had earned the right to vote by taking on stereotypically male roles during WWI.
    (C) Women would help humanize politics.
    (D) Laws were passed that concerned women's rights without the consent of women voters.
    (E) Scientific research proved that women were intellectually capable of understanding politics.

20. The Constitutional Convention of 1787 and the subsequent ratification campaign addressed all the following issues EXCEPT

    (A) the facilitation of interstate trade
    (B) the guarantee of civil rights
    (C) the structure of the central government
    (D) the balance of states' rights and national interests
    (E) the defense of the role of religion in American politics

21. Which of the following shaped United States government policy in South America in the nineteenth and twentieth centuries?

    I.   The Monroe Doctrine
    II.   The Roosevelt Corollary
    III.   The Good Neighbor Policy

  (A) I only
  (B) II only
  (C) I and II only
  (D) II and III only
  (E) I, II, and III

22. The so-called "Tariff of Abominations" (1828) was notable because

  (A) the taxes that it proposed were endorsed by the southern states
  (B) some of the money raised by these tariffs would go to the British treasury
  (C) the revenues would benefit northeastern industries at the expense of some southern states
  (D) the tariff's revenues would be distributed equally to all states
  (E) the tariff was the result of a compromise among all three branches of government

23. The Panic of 1837 was most likely precipitated by all of the following EXCEPT

  (A) unregulated lending practices on the part of Andrew Jackson's "pet banks"
  (B) Andrew Jackson's refusal to re-charter the Bank of the United States
  (C) Andrew Jackson's passage of the Specie Circular denying the use of credit to buy land
  (D) a change in the standard for setting the value of U. S. currency
  (E) overconfidence in the strength of the real estate market

24. Which of the following phrases was coined in the mid-nineteenth century to describe the American desire for westward expansion?

  (A) Social Darwinism
  (B) The Good Neighbor Policy
  (C) Manifest Destiny
  (D) The Silver Standard
  (E) Popular Sovereignty

25. A major cause of the Spanish-American War was

  (A) the expansion of Spanish sea power in the Atlantic
  (B) the historic relationship between the United States and France
  (C) the Cuban insurrection against Spain
  (D) the refusal of the Spanish regime to recognize the independence of Puerto Rico
  (E) the capture of the Alamo by General Santa Ana

RURAL AND URBAN POPULATION IN AMERICA FROM 1940–1970 (in thousands)

Year	Rural	Urban
1940	57,246	74,425
1950	54,230	96,468
1960	54,054	125,269
1970	53,887	149,325

26. Based on the chart above, all of the following can be inferred about the period between 1940 and 1970, EXCEPT

  (A) The percentage of people living in urban areas increased between 1940 and 1970.
  (B) The number of people living in rural areas has decreased since 1940.
  (C) More people lived in rural areas in 1940 than did in 1970.
  (D) Agriculture had ceased to be an important aspect of American life by 1970.
  (E) More people lived in the United States in 1970 than in 1940.

GO ON TO THE NEXT PAGE

27. The ratification of the Nineteenth Amendment led to

    (A) universal suffrage for women
    (B) voting rights for former slaves
    (C) the establishment of a federal income tax
    (D) a ban on the manufacture and sale of alcoholic beverages
    (E) the guarantee of equal protection under law for all Americans

28. The constitutional amendment restricting the presidency to a two-term limit was passed by Congress during the presidency of

    (A) Franklin D. Roosevelt
    (B) Harry S. Truman
    (C) Dwight D. Eisenhower
    (D) Lyndon B. Johnson
    (E) Richard M. Nixon

29. Pair the following men with the ideal that most matches him:

    (A) Marcus Garvey—Talented Tenth; Booker T. Washington—Atlanta Compromise; W. E. B. Du Bois—Back to Africa
    (B) Marcus Garvey—Atlanta Compromise; Booker T. Washington—Talented Tenth; W. E. B. Du Bois—Back to Africa
    (C) Marcus Garvey—Atlanta Compromise; Booker T. Washington—Back to Africa; W. E. B. Du Bois—Talented Tenth
    (D) Marcus Garvey—Back to Africa; Booker T. Washington—Atlanta Compromise; W. E. B. Du Bois—Talented Tenth
    (E) Marcus Garvey—Back to Africa; Booker T. Washington—Talented Tenth; W. E. B. Du Bois—Atlanta Compromise

30. The Constitution gives the Executive Branch of the government the power to do which of the following?

    (A) Appoint Supreme Court justices
    (B) Levy taxes
    (C) Declare wars
    (D) Spend government funds
    (E) Make laws

31. The term "direct primary" refers to an election system in which

    (A) members of the electoral college select the winning candidate
    (B) party leaders determine the order and rank of candidates on the ballot
    (C) members of Congress vote for the House Whip and the Senate Majority Leader
    (D) voters choose the candidates who will run on a party's ticket in a subsequent election
    (E) only one vote is taken and run-off elections are prohibited

32. Which of the following is a right guaranteed by the U. S. Constitution?

    (A) The right to violate unjust laws
    (B) The right to a free public education system
    (C) The right to affordable housing
    (D) The right to petition the government for a redress of grievances
    (E) The right to live on federally controlled land

GO ON TO THE NEXT PAGE

33. The following quote was from a text that helped lead to which of the following?

    "There was never the least attention paid to what was cut up for sausage; there would come all the way back from Europe old sausage that had been rejected, and that was moldy and white—it would be dosed with borax and glycerin, and dumped into the hoppers, and made over again for home consumption."

    (A) The Clayton Antitrust Act
    (B) The Underwood Act
    (C) The Pure Food and Drug Act
    (D) Taft-Hartley Act
    (E) Agricultural Adjustment Act

34. The economic situation known as "stagflation" is associated with which time period?

    (A) 1930s
    (B) 1960s
    (C) 1970s
    (D) 1980s
    (E) 1990s

35. In which of the following ways did some of the American colonies attract new settlers?

    I. By offering certain desirable rights unavailable to people in Europe
    II. By offering free or inexpensive land to settlers
    III. By pooling the resources of all the colonies to pay the passage of new settlers

    (A) I only
    (B) II only
    (C) I and II only
    (D) II and III only
    (E) I, II, and III

36. "There is something very absurd in supposing a continent to be perpetually governed by an island. In no instance hath nature made the satellite larger than its primary planet."

    The above statement is an example of

    (A) the application of natural law to political theory
    (B) the Loyalist policy toward the American colonies
    (C) Federalist writings after the American Revolution
    (D) Puritan political thought
    (E) civil libertarianism in the twentieth century

37. All of the following are American cultural achievements of the 1930s or 1940s EXCEPT

    (A) John Steinbeck's *The Grapes of Wrath*
    (B) Aaron Copland and Martha Graham's *Appalachian Spring*
    (C) Irving Berlin's "God Bless America"
    (D) Thorton Wilder's *Our Town*
    (E) Sid Caesar's "Your Show of Shows"

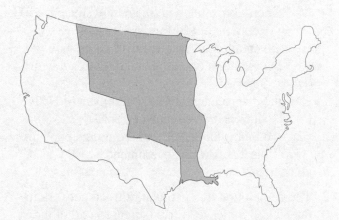

38. The shaded region of the map above represents land acquired from

    (A) Britain
    (B) Spain
    (C) France
    (D) Canada
    (E) the Iroquois Confederacy

GO ON TO THE NEXT PAGE

39. Which of the following parties was formed in opposition to the policies of Andrew Jackson?

    (A) The Republicans
    (B) The Know-Nothings
    (C) The Copperheads
    (D) The Whigs
    (E) The Democratic-Republicans

40. James Fenimore Cooper's *Leatherstocking Tales* novels deal mainly with

    (A) the difficulties faced by the early explorers of the American continent
    (B) the lives of men and women on the North American frontier
    (C) the attitudes of British political figures toward the American colonies
    (D) the settlement of California by Spanish colonists
    (E) the achievements of immigrants in nineteenth-century New York

41. The controversy surrounding the admission of Texas to the United States arose from

    (A) a border dispute with the newly created Republic of California
    (B) the creation of a large, pro-slavery state
    (C) the violation of a long-standing treaty with Spain
    (D) the displacement of large numbers of Native American inhabitants of Texas
    (E) the inclusion of Spanish-speaking people in the Texas state government

42. The completion of a national railroad network in the United States led to an increase in all of the following EXCEPT

    (A) industrial production in the United States
    (B) the proportion of female settlers on the west coast
    (C) cargo traffic on canals and waterways
    (D) revenues for eastern railroad monopolies
    (E) forced migration of Native American peoples

43. "You shall not press down upon the brow of labor this crown of thorns, you shall not crucify mankind upon a cross of gold."

    The statement above made by William Jennings Bryan in 1896 was intended as a defense of

    (A) the American labor movement
    (B) the American farmer
    (C) persecuted religious minorities
    (D) advocates of school prayer
    (E) evolutionary theorists

44. Which of the following works drew attention to the need for reform in the meatpacking industry?

    (A) *Uncle Tom's Cabin*
    (B) *The Scarlet Letter*
    (C) *The Jungle*
    (D) *The Crucible*
    (E) *The Red Badge of Courage*

45. The map below shows an area settled by people who were most likely searching for which of the following?

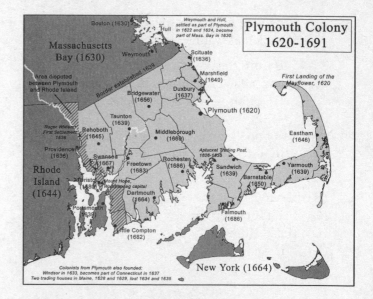

    (A) Freedom from debt
    (B) Economic opportunity
    (C) Separation of church and state
    (D) Affordable land for farming
    (E) Religious freedom

GO ON TO THE NEXT PAGE

46. A provision of the Quota Act of 1924 led to

    (A) an increase in the export of American goods
    (B) a decrease in voter registration
    (C) the creation of affirmative action programs
    (D) a refusal to admit immigrants from Japan
    (E) an increase in tariffs placed on European imports

47. Which of the following was a direct result of the "Red Scare" of 1919 and 1920?

    (A) The passage of the McCarran Act
    (B) The victory of the Bolshevik Party in the Russian Revolution
    (C) The formation of the Congress of Industrial Organizations
    (D) The trial and execution of the Rosenbergs
    (E) The arrest of 4,000 suspected communists

48. "We cannot allow the natural passions and prejudices of other peoples to lead our country to destruction . . . We are on the verge of a war in which the only victor would be chaos and frustration . . . A war which cannot be won without sending our soldiers across an ocean to fight and to force a landing on a hostile coast against armies stronger than our own. We are on the verge of war, but it is not yet too late to stay out."

    The opinions in the speech above were most likely expressed by

    (A) an interventionist
    (B) an isolationist
    (C) a Federalist
    (D) an internationalist
    (E) a Loyalist

49. Which of the following was NOT created during the administration of Franklin D. Roosevelt?

    (A) The Works Progress Administration
    (B) The Tennessee Valley Authority
    (C) The Public Works Administration
    (D) The Interstate Highway System
    (E) The National Recovery Administration

50. The first amendment of the Bill of Rights of the U.S. Constitution guarantees all of the following EXCEPT

    (A) freedom of religion
    (B) freedom of the press
    (C) the right to assemble peacefully
    (D) the right to bear arms
    (E) the right to petition the government

51. Which of the following is an example of the policy known as "dollar diplomacy"?

    (A) The U. S. Congress places limits on interstate trade in order to control local governments.
    (B) The U. S. government offers financial rewards to countries in order to achieve its foreign policy goals.
    (C) American multinational corporations represent U. S. government interests in other countries.
    (D) Government officials sell arms to foreign countries in order to raise money for covert military operations.
    (E) The government abandons the gold standard as a measure of the value of U.S. currency.

52. The purpose of a filibuster is to

    (A) justify the passage of unpopular legislation
    (B) delay or block the passage of a piece of legislation
    (C) explain a piece of legislation for the benefit of voters
    (D) exclude the Executive Branch of government from the legislative process
    (E) override a presidential veto

GO ON TO THE NEXT PAGE

53. The Constitution describes the form and function of all of the following EXCEPT

    (A) the presidency
    (B) the Congress
    (C) the Supreme Court
    (D) the vice presidency
    (E) the cabinet

54. Which sources of information would be most useful in studying the activity of the Underground Railroad?

    (A) Personal accounts and recorded oral histories taken from the "passengers" and "conductors" involved
    (B) North to South timetables of the Union Pacific, dated 1860
    (C) Treaties for the transcontinental railroad
    (D) Letters and diaries belonging to Confederate soldiers
    (E) Public speeches of abolitionists

55. The admission of Missouri in 1820 into the United States was made possible by

    (A) a cash payment to the French, who laid claim to the land
    (B) the admission of Maine, a state which outlawed slavery
    (C) the admission of Texas, a state which laid claim to the Missouri Territory
    (D) the creation of the Confederate States of America
    (E) the opening of the American West

56. All of the following political decisions were results of the debate over slavery and abolition EXCEPT

    (A) the Wilmot Proviso
    (B) the Missouri Compromise
    (C) the Compromise of 1850
    (D) the Kansas-Nebraska Act
    (E) the Civil Rights Act

57. All of the following are associated with American transcendentalism in the nineteenth century EXCEPT

    (A) the essays of Ralph Waldo Emerson and Henry David Thoreau
    (B) a belief in the importance of the human spirit
    (C) utopian communities such as Oneida
    (D) an emphasis on technological progress through industry
    (E) female writers and thinkers, such as Margaret Fuller

58. The *Dred Scott* decision led to the nullification of the

    (A) Missouri Compromise
    (B) Emancipation Proclamation
    (C) Fugitive Slave Law
    (D) Three-Fifths Compromise
    (E) Intolerable Acts

59. The United States exercised which of the following policies in gaining access to the land where the Panama Canal was built?

    (A) The Monroe Doctrine
    (B) The Roosevelt Corollary
    (C) Nativism
    (D) The Frontier Thesis
    (E) Cultural imperialism

60. All of the following campaigned for women's suffrage EXCEPT

    (A) Susan B. Anthony
    (B) Elizabeth Cady Stanton
    (C) Lucretia Mott
    (D) Harriet Beecher Stowe
    (E) Amelia Bloomer

GO ON TO THE NEXT PAGE

61. All of the following contributed to the stock market crash of October 29, 1929, EXCEPT

    (A) the lack of sufficient cash reserves in the banking system
    (B) the overvaluing of the stock market
    (C) the unrestricted purchase of stock on credit
    (D) the speculative investment of large amounts of money
    (E) the lack of insurance for bank depositors

62. The Korean War was considered a "police action" because

    (A) the Supreme Court found the U.S. Army's recruiting practices unconstitutional
    (B) the president did not endorse the participation of American troops
    (C) Congress never formally declared war against North Korea
    (D) the United Nations forced the U.S. government to enter the war
    (E) the war was fought between two sovereign states

63. The successful launch of *Sputnik* in 1957 led to

    (A) an increased interest in the U. S. space program
    (B) a decline in the popularity of Dwight D. Eisenhower
    (C) a decrease in tensions between the Soviet Union and the United States
    (D) a decline in funding for United States defense
    (E) government suspicion of the "military-industrial" complex

64. The term "McCarthyism" has often been used in the late twentieth century to connote

    (A) support for expanding U.S. relations with communist countries
    (B) government actions or investigations based on false accusations or limited evidence
    (C) rallying of pro-American sentiments in times of war
    (D) promotion of violence and drug use in Hollywood entertainment
    (E) restrictive policies that limit media coverage of alternative political viewpoints

65. President Ronald Reagan followed which of the following strategies in response to the economic recession at the beginning of his term?

    (A) Supply-side economics to foster job creation
    (B) Reduction of the federal deficit through increased taxes
    (C) Increased federal spending on public works
    (D) Expansion of unemployment benefits
    (E) Decreased dependence on foreign oil

66. The Oregon Territory was acquired in the 1840s through

    (A) a compromise with the British government
    (B) a treaty with the local Native American inhabitants
    (C) the diplomatic efforts of Lewis and Clark
    (D) a cash transaction with Russia
    (E) an extension of the terms of the Louisiana Purchase

67. Which of the following best describes the philosophy of Progressive reformers in the early 1900s ?

    (A) Individuals and their families are solely responsible for their own well-being.
    (B) Government action should be used to remedy poor social conditions and unfair business practices.
    (C) Religiously based, nonprofit groups should be prohibited from providing community welfare.
    (D) Corporations should be encouraged to support arts and education through philanthropy.
    (E) State and local governments should cede authority to federal programs in the provisions of social welfare.

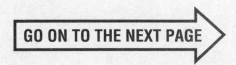

GO ON TO THE NEXT PAGE

68. Which of the following were true about indentured servants?

   I. They worked for a period of several years in exchange for passage to the Americas
   II. They existed mostly in the southern colonies
   III. They were protected from harsh treatment by their masters

(A) I only
(B) I and II only
(C) I and III only
(D) II and II only
(E) All the above

69. U.S. policy toward Native American tribes in the West during the 1880s can best be described as

(A) inconsistent
(B) conciliatory
(C) clearly defined
(D) assimilationist
(E) laissez-faire

70. Which of the following was NOT a factor in the growth of American cities in the late nineteenth century?

(A) A sharp rise in immigration
(B) The lure of newly created jobs in industrial centers
(C) A decline in migration to the frontier
(D) Government incentives to resettle in urban areas
(E) The scarcity of opportunity in rural America

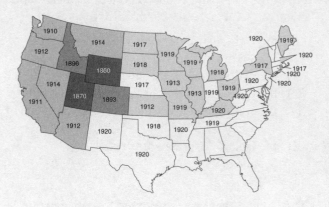

71. The best title for the map above would be

(A) The Admission of States to the Union
(B) The Settlement of North America
(C) The Passage of Woman Suffrage Laws by State
(D) The Repeal of Prohibition Laws by State
(E) The Passage of Desegregation Laws by State

72. The First Continental Congress met in order to

   I. Draft a list of grievances to send to England
   II. Organize boycotts of British Goods
   III. Coordinate colonial militias

(A) I only
(B) II only
(C) I and II only
(D) I, II, and III
(E) None of the above

73. "Television has been far more influential than even Gutenberg's printing press. Books, magazines, and radio have all been described as mass media, but none can compare to the size and shape of television; it is massive. Audiences are drawn from every social class and every demographic. Television focuses and directs these disparate individuals by engaging them in a purely homogenous activity."

    The above statement made by a media critic most likely refers to

    (A) the impact of television as a mass-communication technology on the general public
    (B) the results of government censorship in the mass media
    (C) the difficulties faced by traditional media publishers with the rise of television viewing
    (D) the lack of information available to the average television viewer
    (E) the influence wielded by the media on political affairs

74. All of the following were writers of the Harlem Renaissance EXCEPT

    (A) James Weldon Johnson
    (B) Countee Cullen
    (C) Langston Hughes
    (D) Henry Louis Gates, Jr.
    (E) Zora Neale Hurston

75. The "counterculture" movement of the 1960s can best be described as

    (A) a political and social movement that questioned traditional middle-class values
    (B) a conservative, evangelical movement aiming to increase the religious participation of mainstream Americans
    (C) a series of sit-down demonstrations meant to call attention to the Jim Crow laws and segregation in the South
    (D) a grass roots political organization supporting Barry Goldwater as a third-party presidential nominee
    (E) a series of strikes organized by labor unions in protest of the rising numbers of working women who threatened the jobs of their core members

76. One result of the Marshall Plan of 1948 was

    (A) the shipment of food, raw material, and machinery to postwar Europe
    (B) the airlift of vital supplies to blockaded West Berlin after the Second World War
    (C) the division of Germany into four administrative zones
    (D) the withdrawal of the United States from foreign affairs
    (E) the admission of China to the United Nations

GO ON TO THE NEXT PAGE

77. Which of the following best describes a rationale for the failure of the United States to join the League of Nations after World War I ?

    (A) Communist-controlled Russia would have a central role in the League of Nations.
    (B) The aims of the League of Nations were in direct opposition to the tenets of the Treaty of Versailles.
    (C) Republicans in the Senate were concerned that involvement in the League of Nations would curtail the United States' ability to act in its own best interests.
    (D) President Woodrow Wilson was not wholly supportive of U.S. admission to the League of Nations.
    (E) Great Britain and France refused to join the League of Nations.

78. Rachel Carson's book *Silent Spring* was significant because it

    (A) brought the dangers of DDT and other pesticides to the attention of the American public
    (B) made a decisive case in favor of female suffrage shortly before the ratification of the Nineteenth Amendment
    (C) was the first book by a female author published in the United States
    (D) led to the passage of the strict legislation to protect the ozone layer
    (E) was awarded the Pulitzer Prize in 1968

79. "Laws permitting, and even requiring, their separation in places where they are liable to be brought into contact do not necessarily imply the inferiority of either race to the other . . . ."

    The above passage was probably taken from which of the following Supreme Court rulings?

    (A) *Brown v. Board of Education*
    (B) *Gideon v. Wainwright*
    (C) *Plessy v. Ferguson*
    (D) *Marbury v. Madison*
    (E) *Miranda v. Arizona*

80. All of the following are ideas advocated by *The Federalist Papers* EXCEPT:

    (A) Republican government works best in small communities.
    (B) Wider representation decreases the opportunities for tyranny.
    (C) Individual states will grow increasingly hostile to one another.
    (D) The army should be under federal control.
    (E) A republican government must balance its power among different branches.

81. Which of the following colonies was founded as a refuge for Catholics from religious persecution?

    (A) Georgia
    (B) Virginia
    (C) Pennsylvania
    (D) Maryland
    (E) New York

82. Which of the following reforms is associated with Jacksonian Democracy?

    (A) Improved public education
    (B) Education for women
    (C) The rise of abolitionism
    (D) Improved treatment of the insane
    (E) The creation of child-labor laws

83. The Congressional Reconstruction Acts, enacted after the Civil War, had which of the following effects on Southern states?

    (A) All former slaves were given 40 acres of land and a work animal.
    (B) Constitutional voting laws were changed to enfranchise former slaves as citizens.
    (C) Segregation of public institutions was mandated to appease white constituents.
    (D) Northern citizens were given tax subsidies as an incentive to migrate to the South to help in the rebuilding efforts.
    (E) Radical white supremacist groups, such as the Ku Klux Klan, were outlawed.

GO ON TO THE NEXT PAGE

THE UNDECIDED POLITICAL PRIZE FIGHT.

Reprinted by permission of the Library of Congress

84. The cartoon above could refer to

(A) the onset of the Civil War
(B) continued political competition after the Lincoln-Douglas debates
(C) Lincoln's inability to capture the presidency
(D) the federal government's lack of faith in its citizens
(E) a mistrust of the electoral process

85. Because of New England's geography and poor climate, its 17th century economy became centered on which of the following activities?

(A) Large-scale agriculture of a variety of crops
(B) Subsistence farming
(C) Sea trade, shipping, and fishing
(D) Single-crop production of valuable cash crops
(E) Manufacturing

86. All of the following are examples of post–World War I isolationism in the United States EXCEPT

(A) noninvolvement in the affairs of foreign nations
(B) refusal to join the League of Nations
(C) the "Red Scare"
(D) suspension of trade with European nations
(E) a reduction in military funding

87. The Teapot Dome scandal is an example of

(A) an effort on the part of the Taft administration to weed out government corruption
(B) widespread financial misconduct during the presidency of Warren Harding
(C) efforts made by American colonists to protest unfair taxation
(D) the desire of Congress to be recognized as the most influential branch of government
(E) the methods used by Harry Truman to pass his Fair Deal legislation

88. The North Atlantic Treaty of 1949 established

(A) an alliance among the nations of Western Europe and North America
(B) a return to the isolationism of the 1920s
(C) lend-lease agreements for the supply of war material to the Allied forces
(D) lasting peace with communist nations
(E) the framework for the League of Nations

89. Which of the following is a complete and accurate list of the Axis Powers in World War II ?

(A) The United States, France, and Italy
(B) The United States, Britain, and the Soviet Union
(C) The United States, Britain, and Japan
(D) The United States, Germany, and Italy
(E) Germany, Italy, and Japan

90. Which of the following was an important reason for George H. W. Bush's defeat in the presidential election of 1992?

(A) A weak domestic economy
(B) The Persian Gulf War
(C) Heightened tensions with the Soviet Union
(D) The third party candidacy of Ralph Nader
(E) The Iran-Contra affair

STOP
If you finish before time is called, you may check your work on this test only.
Do not turn to any other test in this book.

Chapter 14
Practice Test 2:
Answers and
Explanations

Practice Test 2 Answer Key
Practice Test 2 Explanations
How to Score Practice Test 2

PRACTICE TEST 2 ANSWER KEY

Question Number	Correct Answer	Right	Wrong	Question Number	Correct Answer	Right	Wrong	Question Number	Correct Answer	Right	Wrong
1.	C	_____	_____	31.	D	_____	_____	61.	E	_____	_____
2.	A	_____	_____	32.	D	_____	_____	62.	C	_____	_____
3.	B	_____	_____	33.	C	_____	_____	63.	A	_____	_____
4.	B	_____	_____	34.	C	_____	_____	64.	B	_____	_____
5.	C	_____	_____	35.	C	_____	_____	65.	A	_____	_____
6.	E	_____	_____	36.	A	_____	_____	66.	A	_____	_____
7.	A	_____	_____	37.	E	_____	_____	67.	B	_____	_____
8.	C	_____	_____	38.	C	_____	_____	68.	B	_____	_____
9.	C	_____	_____	39.	D	_____	_____	69.	A	_____	_____
10.	C	_____	_____	40.	B	_____	_____	70.	D	_____	_____
11.	B	_____	_____	41.	B	_____	_____	71.	C	_____	_____
12.	A	_____	_____	42.	C	_____	_____	72.	C	_____	_____
13.	E	_____	_____	43.	B	_____	_____	73.	A	_____	_____
14.	C	_____	_____	44.	C	_____	_____	74.	D	_____	_____
15.	A	_____	_____	45.	E	_____	_____	75.	A	_____	_____
16.	C	_____	_____	46.	D	_____	_____	76.	A	_____	_____
17.	E	_____	_____	47.	E	_____	_____	77.	C	_____	_____
18.	A	_____	_____	48.	B	_____	_____	78.	A	_____	_____
19.	E	_____	_____	49.	D	_____	_____	79.	C	_____	_____
20.	E	_____	_____	50.	D	_____	_____	80.	A	_____	_____
21.	E	_____	_____	51.	B	_____	_____	81.	D	_____	_____
22.	C	_____	_____	52.	B	_____	_____	82.	A	_____	_____
23.	D	_____	_____	53.	E	_____	_____	83.	B	_____	_____
24.	C	_____	_____	54.	A	_____	_____	84.	B	_____	_____
25.	C	_____	_____	55.	B	_____	_____	85.	C	_____	_____
26.	D	_____	_____	56.	E	_____	_____	86.	D	_____	_____
27.	A	_____	_____	57.	D	_____	_____	87.	B	_____	_____
28.	B	_____	_____	58.	A	_____	_____	88.	A	_____	_____
29.	D	_____	_____	59.	B	_____	_____	89.	E	_____	_____
30.	A	_____	_____	60.	D	_____	_____	90.	A	_____	_____

PRACTICE TEST 2 EXPLANATIONS

1. **C**   The Tea Act of 1773, enacted by Britain a few years before the American Revolution, removed duties (taxes) from the East India Company. The result was a flood of East India tea in the colonies and much lower prices. Colonial merchants protested this infringement of free trade, because high duties had to be paid on all other teas and little to no profit could be made on the East India tea. Choice (C) reflects this situation most accurately. There were protests from the colonists, such as the famous Boston Tea Party, but the colonial militias were yet to be formed, thus eliminating (D). It wasn't until the Intolerable Acts of 1774 and the battles of Lexington and Concord in 1775 that the "armed revolts" began. The trade of coffee (B), and tobacco and sugar (E), were not directly affected by the Tea Act. Choice (A) is completely wrong.

2. **A**   Choice (A), Henry David Thoreau, was a late nineteenth-century American writer and philosopher and is the anti-era choice and the correct answer. Choice (D), Thomas Paine, wrote the pamphlet *Common Sense*, which posed a very influential argument as to why the colonies should separate from England and form an independent government. Samuel Adams (B), Patrick Henry ("Give Me Liberty or Give Me Death") (C), and Thomas Jefferson (E) were all influential public figures in years prior to the American Revolution.

3. **B**   When investors "speculate" on an investment, they risk buying such an investment on the notion that the company or commodity will increase in value over time. "Overspeculation" implies that investors are collectively making overly risky investments, betting on companies that do not have intrinsic value. It can also imply that investors are attempting to make short-term gains rather than build long-term wealth.

4. **B**   This is a factoid question, but you should be able to eliminate effectively to get closer to the final answer, the House of Representatives (B). You should know that Congress makes the law, and that laws are needed to raise revenue. This eliminates the other two branches of federal government, the Executive (C) and the Supreme Court (F). The Internal Revenue Service (A) and the General Accounting Office (D) are bureaucratic agencies involved in the oversight of revenue collection and government spending, but they do not actually make policy changes that affect revenue. So both (A) and (D) should also be eliminated.

5. **C**   The primary difference between Northern and Southern economies prior to the Civil War is that the North was more industrialized and the South was more agricultural (C). Both the North and the South relied on manual labor, and their factory conditions were similar (although there were few factories in the South), thus eliminating choices (A) and (B). It is difficult to compare the different standards of living or employment opportunities, because the types of labor and wages cannot be compared, thus eliminating choices (D) and (E).

6. **E**   This is a factoid question. The Erie Canal was built in New York State and helped ferry goods from New York City to upstate locales.

7. **A**   Pennsylvania (choice I) was founded by William Penn as a Quaker (or Religious Society of Friends) settlement. Virginia (choice II) was the first American settlement and was founded by the London Company for mostly mercantile reasons. Utah (choice III) was settled by Brigham Young and Mormons in the mid–nineteenth century. Choice I only (A) is the correct answer. If you knew the settlement history of any one of these states, you could use POE to eliminate choices.

8. **C**   "Laissez-faire" is a term associated with free market economies. Choice (C) fits best. But if you were unfamiliar with that term, you could use the concept of capitalism in the question to eliminate wrong choices (A), (D), and (E). As for (B), mercantilists were more associated with colonial economic structures.

9. **C**   Think of the era: In the 1870s, women were not allowed to vote and were actively discouraged from entering political organizations, thus eliminating (A) and (B). The viewpoints of French women and American men would not necessarily be reflective of the views of American women, so (D) and (E) could be eliminated. The writings of women of the time (C) would be the best material.

10. **C**   In this question, the answer choices should be connected to the era. Ask yourself: Was this a nineteenth-century development or not? Choices (A), (B), (D), and (E) seem reasonably set in the nineteenth century, but choice (C), assembly-line technique, should jump out as a later innovation. Remember: Henry Ford's company was one of the first to use assembly lines . That was in 1910, when they were used to build Model T's.

11. **B**   You only need to apply the information from the chart to answer this question—the rate of 5.3 from 1891–1900 is the lowest (B). Answer choices (C), (D), and (E) reflect political circumstances that may have influenced immigration but cannot be inferred from the chart.

12. **A**   This is a question based on developments in literature during the early twentieth century, but you can use POE to help narrow the choices. Both these authors sought to portray accurately the harshness and reality of life. Their realist or naturalist writing could be seen as a reaction to the romantic period of literature in the late nineteenth century. Two of Ernest Hemingway's most famous works were *The Sun Also Rises* (1926) and *A Farewell to Arms* (1929). Sinclair Lewis critiqued middle-class values in *Babbitt* (1922).

13. **E** Cross out the EXCEPT and treat each choice as a "Yes" or "No" question: Would the U.S. government do this to aid the economy during the Depression? Also think of the era: The Great Depression started roughly from the Crash of 1929 through the 1930s. You should know that, following Franklin D. Roosevelt's election in 1932, the U.S. government took an activist role in the economy by increasing regulation of market forces and launching public works projects to create jobs. Choices (A), (B), (C), and (D) each reflect this or should at least rank as a "maybe" as you read it. Choice (E) is about the restriction of alcohol known as Prohibition. Nationally enacted by the Eighteenth Amendment in 1919, Prohibition predates the Great Depression of the 1930s. So (E) is the anti-era choice and the correct answer. The Twenty-first Amendment, which repealed Prohibition, was enacted in 1933.

14. **C** These two laws were part of President Lyndon B. Johnson's Great Society initiatives, and they were both signed into law in 1964. You can approach this question by just looking at one of the laws; which of these presidents can be associated with a civil rights act? Johnson is the best choice among these, though Truman (and Eisenhower, but he isn't listed) also presided over some landmark civil rights events—these laws were Johnson's. By the way, the Economic Opportunity Act is sometimes referred to as the antipoverty program, which ties more clearly into Johnson's Great Society vision.

15. **A** The Cuban Missile Crisis, which occurred under the Kennedy administration, and the Berlin Airlift, which occurred under Truman right after World War II, are both examples of Cold War confrontations between the United States and the Soviet Union (A). The Cuban Missile Crisis revolved around the shipment of Soviet-based missiles to be stationed in nearby Cuba, while the Berlin Airlift was a successful airlift of supplies to Soviet-controlled Berlin. Neither led to actual military engagement (B) or was decided upon solely because of weapons technology (E). The policy of détente refers to Nixon and Ford's efforts to ease tensions between the United States and the Soviet Union in the 1970s (C) and Carter's unsuccessful military campaign attempted to free American hostages in Iran in 1979 (D). Use your knowledge of either event to eliminate answer choices and narrow the possibilities.

16. **C** Native American tribes have always been diverse in their customs and cultures, making (C) the best choice. Thinking about the era, you should be able to eliminate the other choices.

17. **E** Answer this EXCEPT question using "Yes" or "No" for each choice. If you remember any colony established for this reason, it's a "Yes" and should be eliminated. Religious freedom (A), commercial interests (B), and trade routes (C) are clearly common reasons for establishing colonies; military advantages were also important, especially given the ongoing tensions among the British, the French, and the Spanish. Manufacturing (E), normally associated with the nineteenth century, is the anti-era choice and the right answer.

18. **A** Think of the era: Britain and France had an intense rivalry and fought many expensive wars, especially the French and Indian War from 1754 to 1763. American colonies were at the whim of British taxes and rules. In this light, only (A) makes sense. Each other choice has the colonial power structure incorrect. The taxes were not imposed by the American colonists on themselves, nor by the French on the colonists. Choice (E) might be a reasonable second choice, but Great Britain was the victor in the French and Indian War, and its large war debts were passed on to American colonists via taxes.

19. **E**   Women argued that their contributions to the economy during WWI, their ability to humanize politics, the fact that laws were passed that concerned them without their consent, and the need for suffrage in the pursuit of equality all merited their right to vote. Women did not cite scientific studies that proved they were intellectually capable of understanding politics.

20. **E**   This question refers to many of the key issues around drafting the Constitution and the intense debates that led to its subsequent ratification. Choices (A), (B), (C), and (D) were key topics of debate and necessary to forming an effective government structure at the time: interstate trade, civil rights of citizens (later amended to the Constitution as the Bill of Rights), the three-branch structure of the federal government, and the balance of state and national interests. Because many colonies were founded on the separation of church and state, the role of religion in a new government was not part of the Constitutional debate; therefore, choice (E) is the "no" in this EXCEPT question and the correct answer.

21. **E**   Beginning in the nineteenth century and continuing in the twentieth, the United States often monitored South American countries for potentially harmful alliances or political situations. President James Monroe established the Monroe Doctrine (choice I) in 1823, which defined this geographic region as a sphere of influence, and President Theodore Roosevelt reaffirmed and expanded the Monroe Doctrine with his Roosevelt Corollary (choice II). The Good Neighbor Policy (choice III), adopted by Franklin D. Roosevelt, advocated recognition of each country's independence and a reduction of U.S. military intervention in Latin America. So choices I, II, and III are all accurate, and (E) is the right answer.

22. **C**   Even if you don't know what the Tariff of Abominations is, you can use the date to clue you into the era (1828). The mid-nineteenth century, or the years preceding the Civil War, are most likely to be associated with conflict between the North and South. Only choices (A) and (C) match this, but (C) fits better into the history of Southern states' disaffection with the Union. Choice (B) is anti-era, because the United States was no longer a colony with fiscal ties to Britain in 1828. Also, choices (A), (D), and (E) are not appropriate because they do not reflect the concept of a "tariff of abomination," meaning a horrible and unfair tax.

23. **D**   For this EXCEPT question, you should look for the anti-era choice, as well as the one that is not like the others. Choices (A), (B), and (C) are all similar and refer to the banking crisis precipitated by Andrew Jackson's policies; beware of these because they are alike and are all reasonable causes for a financial crisis. Choice (E) seems to refer to the overspeculation and extended credit that are common to many "panics," or stock crashes. Choice (D), however, refers to the currency debates (silver standard, gold standards, or nonprecious metal standard) of the late nineteenth century and is a strong anti-era choice.

24. **C**   Western expansion is intimately tied to the concept of Manifest Destiny (C), which stated that it was the natural destiny of the United States to expand to the western edge of North America.

25. **C** A major cause of the Spanish-American War was the Cuban insurrection against Spain (C), which threatened instability in the region and stirred American concern for its national interests. The era is the turn of the twentieth century, when the United States was exerting influence in Mexico, the Caribbean, and other locations in the Western Hemisphere. Use this era knowledge to eliminate choices (A) and (B), which seem more connected to eighteenth-century colonial issues. Choice (D) is incorrect; Puerto Rico was ceded to the United States after the war. Choice (E) refers to an instance in the Mexican-American War earlier in the nineteenth century.

26. **D** Remember on chart questions to rely only on the information supplied. Choices (A), (B), (C), and (E) can all be inferred by the chart. Choice (D) is too strong a statement and cannot be inferred from the numbers. Just because the percentage of rural residents is decreasing doesn't mean that agriculture is no longer important. So (D) is the "no" to the EXCEPT question and the right answer.

27. **A** This is a Trivial Pursuit question, but about a fact that you should memorize. The Nineteenth Amendment allowed universal voting rights for women in 1920 (A). Other answer choices are also constitutional amendments. You can eliminate earlier amendments, such as choices (B) and (E), to improve your chances of guessing.

28. **B** To answer this question, you should know that Franklin D. Roosevelt was elected for an unprecedented four terms. The call to formalize the two-term tradition came during his third administration and was enacted under Harry Truman, the president who immediately followed him. Common sense can lead you to the correct choice.

29. **D** Marcus Garvey's Back to Africa Movement advocated the immigration of African Americans to Africa where they could be free of corrupt white society. Booker T. Washington's Atlanta Compromise argued that African Americans should work hard to earn the respect of whites rather than aggressively pursue equality. W. E. B. Du Bois's Talented Tenth was the idea that a small number of African Americans should become leaders of the community through intellect and skill.

30. **A** The president, who is in the Executive Branch, appoints Supreme Court justices. All the other powers listed in the answer choices are congressional powers. Think of traditional political debates between the president and Congress. They often focus on taxes, what programs to allocate funds to, or the creation of other laws. These powers are not solely rested in the Executive, hence the debate. If you can eliminate one or two choices, guess!

31. **D** This fact-based question can be answered using common sense and a little historical background. The direct primary system came out of election reforms that allowed for voters to "directly" choose a party's candidate for an election (D), rather than have party bosses or others choose for them (B). Choice (A) should be eliminated because the electoral college is an "indirect" system of choosing a president. Members of Congress are not involved in the primary election, unless they are running for office themselves, eliminating choice (C).

32. **D**   Only choice (D), the right to petition the government for a redress of grievances, is constitutionally protected. You can also use knowledge of state versus national government control to help answer this question. Laws related to education and housing tend to be locally determined and vary from state to state, so they cannot be constitutionally guaranteed.

33. **C**   This quote is from Upton Sinclair's *The Jungle*, which exposed horrendous conditions in meat packing factories and the sale of rotten or tainted meat for public consumption. This book led to the passage of the Meat Inspection Act and the Food and Drug Act, and to the founding of the Food and Drug Administration under President Theodore Roosevelt.

34. **C**   *Stagflation* is the term used to describe the economic recession of the 1970s (C), which featured stagnant economic growth plus rising inflation ("stag-flation"), in addition to high unemployment and high fuel prices. You may be able to connect these economic times with President Jimmy Carter to help get the time frame right. Also, if you can identify the term *stagflation* with an economic downturn (it sounds rather depressing, doesn't it?), then you can narrow your choices.

35. **C**   Colonies competed to attract settlers to their region, so the choices that reflect these incentives should be kept. Choice III suggests a cooperative arrangement among the colonies that did not exist, so answer choices (D) and (E) should be eliminated. Both I and II were used at the time, so choice (C) is correct.

36. **A**   The quote uses a scientific metaphor (planets and their smaller satellites) to make a point that the relationship of the American colonies to Britain is "unnatural." Only choice (A) reflects this. A Loyalist would not hold this view, eliminating choice (B). Federalist debates (C) following the American Revolution centered on the balance of power between the states and the new central government. Answer choices (D) and (E) are not in the era of the quote, nor do they relate to its substance.

37. **E**   Connect to the era to help you with this EXCEPT question. Much of the art and literature of the 1930s and 1940s examined, and often celebrated, core American values. The basic goodness of the common man, coupled with realistic descriptions of life's hardships and triumphs, were popular themes. Each of choices (A), (B), (C), and (D), especially Steinbeck and Wilder, fits into the themes of this era. Sid Caesar's "Your Show of Shows" was a television show that was popular in the 1950s. This is the choice (E) that sticks out as "not like the others" and is the anti-era choice.

38. **C**   The shaded region of the map represents land acquired in the Louisiana Purchase from France, choice (C). Knowledge of colonial history can help you eliminate other choices. Britain (A) controlled much of the Northeast, while Spain (B) controlled Mexico and Florida. Canada (D) never had colonial ownership in the U.S. region. These answer choices can be eliminated.

39. **D**   Andrew Jackson was elected as a Democrat, but his policies were very controversial and spurred the creation of a third-party faction, the Whigs (D). This is a fact-based question, but you should be able to eliminate some choices and guess. Choice (A) refers to a later party, while (E) was one of the first two established political parties. Both answer choices should be eliminated. The Whig Party would be a good guess because it is the more well-known of the remaining choices.

40. **B**   James Fenimore Cooper's work dealt with the lives of frontier settlers, the natural environment of the American frontier, and the implications of human impact on that environment (B). His work was one of the first truly American-based works of literature. Within the books of the *Leatherstocking Tales*, notably *The Deerslayer* (1841) and *The Pioneers* (1823), the hero Natty Bumpo was featured along with his Mohican guide Chingachgook. To help with guessing, you might be able to associate Cooper as an American writer or realize the "Leatherstocking" title relates to rugged frontier clothing, and thus eliminate choices (C), (D), or (E).

41. **B**   For this question, any of the answer choices seem reasonable, but if you think of the era of the question, it's easy to identify (B) as the right answer. A major issue in adding new states to the United States prior to the Civil War was whether the new state would be "slave" or "free." From 1800 to 1865, new states were admitted only if they could be balanced to maintain the uneasy compromise on the question of slavery. The annexation of Texas, especially as a large state, threatened to disrupt that balance. Any questions on this subject should instantly ring a bell on the question of slavery. In this case, Oregon was admitted as a "free state" to the United States a few months later via a treaty with Great Britain.

42. **C**   Remember to cross out the EXCEPT and treat this as a "Yes" or "No" question. What could a national railroad network lead to? Better railroads could easily lead to an increase in industrial production, the movement of settlers, revenues for railroad owners, and the displacement of Native Americans. The effect of improved railroad use on canal traffic would more likely be a reduction than an increase. So, choice (C) is the odd one out and the correct answer.

43. **B**   This quote question gives you information in the quote itself and in the name of the speaker. William Jennings Bryan was a famous orator, especially known for his leadership in the Populist movement and in defense of American farmers and their interests. If you remember this fact about Bryan, choice (B) will jump out. Otherwise, you can still eliminate choices by using the text of the quote, which refers to the oppression of laborers by some monetary policy, namely the gold standard. This would limit the best choices to (A) or (B). Bryan was also involved in the Scopes trial, which focused on whether the theory of evolution could be taught in school (E), but he was against evolutionists and the substance of the quote has nothing to do with this topic.

44. **C**   Upton Sinclair's *The Jungle* (C) drew attention to the deplorable conditions in Chicago's meatpacking industry and lead to progressive reforms. This is a factoid question, so it helps if you know something about any of these novels. Eliminate any choices that you know are not related to the subject of the question. *Uncle Tom's Cabin* (A) by Harriet Beecher Stowe was an abolitionist piece opposing slavery. *The Scarlet Letter* (B) by Nathaniel Hawthorne dealt with issues of Puritan society. The subject of *The Crucible* by Arthur Miller (D) was the witch trials of Salem, but its themes about how hysteria and unfounded suspicions can erode a community were a metaphor for the widespread fear of communism in the 1950s. *The Red Badge of Courage* by Stephen Crane (E) was a naturalistic story of a Civil War soldier.

45. **E**   The Plymouth Colony shown on this map was founded by the Pilgrims who were a group of Separatists, which means that they felt the Anglican church was too corrupt to be purified, and therefore wanted to separate from it. The Pilgrims settled in the New World, where they could practice their religion freely.

46. **D**   The Quota Act of 1924 restricted all immigration, setting new limits on European immigration and totally prohibiting immigration from Asia, including Japan (D). Think of the era of the 1920s: America was growing increasingly isolationist, conservative, and wary of immigration. U.S. involvement in World War I had caused severe military losses and stirred nationalistic desires to remain isolated from the troubles of the rest of the world. Other answer choices do not connect to the era.

47. **E**   The "Red Scare" refers to widespread fears of a communist revolution in the United States, prompted by the 1917 success of the Bolsheviks in Russia. Choice (E) reflects the official response to public worries. Federal and state law enforcement agencies were put on guard to prevent radical uprisings. The "Palmer Raids," authorized by Attorney General A. Mitchell Palmer, resulted in the arrest of more than 4,000 suspected communists, many held in violation of their civil rights. Choice (B) should be eliminated because it is a cause, not a result, of the Red Scare. Choices (A) and (D) are worthy guesses, but these events were related to the fears of communism in the 1950s. Choice (C) is not related to communism.

48. **B**   If you read just the first and last line of this quote, you can identify that the speaker is against entering a war. Realizing this, you can eliminate choices (A) and (D) and should note that choice (B), the correct answer, looks like a good match. Although a Loyalist would be against a war with England, the quote refers to sending soldiers across the ocean, which was not the case in the American Revolution.

49. **D**   The Interstate Highway system was created under Eisenhower's administration, while the others were New Deal programs, so choice (D) is the correct answer. If you didn't know that, you could still eliminate any programs you know were created by the New Deal or can associate with Franklin D. Roosevelt, and then guess.

50. **D**   The right to bear arms is in the Second Amendment to the Constitution and is therefore the odd one out in this set of answer choices. Guaranteed rights to religion, peaceful assembly, government petition, and the freedom of the press are all First Amendment protections.

51. **B**   "Dollar diplomacy" refers to using economic incentives and monetary policy to secure international alliances rather than military force or war (B). Choices (A) and (E) should be eliminated because they are not related to the international affairs suggested by the word *diplomacy* in the phrase. Choices (C) and (D) put U.S. diplomacy in a very harsh and controversial light. Unless you are sure that such a choice is correct, it would be better to take another guess.

52. **B**   A filibuster is a stalling technique used to delay or block the passage of a piece of legislation (B). If you don't know this definition, try to eliminate unlikely choices and guess. Choice (C) can be eliminated because there is no formal process for explaining legislation to voters.

53. **E**   Use the "one of these things is not like the others" technique to help with this question. The heads of the three branches of the federal government (president, Congress, and the Supreme Court) were defined in the Constitution and clearly "go together." You might then guess between the remaining choices or peg the vice president with the group it clearly resembles. The odd choice is the cabinet (E), which is the correct answer. The cabinet was created through executive tradition rather than the Constitution.

54. **A**   The Underground Railroad was the secret system used to help runaway slaves escape to free states, territories, or countries. It was really a network of people working together, although the system often employed the language of the railroad, including such terms as "passengers" and "conductors." It was not an actual railroad or a type of transportation, eliminating choices (B) and (C). Also, because it was secret, you would not be able to find references about it in public speeches, eliminating choice (E). Choice (A) is the best choice; personal accounts, handed down through families, or oral histories from the actual participants would be needed to identify places, locations, and strategies used in the Underground Railroad system. Even though the participants would now be deceased, information might be obtained from family records or from recorded or written accounts taken early in the twentieth century.

55. **B**   This question again refers to the sectional strife caused by the balance of slave and free territories. The Missouri Compromise of 1820 allowed Missouri to be admitted if Maine was admitted concurrently (B). The other answer choices don't address this issue.

56. **E**   The answer to this EXCEPT question is the anti-era choice. The Civil Rights Act was enacted in the twentieth century, nearly 100 years after the various political compromises to balance the slavery question, and is the correct answer (E). You may be unsure about what the Wilmot Proviso is, but the other choices (B), (C), and (D) are clearly from the pre–Civil War era.

57. **D**   Use the "one of these things is not like the others" technique to help with this question. Ralph Waldo Emerson and Henry David Thoreau should jump out at you as two of the key figures of the time, and then you can connect their works *Walden* and *On Nature*, which celebrated the human spirit and natural things. With this knowledge, choices (A), (B), and (C) go together and choice (D), the correct

answer, seems the odd one out. Choice (E) is a decent guess, because you might think it is anti-era. But Margaret Fuller and Elizabeth Palmer Peabody were two examples of female transcendentalists.

58. **A**   The Dred Scott Supreme Court decision permitted slaves to be transferred as owned property between free and slave states, thus violating the terms of various sectional compromises, such as the Missouri Compromise (A). If you can connect the question to the era preceding the Civil War, you should be able to eliminate choices (D) and (E) because they were earlier in history, and choice (B) was declared during the Civil War and was never nullified.

59. **B**   Roosevelt's corollary to the Monroe Doctrine was a policy used to rationalize U.S. involvement in Latin and Central America, including the movement to connect the Caribbean to the Pacific Ocean via the Panama Canal (B). The Monroe Doctrine (A) is from an earlier time period, and the other answer choices refer to policies or movements that are not explicitly tied to Latin America or to the Panama Canal.

60. **D**   In this EXCEPT question, the odd one out is the right answer. Harriet Beecher Stowe wrote *Uncle Tom's Cabin* and spoke out about slavery, while the other women were associated with the women's suffrage movement.

61. **E**   In this EXCEPT question, you have to identify possible causes to the 1929 stock market crash. Choices (A), (B), (C), and (D) are closely tied to the cash flow and overspeculation associated with the crash. Choice (E), on the other hand, was a characteristic of the national banking system and not directly related to the crash. Because banks lacked insurance, the stock market crash had wide and often disastrous economic effects, even for people not invested in the stock market. Choice (E) may have worsened the effects of the stock market crash, but it was not a cause.

62. **C**   "Police action" is one good way to describe a war you don't want to call a war—just like the Korean conflict in the 1950s. The early years of the Cold War demanded delicacy, and the outright declaration of war over the actions of the North Koreans might have provoked the communist leadership of Russia or China—Truman wasn't ready to risk that. The president doesn't need a congressional declaration of war to send troops for purposes other than combat, so when the UN asked its member nations to help Korea, Truman sent U.S. troops as "peacekeepers" and "advisers." Even if you didn't know that, there are opportunities to do some POE here. If you're familiar with U.S. government at all, you know the president is the only one who can send troops, so cross out (B). Also, the UN can't really *force* a member state to do anything. So the answer isn't (D)—cross it out. With (A), (C), and (E) remaining, it's worth your time to guess.

63. **A**   Use the era of 1957 to connect the question to Cold War sentiments. The launch of *Sputnik*, a Russian satellite, in 1957 spurred American support for a competitive space program (A), heating up the "space race" between the two nations. Americans were fearful of falling behind the communist power in scientific and military prowess. The other answer choices represent opinions opposite to the popular sentiments on this Cold War incident.

64. **B** To answer this question, you have to understand the meaning of the term "McCarthyism" in the context of the late twentieth century. Senator Joe McCarthy headed many of the anticommunist efforts in Congress in the 1940s and 1950s. But he was ultimately censured by the Senate and criticized for being too zealous and for making false claims with little evidence. Thus, (B) best captures the more general meaning of the phrase when applied to current political situations. Choice (A) can be eliminated because McCarthy wouldn't be associated with progressive policies toward communist nations. Choices (C) and (D), while reminiscent of Cold War mentality or Hollywood blacklisting, are not as clearly associated with McCarthy-like tactics in twentieth-century politics.

65. **A** To answer this question, you can use your knowledge of Ronald Reagan or your understanding of his Republican economic policies. In general, Democrats are often considered the "tax-and-spend" party whereas Republicans are characterized as the "anti-tax" party and are known for their willingness to make cuts in social spending. Economically, politically, and socially, there are pluses and minuses to each approach, but this simplistic rubric can help you remember which policies would better suit Republicans and Democrats. Reagan was a champion of "supply-side" economics, also known as the "trickle-down" theory, which holds that tax cuts to the rich and to corporations actually help the poor because they spur economic growth and job creation (A). Choices (B), (C), and (D) all describe policies that fit more within the Democratic politics of taxing or spending. Choice (E) is reminiscent of Democratic President Jimmy Carter's policy in the recession during his term.

66. **A** The Oregon Territory was acquired through a compromise with the British government, which also held claims to the land. Use the era of the 1840s to eliminate choices dealing with Native American treaties (B) and Lewis and Clark (C), both of which preceded the era.

67. **B** During the Progressive era of the early 1900s, reformers demanded more accountability from businesses and more action from local, state, and national government on social issues. A core tenet of their philosophy was that government regulation could better protect and help citizens, making (B) the best choice. Choice (A) should be eliminated because the Progressive reformers sought to help individuals and families in poor conditions. Progressive reformers were in favor of locally based religious groups providing a key role in community welfare, and would not have wanted their efforts restricted (C). In the late twentieth century, there has been debate about whether religious organizations should have access to federal funding, but that is not within the era of the question. Both choices (D) and (E) are opposed to what Progressive reformers would have thought.

68. **B** Indentured servants were workers who agreed to work for a certain number of years in exchange for transportation to the Americas. Indentured servitude thrived in the southern colonies as they were agrarian in nature and needed a large labor force. Indentured servants were not protected from harsh treatment by their masters. In fact, some masters treated their indentured servants worse than their slaves since the slaves were seen as a perpetual investment while indentured servants were not.

69. **A** It is important to place the era of the 1880s as after the Civil War and after the bulk of western expansion had occurred. At this time, much of the displacement of the Native American tribes had already taken place as U.S. troops forced tribes into the reservation system. Inconsistent U.S. policy

toward Native Americans was the result of various government agencies working at cross-purposes (A). For instance, a reform movement to have better relations with the tribes gained support in the Department of the Interior in the 1880s, but at the same time, the Department of War directed military aggression against the tribes. Choice (C) may have captured earlier U.S. policy, but is anti-era for this question. Choices (B) and (D) are not accurate for the era either, although they may describe more twentieth-century policies.

70. **D** Think of the era: The late nineteenth century marked the beginning of the industrial age that led to the growth of cities. The population grew for many reasons, including the availability of jobs in urban areas, new immigration, and the decline of opportunities at the frontier and in farming. There were no government incentives to populate the cities in this era, though, so choice (D) is the correct answer.

71. **C** Look at the dates on the map to connect to the era: around 1918, 1919, 1920, mainly, with a few earlier dates. Then look for the answer choice that best matches the Progressive era. Choices (A), admission of states to the Union, and (B), settlement of North America, would have dates earlier than 1865. The passage of desegregation laws (E) would be associated with the Civil Rights movement in the 1950s and 1960s. Choices (C) and (D) are closest to the time frame, but the women's voting movement is best (C). Remember the Nineteenth Amendment was ratified in 1920, and many states gave women the right to vote earlier. (Wyoming and a few other frontier states were early adopters of the movement in order to encourage women to move west.) It also helps if you know that the southeastern states at first rejected the Nineteenth Amendment, which is why those states have no dates on the map. (Eventually, all the states formally ratified the amendment, even though it was purely a symbolic gesture after Tennessee's ratification provided the three-fourths majority necessary to make it a law.) Choice (D) can be eliminated if you remember that the beginning of Prohibition laws were in the 1910s and 1920s, but the repeal of those laws came later in the 1930s.

72. **C** The First Continental Congress met to create a list of grievances to send to the King of England and Parliament. Its other main purpose was to organize a boycott of British goods. The delegates did not yet plan military action as they hoped to reach some sort of agreement with Great Britain so III is incorrect.

73. **A** Key parts of this quote are that television is "more influential than Gutenberg's printing press" and that it has a mass audience of viewers, making (A) the best choice. Don't read anything into the quote that is not explicitly stated. There is nothing in the quote about the political ramifications of television or the level of information it brings, eliminating choices (B), (D), and (E). Choice (C) also goes beyond the scope of the quote.

74. **D** This is a fact-based question, but you can connect to the era of the Harlem Renaissance (1920s and 1930s) to help eliminate choices or find the "odd one out" in this EXCEPT question. Zora Neale Hurston and Langston Hughes are among the most famous writers of this period, so they should be eliminated. Henry Louis Gates, Jr., is also a famous name, but he is a contemporary writer on African American studies and culture. As the only modern name, choice (D) is the "odd one out" and the correct answer.

75. **A** Choice (A) best describes the "counterculture" movement of the 1960s. The "counter" part of the term refers to the fact that its followers were reacting against the mainstream culture of their parents and other authority figures. Connecting to the era of the 1960s should give you enough information to eliminate anti-era choices (B) and (E). Lunch counter demonstrations are better associated with the Civil Rights movement starting in the 1950s (C). Choice (D) might be a decent guess, but Barry Goldwater was a conservative Republican presidential candidate in 1964.

76. **A** The Marshall Plan of 1948 was a major American diplomatic policy that supported the rebuilding of Europe after World War II through the supply of food and economic goods, making choice (A) the best answer. By connecting to the post–World War II era, indicated by the 1948 date, you should be able to eliminate choices (D) and (E) as anti-era. Choices (B) and (C) are accurate, making them decent guesses, but were not part of the Marshall Plan.

77. **C** President Woodrow Wilson was the great champion of the League of Nations, which was part of the Treaty of Versailles after World War I, but he could never get enough Republicans in the Senate to support U.S. involvement in the organization. Republicans were concerned that an alliance with European nations could lead the United States into another war. With any of this information, you can pick choice (C) as the best answer and eliminate choices (B) and (D). Great Britain and France (E) agreed to participate in the League of Nations, and communist-controlled Russia (A) was never invited to participate, so these choices are wrong.

78. **A** Rachel Carson's book *Silent Spring* should be connected to the environmental movement of the late 1960s and 1970s. It was one of the first popular works to raise concern over the widespread use of DDT and, by extension, other chemicals and toxins that could hurt the environment, the ecological food chain, and people (A). Choices (B) and (C) are anti-era, and choice (E), while an honor, is not really a significant contribution. Choice (D) is an okay guess, but despite the popularity of the environmental movement, there has not been "strict" legislation in the United States to protect the ozone.

79. **C** The quote is from a court ruling justifying the "separate but equal" standard for segregating races in public institutions. *Plessy v. Ferguson* (1896), the correct answer (C), is a good Supreme Court case to know, because this ruling justified the racist segregation of the South for many years after the Civil War. You may be able to eliminate some choices and guess: *Brown v. the Board of Education* (1954) overturned the *Plessy* decision and was the basis for the integration of schools, and the *Miranda v. Arizona* ruling concerns rules of fair arrest and the familiar "Miranda" rights that you hear in police dramas all the time: "You have the right to remain silent. You have the right to an attorney…."

80. **A** You should connect to the era and remember that The Federalist Papers were arguments supporting the establishment of a stronger national government and a new Constitution, and then answer "Yes" or "No" for each answer choice. Choices (B), (D), and (E) all refer to characteristics or benefits of a national government, whereas choices (A) and (C) are opposing opinions concerning small government. Choice (A) is the "odd one out" as the only choice that refers to the benefits of a smaller government, an opinion not voiced by the Federalists.

81. **D** George Calvert—Lord Baltimore, the original English proprietor of Maryland—received a royal grant that he used to establish the colony of Maryland as a refuge for persecuted Catholics.

82. **A** Again use the era of Andrew Jackson to help with this question. Choices (B) and (E) can be eliminated, as these were concerns of the Progressive Era. Choices (C) and (D) are a little tougher—these issues do date to the mid-nineteenth century, but they are less associated with the spirit of *Jacksonian* Democracy than improved public education was. If you could eliminate (B) and (E), though, it was worth your time to guess. Choice (A) is the best answer. It fits Jackson's persona of a man of the people and a supporter of direct representation, which philosophically depended on basic education for American citizens as voters and participants in the political process.

83. **B** One of the effects of the Reconstruction acts was to change voting laws so that freed slaves could vote, or be enfranchised (B). These changes spurred the creation of white supremacist groups and local laws to hinder the voting process for African Americans, such as the poll tax and literacy requirements. Use the era, and your knowledge that Congressional Republicans wanted to punish rather than appease the South right after the Civil War, to lead you to the best answer. Choice (C) can be eliminated. Choice (A), providing 40 acres and a mule to freed slaves, was discussed in Congress but never enacted.

84. **B** Look for clues in the cartoon to connect to the era and the subject: The political prize is the White House and one of the fighters is Abraham Lincoln. The Lincoln-Douglas debates of 1858, which dealt with the questions of slavery and the future of the Union, were still relevant to the election of 1860. Lincoln and Douglas squared off again, this time for the presidency, making (B) the best answer. Choice (C) can be eliminated, because Lincoln did win the presidency. There is nothing in the picture that refers to the topics of answer choices (D) and (E), so they too can be eliminated. Although choice (A) is in the right era, the cartoon is earlier than the onset of the Civil War. Furthermore, the gentleman's fistfight is too mild a metaphor for a possible war between the states.

85. **C** New England's geography was ill-suited to large-scale agriculture. As a result, the early economy of the region grew up around its access to the ocean and consisted largely of sea trade, shipping, and fishing.

86. **D** Remember to cross out the EXCEPT and answer the question about American isolationism with "Yes" and "No." Choices (A), (B), and (C) are all easily connected to a time of isolation, as is a reduction of military funding (E). Suspension of trade with Europe (D), though, doesn't make sense. Considering our economic and cultural ties with many European nations, this is too extreme to be true, even in a time of relative isolation.

87. **B** The Teapot Dome scandal occurred during Warren Harding's presidential administration in the early 1920s (B). One of many scandals under Harding's watch, this one involved the secretary of the interior accepting bribes and then allowing the "leasing" of national land for private oil drilling. It's helpful to remember that President Harding is often associated with the scandals of his administration.

88. **A**   Recognize the era of the question: 1949 is immediately following World War II and just prior to the Cold War. Choice (A) is the one that best reflects the relationship of the United States and its Western European allies. They established the North Atlantic Treaty Organization, better known as NATO, in 1949. Both choices (B) and (E) are anti-era, and would be more true in the era after World War I. Choice (D) should be eliminated, because the United States never entered such a treaty, and certainly wouldn't in the Cold War era. Choice (C) would be a decent guess, but actually describes U.S. support efforts before entering World War II.

89. **E**   For this question, it helps to know who was on which side in World War II and then use what you know to eliminate wrong choices. Germany was clearly one of the enemies and so was Japan. Only (E) reflects that alliance. The United States was part of the Allied forces, so you can use that to eliminate answer choices as well.

90. **A**   Despite a host of foreign policy successes, including a resounding victory in the Persian Gulf War and successfully managing the breakup of the Soviet Union, George H. W. Bush's 1992 re-election bid failed. This was largely due to both the weakness of the domestic economy in the months preceding the election, and the third-party candidacy of Ross Perot.

HOW TO SCORE PRACTICE TEST 2

When you take the real exam, the proctors will collect your test booklet and bubble sheet and send your answer sheet to the processing center where a computer looks at the pattern of filled-in ovals on your answer sheet and gives you a score. We couldn't include even a small computer with this book, so we are providing this more primitive way of scoring your exam.

Determining Your Score

STEP 1 Using the Answer Key at the beginning of this chapter, determine how many questions you got right and how many you got wrong on the test. Remember, questions that you do not answer don't count as either right answers or wrong answers.

STEP 2 List the number of right answers here.

(A) _____

STEP 3 List the number of wrong answers here. Now divide that number by 4. (Use a calculator if you're feeling particularly lazy.)

(B) _____ ÷ 4 = _____

STEP 4 Subtract the number of wrong answers divided by 4 from the number of correct answers. Round this score to the nearest whole number. This is your raw score.

(A) _____ – (B) _____ = (C) _____

STEP 5 To determine your real score, take the number from Step 4 above and look it up in the left column of the Score Conversion Table on the next page; the corresponding score on the right is your score on the exam.

PRACTICE TEST 2
SCORE CONVERSION TABLE

Raw Score	Scaled Score	Raw Score	Scaled Score	Raw Score	Scaled Score
95	800	55	680	15	440
94	800	54	670	14	430
93	800	53	670	13	430
92	800	52	660	12	420
91	800	51	660	11	420
90	800	50	650	10	410
89	800	49	640	9	400
88	800	48	640	8	400
87	800	47	630	7	390
86	800	46	630	6	390
85	800	45	620	5	380
84	800	44	610	4	370
83	800	43	610	3	370
82	800	42	600	2	360
81	800	41	600	1	360
80	800	40	590	0	350
79	800	39	580	−1	340
78	800	38	580	−2	340
77	800	37	570	−3	330
76	800	36	570	−4	330
75	800	35	560	−5	320
74	790	34	550	−6	320
73	790	33	550	−7	310
72	780	32	540	−8	300
71	770	31	540	−9	300
70	770	30	530	−10	290
69	760	29	520	−11	290
68	760	28	520	−12	280
67	750	27	510	−13	270
66	740	26	510	−14	270
65	740	25	500	−15	260
64	730	24	490	−16	260
63	730	23	490	−17	250
62	720	22	480	−18	240
61	720	21	480	−19	240
60	710	20	470	−20	230
59	700	19	460	−21	230
58	700	18	460	−22	220
57	690	17	450	−23	210
56	690	16	450	−24	210

Chapter 15
Practice Test 3

U.S. HISTORY
SUBJECT TEST 3

Your responses to the U.S. History Subject Test questions must be filled in on Test 3 of your answer sheet (the answer sheet at the back of the book). Marks on any other section will not be counted toward your U.S. History Subject Test score.

When your supervisor gives the signal, turn the page and begin the U.S. History Subject Test.

U.S. HISTORY SUBJECT TEST 3

Directions: Each of the questions or incomplete statements below is followed by five suggested answers or completions. Select one that is best in each case and then fill in the corresponding oval on the answer sheet.

1. Each of the following European nations launched major colonization attempts along the eastern seaboard of North America in the late sixteenth-century EXCEPT

   (A) Spain
   (B) England
   (C) Italy
   (D) France
   (E) The Netherlands

2. Which of the following was the most important "cash crop" grown for sale in the Virginia colony in the seventeenth and eighteenth centuries?

   (A) Pumpkins
   (B) Potatoes
   (C) Tea
   (D) Tobacco
   (E) Sugar

3. What is the term for the seventeenth- and eighteenth-century British policy that avoided strict enforcement of parliamentary laws in order to encourage the obedience of the American colonies?

   (A) Salutary Neglect
   (B) The 10% Plan
   (C) Calvinism
   (D) The Gag Rule
   (E) The Great Compromise

4. One effect of the Nullification Crisis during the presidency of Andrew Jackson was

   (A) a burgeoning of interest in westward expansion
   (B) the emergence of the two-party system
   (C) a decrease in the power of the executive branch of government
   (D) the expansion of voting rights to Native Americans
   (E) the establishment of federal supremacy over the states

5. Which of the following lists the admission of states into the union in the correct chronological order (from first to last)?

   (A) New Jersey, Arizona, New York, Virginia
   (B) Virginia, Ohio, Nebraska, Wyoming
   (C) California, Rhode Island, Florida, Mississippi
   (D) Texas, North Dakota, Connecticut, Massachusetts
   (E) Delaware, Pennsylvania, Michigan, Maryland

6. Alexander Hamilton conceived of the First Bank of the United States in order to

   (A) prevent predatory lending practices on the part of private banks
   (B) standardize American currency and deal with Revolutionary War debt
   (C) provide an alternative to George Washington's own plan for a national bank
   (D) ensure that American farmers had adequate access to subsidized loans
   (E) decrease the extent of the powers of the federal government

7. Which of the following was a goal of the Know-Nothing Party in the 1850s?

   (A) To reduce the influence of university-educated elites on American politics
   (B) To encourage an influx of skilled immigrants from Europe
   (C) To develop alternatives to the two-party system
   (D) To create a political haven for Native Americans and other minorities
   (E) To limit the influence of immigrants on American society and thus "purify" the nation

GO ON TO THE NEXT PAGE

AN AWFUL BLOT.
Copyright, LIFE PUBLISHING CO.

8. The political movement depicted in the cartoon above eventually led to which of the following federal regulations?

(A) The Erdman Act of 1898
(B) The Emergency Quota Act of 1921
(C) The Social Security Act of 1935
(D) The Fair Labor Standards Act of 1938
(E) The Taft-Hartley Act of 1947

9. "I believe it must be the policy of the United States to support free peoples who are resisting attempted subjugation by armed minorities or by outside pressures."

The quote above most likely represents which of the following American foreign policies?

(A) The Monroe Doctrine
(B) The Truman Doctrine
(C) The Carter Doctrine
(D) The Powell Doctrine
(E) The Rumsfeld Doctrine

10. Which of the following American novels is known for exposing the realities of urban poverty and the unsanitary conditions of the meatpacking industry?

(A) Upton Sinclair's *The Jungle*
(B) Joseph Heller's *Catch-22*
(C) Harriet Beecher Stowe's *Uncle Tom's Cabin*
(D) John Steinbeck's *The Grapes of Wrath*
(E) Richard Wright's *Native Son*

GO ON TO THE NEXT PAGE

12. Which of the following best characterizes the main topic of discussion during the Lincoln-Douglas debates?

   (A) The expansion of slavery into the territories
   (B) The prohibition of the manufacture and sale of alcohol
   (C) The secession of South Carolina
   (D) The role of the vice presidency
   (E) The issue of reparations due to former slaves and their families

13. Joseph Smith was the founder of which nineteenth-century religious movement that began during the Second Great Awakening?

   (A) The Shakers
   (B) The Unitarians
   (C) The Mormons
   (D) The Adventists
   (E) The Jehovah's Witnesses

14. Which of the following best describes the type of person derisively referred to as a "carpetbagger" immediately after the Civil War?

   (A) A freed slave who moved from the South to a northern state
   (B) A Southern politician who had switched allegiances during the war
   (C) A representative of the federal government who reneged on promises made before the war
   (D) A pioneer who packed up and moved west immediately following the end of hostilities
   (E) A Northerner who moved south in order to profit from the postwar instability

"The Bostonians paying the excise-man, or tarring & feathering"

11. The 1774 print shown above most likely depicts which of the following?

   (A) The colonists expressing their gratitude to the British monarchy
   (B) The colonists expressing their dissatisfaction with the system of direct taxation imposed by the British
   (C) The colonists enjoying the festivities associated with the arrival of a ship in the port of Boston
   (D) The colonists protesting the unjust treatment of Native Americans in New England
   (E) The colonists publicly humiliating a man accused of being a heretic

GO ON TO THE NEXT PAGE

15. Why, despite President Woodrow Wilson's strong support for the move, did the United States not join the League of Nations immediately following World War I?

(A) The governments of England and France blocked the United States from joining.
(B) There was not enough support among high-ranking military officers.
(C) The financial debts incurred during the war prevented Wilson from taking action.
(D) The idea of joining the League of Nations sparked widespread protests among veterans.
(E) There was strong opposition in the Senate to becoming entangled in further European affairs.

16. Each of the following was provided to returning World War II veterans under the G.I. Bill EXCEPT

(A) low-cost mortgages
(B) low-interest loans
(C) stipendiary support for higher education
(D) free health insurance
(E) unemployment compensation

17. The primary intention of the Bay of Pigs Invasion was to

(A) promote American oil interests in Venezuela
(B) safeguard American expatriates in Nicaragua
(C) overthrow the government of Jacobo Arbenz Guzmán in Guatemala
(D) prevent a coup attempt against Maximiliano Hernández Martínez in El Salvador
(E) overthrow the government of Fidel Castro in Cuba

18. Which two campaign promises made by President Ronald Reagan dominated his presidential agenda?

(A) Ending the "tax and spend" policies of his liberal predecessors and winning the Cold War
(B) Increasing taxes on the top 10% of Americans and rebuilding diplomatic ties with Latin America
(C) Rebuilding trust and cooperation among the dissenting factions within the Congress and raising teacher pay nationwide
(D) Creating a strong environmental conservation program and shoring up American influence in the United Nations
(E) Reforming immigration policy and creating conditions more favorable to labor unions

19. In the 1990s, President Clinton became only the second president ever to be impeached for which of the following reasons?

(A) Accusations of tax fraud
(B) Accusations of perjury and obstruction of justice
(C) Accusations of treason against the United States
(D) Accusations of vote tampering
(E) Accusations of dereliction of duty

20. The Quaker community faced hardship in England for each of the following reasons EXCEPT

(A) a refusal to bear arms or otherwise participate in England's wars
(B) a refusal to bow down to nobles or doff hats to those of higher social classes
(C) a refusal to pay taxes that would assist in military spending
(D) a refusal to participate in worship services without a trained minister serving as an intermediary
(E) a refusal to swear allegiance to the British monarchy and its institutional power

GO ON TO THE NEXT PAGE

21. The Salem Witch Trials in seventeenth-century Massachusetts were influenced by all of the following factors EXCEPT

    (A) a strong belief in the pervasive influence of supernatural forces
    (B) a lack of judicial due process
    (C) ongoing feuds and distrust in the local community
    (D) widespread economic prosperity
    (E) mass hysteria fueled by overzealous religious faith

22. Which of the following was one of the principal reasons that led to Bacon's Rebellion in 1676?

    (A) A distrust in the judiciousness of the Virginia colony's economic policies
    (B) A desire to align the colony's militia with those of neighboring colonies
    (C) A widespread skepticism regarding the fairness of cotton prices
    (D) A sense of anger stemming from the colonists' limited opportunities for social advancement
    (E) A failure of the Virginia political establishment to protect frontier settlements from Native American attacks

23. One purpose of the Navigation Acts was to

    (A) restrict colonial trade to England's benefit
    (B) enable the colonies to trade freely with the French and Spanish
    (C) promote fair market prices for staple goods that would be mutually beneficial to England and the colonies
    (D) encourage sea-based exploration of new territories in the Caribbean
    (E) protect the colonial shipping industry from pirates and other marauders

24. Which of the following was one of the most important political ramifications of the Treaty of Paris, which ended the French and Indian War in 1763?

    (A) Britain ceded all of its territory north of the Mason-Dixon line to France.
    (B) Britain ceded all of its territory west of the Missouri River to France.
    (C) France ceded all of its territory east of the Mississippi River to Britain.
    (D) Britain ceded all of its territory south of the 49th parallel to France.
    (E) France ceded all of its territory north of the 49th parallel to Britain.

GO ON TO THE NEXT PAGE

THE PROPAGATION SOCIETY.——— MORE FREE THAN WELCOME.

Pope: My friend we have concluded to take charge of your spiritual welfare, and your temporal estate, so that you need not be troubled with the care of them in future; we will say your prayers and spend your money, while you live, and bury you in the Potters Field, when you die. Kneel then! And kiss our big toe in token of submission.

Brother Jonathan: No you don't, Mr. Pope! You're altogether too willing; but you can't put "the mark of the Beast" on Americans.

Young America: You can neither coax, nor frighten our boys, Sir! We can take care of our own worldly affairs, and are determined to "Know nothing" but this book, to guide us in spiritual things.

First bishop: I cannot bear to see that boy, with that horrible book.

Second bishop: Only let us get a good foothold on the soil, and we'll burn up those Books and elevate this Country to the Same degree of happiness and prosperity, to which we have brought Italy, Spain, Ireland and many other lands.

Third bishop: Sovereign Pontiff! Say that if his friends, have any money, when he dies; they may purchase a hole, for him in my cemetery, at a fair price.

Fourth bishop: Go ahead Reverend Father; I'll hold our boat by this sprig of shamrock.

25. The sentiments expressed in the cartoon above most likely reflect which of the following?

(A) Mercantilism
(B) Nativism
(C) Transcendentalism
(D) Romanticism
(E) Realism

26. Which of the following developments paved the way for pioneers to settle the American West from Texas to the Pacific Ocean?

(A) The end of the Mexican-American War in 1848
(B) The Louisiana Purchase in 1803
(C) The Texas Annexation of 1845
(D) The end of the Spanish-American War in 1898
(E) The military stalemate at the end of the War of 1812

GO ON TO THE NEXT PAGE

27. One effect of the Kansas-Nebraska Act of 1854 was to

    (A) end slavery in the western territories
    (B) drive a wedge between Native Americans and those who wished to settle the frontiers
    (C) overturn the Missouri Compromise of 1820 by granting settlers popular sovereignty
    (D) end slavery in the Mid-Atlantic states
    (E) unify the Democratic and Whig parties

NO LACK OF BIG GAME
The President Seems to Have Scared Up Quite a Bunch of Octopi.

28. The cartoon above illustrates which of the following legislative agendas of President Theodore Roosevelt?

    (A) The dissolution of monopolistic corporations
    (B) The expansion of national parks and forests
    (C) The regulation of railways and interstate commerce
    (D) The promotion of civil rights protections for all Americans
    (E) The bolstering of American military prowess

29. One purpose of "muckraking" journalism in the early twentieth century was to

    (A) report on foreign policy and overseas military involvement
    (B) report on the economic difficulties brought about by the stock market crash
    (C) report on political and corporate corruption
    (D) report on athletic events and popular culture
    (E) report on religious topics of interest to immigrant communities

30. To whom was President Richard Nixon referring when he appealed to the "silent majority" in the late 1960s?

    (A) Those Americans who wished to see the passage of more liberal policies toward the legalization of drugs
    (B) Those Americans who did not agree with Nixon's strategy of political realism
    (C) Those Americans who actively campaigned for a return to traditional American values
    (D) Those Americans who had died in the Korean War and Vietnam
    (E) Those Americans who did not take an active role in politics but were supportive of Nixon's conservative policies

31. Which of the following quotes best exemplifies the American colonists' reaction to the Stamp Act of 1765?

    (A) "We must consider that we shall be as a city upon a hill."
    (B) "He that will not work shall not eat."
    (C) "I am not a Virginian, but an American."
    (D) "Taxation without representation is tyranny."
    (E) "My country is the world, and my religion is to do good."

32. The First Continental Congress petitioned King George III to do which of the following?

    (A) End the enforcement of the Intolerable Acts
    (B) Recognize Massachusetts as an independent political entity
    (C) Intervene on behalf of frontier settlers besieged by violent schisms
    (D) Grant the colonies financial support through loans and paper money
    (E) Establish George Washington as the military leader of the colonies

33. Each of the following helps to explain why the American colonists encountered great difficulties during the first year of the Revolutionary War EXCEPT:

    (A) Not all of the colonists initially favored independence.
    (B) The colonial forces lacked the funding and training to match the British "redcoats" in open battle.
    (C) The colonial forces had had less than half of the troop strength of the British army.
    (D) Britain promised freedom to any slave who helped to fight to restore British authority in the colonies.
    (E) Early military losses resulted in a decline in morale among American troops.

34. Which of the following was a major reason behind the split between Federalists and Anti-Federalists in the era immediately following the Revolutionary War?

    (A) A disagreement about whether the United States should have a separation of powers within the federal government
    (B) A disagreement about whether the United States should have a strong central government or a more limited one
    (C) A disagreement about whether the United States government should be based upon the will of the people
    (D) A disagreement about whether the United States should be entirely independent of the British monarchy
    (E) A disagreement about whether it was necessary to set up checks against the possibility of future political corruption

35. The intention of the Monroe Doctrine was to

    (A) provide the United States with a legal means to intervene in European colonial activities in Africa
    (B) keep the western hemisphere free from European influence and military intervention
    (C) maintain a solid military alliance between the United States and France
    (D) limit European abolitionists' influence on attitudes in the United States
    (E) pave the way for more widespread cooperation between American and Spanish naval forces

GO ON TO THE NEXT PAGE

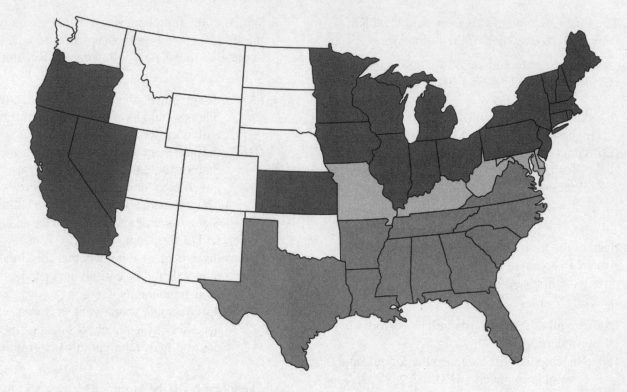

36. The map above most likely shows which of the following?

    (A) Divisions among cotton-producing and non-cotton-producing states and territories in the late seventeenth century
    (B) Divisions among states and territories that had granted women the right to vote circa 1890
    (C) Divisions relating to fiscal policy among states and territories circa 1930
    (D) Divisions relating to support for the temperance movement among states and territories circa 1920
    (E) Divisions of allegiance among states and territories in 1861

37. Which of the following men was NOT an Industrial Era business leader?

    (A) Andrew Carnegie
    (B) John D. Rockefeller
    (C) Cornelius Vanderbilt
    (D) Howard Schultz
    (E) J. P. Morgan

38. The primary purpose of President Woodrow Wilson's "Fourteen Points" speech was to

    (A) justify an isolationist foreign policy vis-à-vis Latin America
    (B) bolster the strength of the Federal Reserve
    (C) weaken his political enemies on the topic of immigration from Italy and Ireland
    (D) counter the accusation that he was "weak" on the topic of communism
    (E) argue that World War I was fought for a moral cause and to encourage postwar peace in Europe

GO ON TO THE NEXT PAGE

WOMANS HOLY WAR.
Grand Charge on the Enemy's Works.

39. The movement depicted in the cartoon above was influential in the passage of which of the following Amendments to the Constitution?

(A) The Fourth Amendment
(B) The Eighth Amendment
(C) The Fifteenth Amendment
(D) The Eighteenth Amendment
(E) The Twenty-sixth Amendment

40. Which of the following best characterizes the literature of the Beat Generation?

(A) A rejection of mainstream American values and an embrace of experimentation with drugs and alternative sexualities
(B) An embrace of nature and the conservation movement
(C) An emphasis upon intuitive thought and the power of human reasoning
(D) An attempt to apply objectivity and detachment to the study of human beings and animals
(E) A return to conservative and classical themes

41. Each of the following was a characteristic of the religious ideals of the First Great Awakening EXCEPT

(A) an emphasis on ritual and hierarchy
(B) an emphasis on evangelism
(C) an emphasis on personal revelation
(D) an emphasis on the need for salvation
(E) an emphasis on commitment to personal morality

42. Which of the following best describes the pattern of "triangular trade" employed by British mercantilists in the years prior to the American Revolution?

(A) Rum to New England; slaves to Africa; molasses to the Caribbean
(B) Slaves to New England; rum to Africa; molasses to the Caribbean
(C) Molasses to New England; rum to Africa; slaves to the Caribbean
(D) Slaves to New England; molasses to Africa; rum to the Caribbean
(E) Molasses to New England; slaves to Africa; rum to the Caribbean

GO ON TO THE NEXT PAGE

43. In what way was the Rhode Island colony unique among American colonies in the seventeenth century?

    (A) It provided religious freedom to persecuted groups such as Quakers and Jews.
    (B) It was initially claimed as a Dutch territory.
    (C) It was founded by a Puritan religious leader.
    (D) Its economy was based upon agriculture, fishing, and sea trade.
    (E) It was the home of what became a major American university.

44. The Quakers, Mennonites, and Amish all adhere to which of the following principles?

    (A) Agnosticism
    (B) Deism
    (C) Dogmatism
    (D) Militarism
    (E) Pacifism

45. Which of the following were characteristic of the Republican promise of a "return to normalcy" in the 1920s?

    (A) An attempt to rid the government and corporations of corruption and abuses
    (B) An environment hospitable to big business and an isolationist foreign policy
    (C) An aggressive movement to break up monopolistic business practices
    (D) An emphasis upon educational reform
    (E) An increase in tax rates upon the wealthiest Americans

46. "The only thing we have to fear is . . . fear itself—nameless, unreasoning, unjustified terror which paralyzes needed efforts to convert retreat into advance."

    President Franklin D. Roosevelt made the proclamation above in his inaugural address in reference to which national crisis?

    (A) The Red Scare
    (B) The sinking of the ship *Titanic*
    (C) The polio epidemic
    (D) The Great Depression
    (E) The Japanese attack on Pearl Harbor

47. Which of the following is one of the most long-lasting achievements of the Eisenhower administration?

    (A) The formation of the interstate highway system
    (B) The successful implementation of progressive minimum wage laws
    (C) A vigorous public rebuttal of McCarthyism
    (D) An opening up of U.S. trade relations with China
    (E) Ending the war in Vietnam

48. The United States built up huge arsenals of nuclear weapons during the 1950s and 1960s because of the belief that

    (A) nuclear technology would be beneficial in the field of medicine
    (B) a strong nuclear arsenal would be the only way to deter terrorist attacks by non-state actors
    (C) if both the United States and the Soviet Union had huge arsenals of devastating weapons, neither side would actually use them
    (D) using nuclear weapons would be a more humane way of conducting warfare in the modern era
    (E) an arms race would have salutary effects upon the American industrial economy

GO ON TO THE NEXT PAGE

49. Which of the following is the best description of the "domino theory"?

   (A) If one country develops financially profitable technology, then other countries will copy that technology.
   (B) If one country raises its tax rates, then other countries will lower their tax rates.
   (C) If one country falls to communist influence, then the surrounding countries will follow.
   (D) If one country elects a left-leaning leader, then the surrounding countries will follow.
   (E) If one country builds up its military capabilities, then other countries will rush to match those capabilities.

50. Each of the following was a devastating effect of the European colonization of the Americas EXCEPT

   (A) the introduction of unknown diseases
   (B) the decimation of native populations through war
   (C) the displacement of native populations from their ancestral lands
   (D) the widespread enslavement of native populations for work on plantations
   (E) the killing off of nearly the entire buffalo population

51. In which of the following geographical areas were women the most numerically strong during the colonial period?

   (A) The Jamestown Colony
   (B) The frontier regions
   (C) The Plymouth Colony
   (D) The Massachusetts Bay Colony
   (E) New York

52. Membership in the General Court of the Massachusetts Bay Colony was initially restricted to which of the following groups?

   (A) Puritan men and women
   (B) Adults over the age of 21
   (C) Landholding men and women
   (D) Puritan men
   (E) Landholding Puritan men

53. Each of the following philosophers significantly influenced the political thinking of the framers of the Constitution EXCEPT

   (A) Jean-Jacques Rousseau
   (B) John Locke
   (C) Thomas Hobbes
   (D) Voltaire
   (E) Henry David Thoreau

54. James Baldwin, Langston Hughes, and Zora Neale Hurston are all prominent representatives of which of the following American literary movements?

   (A) The Harlem Renaissance
   (B) Transcendentalism
   (C) Realism
   (D) Dadaism
   (E) The Southern Agrarians

GO ON TO THE NEXT PAGE

THE "RAIL SPLITTER" AT WORK REPAIRING THE UNION.

55. Which two American leaders are depicted attempting to repair the Union in the cartoon above?

(A) Andrew Jackson and Abraham Lincoln
(B) Andrew Mellon and Abraham Lincoln
(C) Andrew Johnson and Abraham Lincoln
(D) Andrew Carnegie and Abraham Lincoln
(E) Andrew "Dice" Clay and Abraham Lincoln

56. The election of 1824 is notable in part because

(A) it was the first time that women were permitted to vote nationwide
(B) it was the first election to use a "winner-take-all" system
(C) it coalesced the entire country around a unified political front
(D) it returned the country to factional two-party politics
(E) it marked the end of the Whig Party's political power

GO ON TO THE NEXT PAGE

57. The 1943 sign pictured above most likely reflects which of the following?

(A) Jim Crow laws in the southern United States
(B) World War II–era recruitment of African American soldiers
(C) The racial integration of public schools
(D) New Deal programs designed to benefit the urban poor
(E) The ideals of the voting rights movement

58. Which of the following was a primary reason for which President Harry Truman decided to order the use of the atomic bomb in Hiroshima and Nagasaki?

(A) He believed that a successful bombing campaign would enable U.S. forces to invade the Japanese mainland more easily.
(B) He believed that the massive scale of destruction would force Japan to surrender.
(C) He believed that the Germans would surrender for fear that similar military action would take place on German soil.
(D) He believed that the Allies would follow the American action by dropping subsequent bombs of their own.
(E) He believed that bombing Hiroshima and Nagasaki would wipe out most of Japan's weapons capabilities.

59. Which of the following was an important advancement in civil rights that took place during the presidency of Harry Truman?

(A) The desegregation of the American military
(B) The overturning of *Plessy v. Ferguson*
(C) The Montgomery Bus Boycott
(D) The establishment of the Southern Christian Leadership Conference
(E) The establishment of the Student Nonviolent Coordinating Committee

60. Married women in colonial America were

(A) able to vote
(B) able to hold public office
(C) able to serve on juries
(D) able to make contracts without their husbands' approval
(E) able to engage in business outside the home

GO ON TO THE NEXT PAGE

61. In what way was Thomas Paine's pamphlet *Common Sense* influential on the course of American history?

    (A) It played a key role in changing the attitudes of Southern plantation owners toward the morality of slavery.
    (B) It promulgated the ideal of Manifest Destiny.
    (C) It inspired people in the thirteen colonies to fight for independence from Britain.
    (D) It exposed the unjust labor conditions of American farmers.
    (E) It exploited American fears concerning waves of mass immigration.

62. President George Washington's Farewell Address was notable for setting which of the following precedents?

    (A) A refusal to participate in economic agreements with European nations
    (B) A two-term limit on the American presidency
    (C) A tradition of farmer-politicians that lasted a century
    (D) A requirement that all presidents serve in the military before entering politics
    (E) A belief in the necessity of multiple political parties

63. *Marbury v. Madison* is considered a landmark Supreme Court ruling for which of the following reasons?

    (A) It established the rules by which the federal government is able to tax the states.
    (B) It helped to differentiate between the separate spheres of influence of the executive and judicial branches of government.
    (C) It clarified the issue of when an individual is legally granted the right to privacy.
    (D) It laid out the circumstances under which it is permissible for a company to operate across state lines.
    (E) It refined the definition of "freedom of speech."

64. Which of the following was a result of President Andrew Jackson's policies toward Native Americans?

    (A) The transplantation of several Native American tribes away from their homelands to federal territories west of the Mississippi River
    (B) An upsurge in support for his presidency among the Native American electorate
    (C) A peaceful resolution to issues of Native violence that had plagued New England for centuries
    (D) The relocation of Native American tribes from the Southwest to the Mid-Atlantic region
    (E) A backlash against his presidency among non-Native whites in the South

65. From which countries did the majority of "New Immigrants" to the United States arrive in the years following the Civil War?

    (A) England, Scotland, Wales, and Ireland
    (B) Denmark, Norway, Finland, and Sweden
    (C) Italy, Greece, Russia, and China
    (D) Germany, Belgium, Luxembourg, and the Netherlands
    (E) Mexico, Honduras, El Salvador, and Guatemala

66. Which of the following best describes the time period when the Whig party started to decline in numbers and influence?

    (A) The 1790s
    (B) The 1820s
    (C) The 1830s
    (D) The 1850s
    (E) The 1890s

GO ON TO THE NEXT PAGE

67. "If there is no struggle, there is no progress. Those who profess to favor freedom, and deprecate agitation, are men who want crops without plowing up the ground, they want rain without thunder and lightning."

The 1857 quote above can best be viewed as an expression of which of the following?

(A) The environmental movement
(B) The anti-war movement
(C) The women's suffrage movement
(D) The gay rights movement
(E) The abolitionist movement

68. The image of the fashionably dressed "flapper" holding a cigarette in the illustration above most likely comes from which era of American history?

(A) The Roaring Twenties
(B) The Era of Good Feelings
(C) The Gilded Age
(D) The Disco Age
(E) The Gay Nineties

69. "We conclude that the doctrine of 'separate but equal' has no place. Separate educational facilities are inherently unequal."

The sentiment expressed in the quote above most likely comes from which of the following Supreme Court rulings?

(A) *Dred Scott v. Sandford*
(B) *Gibbons v. Ogden*
(C) *Miranda v. Arizona*
(D) *Brown v. Board of Education*
(E) *McCulloch v. Maryland*

70. Thomas Jefferson's establishment of the University of Virginia was innovative because

(A) it contained a prominent School of Divinity
(B) students were able to bring their families to campus
(C) it was the first institution of higher education in the state of Virginia
(D) higher education was separated from religious doctrine
(E) tuition was free to all students

71. Which of the following best characterizes the role of indentured servants during the colonial period?

(A) Captives from Africa forced to work on plantations
(B) Immigrants from the Caribbean who lacked sufficient job prospects
(C) Poor or indebted Europeans obligated to work for colonial employers
(D) Native Americans who performed menial household duties in the employ of frontier settlers
(E) Free men and women who worked their way up the pay ladder through a system of meritocracy

GO ON TO THE NEXT PAGE

72. The trail from St. Louis to the Pacific Ocean indicated on the map above most likely reflects which of the following?

    (A) The Powell Geographic Expedition of 1869
    (B) The expedition of Meriwether Lewis and William Clark in 1804
    (C) Roald Amundsen's search for the Northwest Passage in 1903
    (D) Henry Morton Stanley's search for David Livingstone in 1871
    (E) The Hayden Geological Survey of 1871

73. Which of the following women was banished from the Massachusetts Bay Colony after she challenged the ruling Puritan authorities?

    (A) Rosa Parks
    (B) Anne Hutchinson
    (C) Abigail Adams
    (D) Louisa May Alcott
    (E) Clara Barton

74. The region of the Ohio River Valley was disputed territory among which groups in the middle of the eighteenth century?

    (A) The French and the British
    (B) The French and the Spanish
    (C) The British and the Spanish
    (D) The British and the Dutch
    (E) The French and the Dutch

75. The Roosevelt Corollary to the Monroe Doctrine reflected President Theodore Roosevelt's belief that in matters of foreign policy, the United States should

    (A) "rest on the traditional American values of restraint and empathy"
    (B) "keep the United States free from political connections with every other country"
    (C) "cultivate peace and harmony with all"
    (D) "steer clear of permanent alliances"
    (E) "speak softly, and carry a big stick"

76. Benjamin Franklin is noted for all of the following achievements EXCEPT

    (A) participating in the drafting of the Declaration of Independence
    (B) an abiding interest in scientific experimentation
    (C) founding the Democratic Party
    (D) serving as a diplomatic representative of the United States abroad
    (E) establishing a lending library

77. The utopian community of Shakers in the eighteenth century was unique in part because of its belief in

    (A) divine revelation
    (B) the equality of the sexes
    (C) the influence of supernatural forces
    (D) pacifism
    (E) evangelization

GO ON TO THE NEXT PAGE

78. "I refuse to accept the view that mankind is so tragically bound to the starless midnight of racism and war that the bright daybreak of peace and brotherhood can never become a reality…I believe that unarmed truth and unconditional love will have the final word."

The quote above most likely comes from which of the following sources?

(A) Martin Luther King, Jr.'s acceptance speech at the Nobel Prize ceremony, 1964
(B) Malcolm X's speech, "The Ballot or the Bullet," 1964
(C) Jesse Jackson's Democratic National Convention address, 1984
(D) President John F. Kennedy's inauguration speech, 1961
(E) President Lyndon Johnson's speech, "The American Promise," 1965

79. The poster above most likely reflects the ideals of which of the following federal programs?

(A) The Square Deal
(B) The Occupy Movement
(C) The Pacifist Movement
(D) The Tea Party Movement
(E) The New Deal

80. Which of the following was NOT a primary reason for the trouble endured by the Jamestown settlement in the early 1600s?

(A) A lack of reliable sources for clean drinking water
(B) Periodic warfare with neighboring Powhatan tribes
(C) The spread of disease through mosquitoes and other pests
(D) Insurrection among the slaves
(E) Poor farming conditions due to swampland

GO ON TO THE NEXT PAGE

81. The Iroquois tribes in what is now the state of New York lived in which type of dwelling during the colonial period?

    (A) Conical teepees made of buffalo hide and wooden poles
    (B) Semi-subterranean lodges made of earth and reeds
    (C) Large longhouses made of wooden frames and bark
    (D) Multistory adobe houses made of clay and straw
    (E) Beehive-shaped houses made of wooden frames and grass

82. Which of the following was NOT a major crop in colonial New England?

    (A) Corn
    (B) Wheat
    (C) Rye
    (D) Squash
    (E) Beans

83. The Gold Rush of 1848–1855 spurred a massive jump in the population of which American city?

    (A) New York
    (B) Washington, D.C.
    (C) St. Louis
    (D) San Antonio
    (E) San Francisco

84. The Federalists conceded the Bill of Rights to the Anti-Federalists in response to the latter's concern that

    (A) the Constitution lacked sufficient provisions to protect individual liberties
    (B) the Constitution did not adequately define the role of the vice presidency
    (C) the Constitution did not specify term limits for the presidency
    (D) the Constitution placed too much of an emphasis upon individual liberties
    (E) the Constitution did not adequately protect the interests of the merchant class

85. "We are assembled to protest against a form of government existing without the consent of the governed—to declare our right to be free as man is free, to be represented in the government which we are taxed to support."

    The 1848 quote above most likely comes from which of the following sources?

    (A) Helen Keller, "Strike Against War"
    (B) Mother Jones, "Labor Speech to Coal Miners"
    (C) Elizabeth Cady Stanton, "Seneca Falls Keynote Address"
    (D) Margaret Sanger, "The Morality of Birth Control"
    (E) Sojourner Truth, "The Spirit Calls Me"

86. The "Triple Entente" refers to the alliance among which nations in the period immediately before World War I?

    (A) The United States, Great Britain, and France
    (B) The United States, France, and Russia
    (C) Germany, Austria-Hungary, and Italy
    (D) Great Britain, France, and Russia
    (E) Great Britain, Germany, and the United States

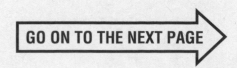

87. The "Instructions to All Persons of Japanese Ancestry" from April 1942 pictured above most likely preceded which of the following events?

(A) The Japanese bombing of Pearl Harbor
(B) The admission of Hawaii into the union
(C) The internment of Japanese-Americans in California
(D) The segregation of Asian students in American public schools
(E) The issuance of labor permits for Japanese migrant laborers

88. In the years since 1910, the African American population has shifted from

(A) mostly urban to mostly suburban
(B) mostly rural to almost entirely urban
(C) almost entirely suburban to mostly rural
(D) almost entirely urban to almost entirely rural
(E) mostly suburban to almost entirely urban

89. Which of the following American military engagements was NOT preceded by a formal declaration of war by Congress?

(A) The War of 1812
(B) The Spanish-American War
(C) World War I
(D) World War II
(E) The Korean War

90. In 1791, why did Thomas Jefferson and James Madison oppose Alexander Hamilton's proposal for high protective tariffs as a means of generating revenue for the federal government?

(A) They did not think that Hamilton's plan would survive a presidential veto.
(B) They wanted to delay the plan until such time as the United States had a more stable national currency.
(C) They had planned a similar proposal of their own and didn't approve of Hamilton's rates of taxation.
(D) They were concerned that Hamilton's plan would undermine the authority of the federal government.
(E) They worried that such a move would render industries overly reliant upon federal aid.

STOP

If you finish before time is called, you may check your work on this test only.
Do not turn to any other test in this book.

Chapter 16
Practice Test 3:
Answers and
Explanations

PRACTICE TEST 3 ANSWER KEY

Question Number	Correct Answer	Right	Wrong	Question Number	Correct Answer	Right	Wrong	Question Number	Correct Answer	Right	Wrong
1.	C	____	____	31.	D	____	____	61.	C	____	____
2.	D	____	____	32.	A	____	____	62.	B	____	____
3.	A	____	____	33.	C	____	____	63.	B	____	____
4.	E	____	____	34.	B	____	____	64.	A	____	____
5.	B	____	____	35.	B	____	____	65.	C	____	____
6.	B	____	____	36.	E	____	____	66.	D	____	____
7.	E	____	____	37.	D	____	____	67.	E	____	____
8.	D	____	____	38.	E	____	____	68.	A	____	____
9.	B	____	____	39.	D	____	____	69.	D	____	____
10.	A	____	____	40.	A	____	____	70.	D	____	____
11.	B	____	____	41.	A	____	____	71.	C	____	____
12.	A	____	____	42.	C	____	____	72.	B	____	____
13.	C	____	____	43.	A	____	____	73.	B	____	____
14.	E	____	____	44.	E	____	____	74.	A	____	____
15.	E	____	____	45.	B	____	____	75.	E	____	____
16.	D	____	____	46.	D	____	____	76.	C	____	____
17.	E	____	____	47.	A	____	____	77.	B	____	____
18.	A	____	____	48.	C	____	____	78.	A	____	____
19.	B	____	____	49.	C	____	____	79.	E	____	____
20.	D	____	____	50.	D	____	____	80.	D	____	____
21.	D	____	____	51.	B	____	____	81.	C	____	____
22.	E	____	____	52.	E	____	____	82.	B	____	____
23.	A	____	____	53.	E	____	____	83.	E	____	____
24.	C	____	____	54.	A	____	____	84.	A	____	____
25.	B	____	____	55.	C	____	____	85.	C	____	____
26.	A	____	____	56.	D	____	____	86.	D	____	____
27.	C	____	____	57.	A	____	____	87.	C	____	____
28.	A	____	____	58.	B	____	____	88.	B	____	____
29.	C	____	____	59.	A	____	____	89.	E	____	____
30.	E	____	____	60.	E	____	____	90.	E	____	____

PRACTICE TEST 3 EXPLANATIONS

1. **C**   Spain (A), England (B), France (D), and the Netherlands (E) were important colonizers of North America in the sixteenth century. Many Italian explorers, such as Christopher Columbus, worked for the governments of other countries, but the Italian states (C) were politically fragmented during the Age of Exploration and did not play a major role in the European expansion to the New World.

2. **D**   The early American colonists observed the Native Americans growing tobacco and quickly realized that tobacco cultivation would be a very profitable venture. Pumpkins (A) and potatoes (B) were widely known in the early colonies, but were not nearly as profitable as tobacco. During the Colonial period, tea (C), and sugar (E) were primarily imported from other English colonies in Asia and the Caribbean.

3. **A**   "Salutary Neglect" is the term for the British policy of not strictly enforcing trade laws and other regulations in the American colonies. This policy ultimately had the effect of strengthening the push for independence, since the colonists were left to govern themselves largely independent of Britain's power and gained increasing self-control in the pre-Revolutionary years. The "10% Plan" (B) was part of Abraham Lincoln's policy of Reconstruction after the Civil War. "Calvinism" (C) is a major Protestant theological tradition endorsed by the Puritans and other American religious groups. A "Gag Rule" (D), generally speaking, refers to the limiting or forbidding of discussion of a certain topic. The main usage of the term "gag rule" in U.S. history refers to the attempts of pro-slavery politicians to block abolitionist legislation.

4. **E**   The doctrine of nullification held that states had the right to negate any federal laws that were perceived to overreach. In 1832, the South Carolina legislature declared several federal tariffs null and void, and President Jackson responded aggressively in exerting the power of the federal government.

5. **B**   The dates of entry into the union of the states in question were Virginia in 1778, Ohio in 1803, Nebraska in 1867, and Wyoming in 1890. The main clue that this answer is correct is that statehood, generally speaking, moved from east to west chronologically.

6. **B**   After the Revolutionary War, the United States faced a number of economic challenges. As George Washington's Secretary of the Treasury, Alexander Hamilton established the Bank of the United States as part of his broader fiscal and monetary program to normalize American currency and deal with both state and federal debts.

7. **E**   The Know-Nothing party in the 1850s reflected both nativist (anti-immigrant) and anti-Catholic sentiment and its leaders played upon popular fears about (mainly) German and Irish immigrants being "controlled" by the Pope in Rome. The Know-Nothing movement was also linked to the temperance movement, since many German and Irish immigrants drank alcohol.

8. **D**   In the early 1900s, American Progressives frequently railed against unfair labor practices, including the widespread use of child labor. Among other things, the Fair Labor Standards Act introduced the 40-hour workweek and prohibited minors from most forms of employment (outside of agriculture). The Erdman Act (A) dealt with labor disputes within the railroad industry and allowed railroad workers

to organize into unions. The Emergency Quota Act (B) placed numerical limits on immigration into the United States and established quotas for immigrants from certain countries. The Social Security Act (C), originally designed to provide economic security during the Great Depression, established a system of financial benefits to retirees and the elderly. The Taft-Hartley Act (E), also known as the Labor Management Relations Act, restricted the activities and power of labor unions.

9. **B** This quote comes from a 1947 speech to Congress by President Harry Truman and is a broad articulation of the Truman Doctrine's goal of stopping Soviet expansion and the spread of communism around the globe. The Monroe Doctrine (A), from the early nineteenth century, dealt with U.S. foreign policy toward Latin America. The Eisenhower Doctrine (C), articulated in 1957, permitted Middle Eastern countries to request American economic or military assistance if they were threatened. The Powell Doctrine (D) refers to General Colin Powell's articulation of the appropriateness of using American military might in the run-up to the 1990–1992 Gulf War. The Rumsfeld Doctrine (E) refers to President George W. Bush's Defense Secretary Donald Rumsfeld's belief in transforming the American military into a smaller, more nimble, and technologically advanced force.

10. **A** Upton Sinclair's 1906 novel *The Jungle* portrays the lives of poor immigrants working in the meatpacking industry in Chicago and is considered important because of its depiction of exploitation and the helplessness of the urban poor in the early twentieth century. *Catch-22* (B) is a satirical anti-war novel from 1961. *Uncle Tom's Cabin* (C) is an 1852 anti-slavery novel. *The Grapes of Wrath* (D) is a 1939 realist novel depicting struggling families during the Great Depression. *Native Son* (E) is an African American protest novel from 1940.

11. **B** This print depicts the tarring and feathering (public humiliation) of Boston Commissioner of Customs James Malcolm. One can see that tea is being forced down the throat of the "excise man" (tax collector) while the Boston Tea Party takes place in the background.

12. **A** The Lincoln-Douglas debates, which took place in 1858, concerned the matter of slavery—particularly slavery in the territories. Abraham Lincoln was then the Republican candidate for the Illinois Senate and his Democratic opponent was Stephen Douglas. Among other topics, Lincoln and Douglas discussed the issue of popular sovereignty (the idea that the people of a given state or territory could decide for themselves whether to allow slavery).

13. **C** Joseph Smith founded the Latter-Day Saint movement, commonly known as Mormonism, in the late 1820s. During the Second Great Awakening, Smith claimed to have received a special revelation from God, and that vision is recorded in the Book of Mormon.

14. **E** During the Reconstruction era after the Civil War, many Northerners moved to the Southern states in order to profit from the postwar instability. These Northerners were called "carpetbaggers" because of the carpet bags (a type of luggage) they carried at the time. In later years, "carpetbagger" came to refer to anyone who opportunistically exploited others.

15. **E** After World War I, the Congress, and in particular the Senate, was hesitant to become involved in further entanglements abroad. The period after World War I saw an isolationist tendency among many politicians, and thus despite Wilson's strong urging, the United States did not join the League of Nations.

16. **D** The Servicemen's Readjustment Act, commonly known as the G.I. Bill, was signed by President Roosevelt in 1944 and was intended to assist veterans in their transition back to civilian life. All of the items listed in the answer choices except free health care (D) were part of the program.

17. **E** The Bay of Pigs fiasco was a failed attempt by the CIA under President John F. Kennedy to overthrow the regime of Cuban leader Fidel Castro with the help of Cuban exiles.

18. **A** President Reagan's economic policies, sometimes referred to as "Reaganomics," emphasized a "trickle down" ideal in which wealthy, upper-class prosperity would indirectly benefit the poor. A key component of this philosophy was the notion that a smaller role for the government and a decrease in taxes would benefit the nation's economy. Reagan also focused heavily on winning the Cold War, and during his presidency the Pentagon's budget increased dramatically.

19. **B** After the Monica Lewinsky scandal, in which it was discovered that President Clinton had a sexual relationship with one of his White House interns, he was impeached by the Congress for his handling of the scandal. The charges brought against him were perjury (lying under oath) and obstruction of justice. He was acquitted on both charges.

20. **D** The Quakers explicitly taught that it was NOT necessary to have a formally trained minister who would act as an intermediary between the people and God. This stance highly angered the hierarchical power structure of the Anglican Church. The other answer choices were characteristic traits of Quakers.

21. **D** The time of the Salem Witch Trials was not particularly economically prosperous. On the contrary, the colonists were beset with troubles and many inhabitants of Salem were economically deprived.

22. **E** Bacon's Rebellion was an attack against the rule of Virginia Governor William Berkeley, led by Nathaniel Bacon. There were numerous reasons for this rebellion, but chief among them was the frustration of many frontier settlers due to the fact that the colonial government did not respond strongly to settlers' concerns about their safety in the face of ongoing attacks by Native American tribes.

23. **A** The Navigation Acts, passed between 1651 and 1673, were part of a broader British attempt to achieve a favorable balance of trade by which Americans would produce raw goods and export them to England, where those goods would be manufactured into products that could be sold across Europe. English ships and companies were usually the benefactors of this arrangement.

24. **C** At the end of the French and Indian War, France chose to cede its territory east of the Mississippi River in favor of holding on to several territories in the Caribbean. This change in the political map had long-lasting consequences in the subsequent history of the United States and in Anglo-French relations.

25. **B** One can tell from the cartoon that immigrants dressed in the garb of Catholic clerics are coming to the shores of the United States. This image reflects the anti-Catholic sentiment of the Nativist movement, which sought to minimize the influence of Catholic immigrants from Europe on American society and politics.

26. **A**   At the end of the Mexican-American War, the peace treaty known as the Treaty of Guadalupe Hidalgo granted the United States a vast swath of land ranging from Texas west to the Pacific Ocean (modern-day California).

27. **C**   The Kansas-Nebraska Act created the territories of Kansas and Nebraska and granted settlers of those territories the freedom to determine whether or not to allow slavery within their borders (popular sovereignty). This decision had the effect of overturning the Missouri Compromise, which prohibited slavery in the northern parts of what was then the Louisiana Purchase territory.

28. **A**   The cartoon depicts President Roosevelt fighting the coal, beef, and oil trusts. Roosevelt's actions helped to limit the influence of large, monopolistic corporations and earned him the nickname "trust buster." Answers (B) and (C) are also characteristic concerns of Roosevelt's presidency, but have nothing to do with the cartoon in question.

29. **C**   So-called "muckraking" journalists were primarily interested in reform, and during the Progressive Era they were actively involved in investigations that exposed corrupt business practices and political scandals.

30. **E**   Generally speaking, a "silent majority" refers to a large group of people who do not express their opinions publicly. President Nixon used the term to appeal to those Americans who were not pleased with the cultural liberalization that took place in the 1960s but were not especially vocal about their discontent.

31. **D**   By means of the Stamp Act, the British parliament imposed a direct tax on the American colonies, mainly through the requirement that certain printed material carry a valid revenue stamp. This legislation was extremely unpopular in the colonies, as many Americans viewed it as unfair that the British would tax them without the consent of American representation in parliament.

32. **A**   The First Continental Congress assembled in 1774 in large part due to anger over the "Intolerable Acts," a series of punitive measures taken by Britain in an attempt to reduce the colonies' autonomy after the events of the Boston Tea Party. One of the acts of the First Continental Congress was to petition King George III to cease enforcing these trade blockades.

33. **C**   The colonists did, in fact, have almost the same number of troops as did the British. The problem was not that the Americans didn't have sufficient numbers, but rather that they were poorly trained and lacked the funding necessary to go head-to-head with the well-seasoned British veterans (who also had the significant advantage of being backed by a powerful navy). The tide of the war began to turn after a series of decisive battles and after France joined the American side in 1778.

34. **B**   The Federalists and the Anti-Federalists agreed upon a great many topics, but their principal disagreement was over the issue of how large and strong the federal government should be. The Federalists favored a strong central government, while the Anti-Federalists favored a more limited central government.

35. **B**   The Monroe Doctrine, which dominated American foreign policy for many decades, began in the 1820s with a statement stipulating that any European attempt to further interfere in North or South American affairs would be viewed as an act of aggression requiring the United States to respond. The goal of this doctrine was to create separate spheres of influence so that the United States could pursue its own goals in the western hemisphere without European involvement.

36. **E**   The map shows the current boundaries of the 48 contiguous states, but the shaded distinctions illustrate which areas were part of the Union and which areas were part of the Confederacy during the Civil War. The principal clue is the north-versus-south distinction among the eastern states.

37. **D**   Howard Schultz is the founder of Starbucks, the coffee company founded in 1971 in Seattle. Andrew Carnegie (A) led the late nineteenth-century expansion of the American steel industry. John D. Rockefeller co-founded the Standard Oil Company in 1870. Cornelius Vanderbilt (C) was an entrepreneur who made his wealth through the railroad and shipping industries in the nineteenth century. J. P. Morgan (E) was a banker who formed General Electric in 1892.

38. **E**   President Wilson's 1918 statement commonly known as the "Fourteen Points" presented a series of policies regarding the justification for American involvement in World War I.

39. **D**   The cartoon depicts a crusading woman, part of the temperance movement, destroying barrels of alcohol. The Eighteenth Amendment declared illegal the production, transportation, and sale of alcohol, ushering in the era of Prohibition. The Fourth Amendment (A) prohibits unreasonable search and seizure; the Eighth Amendment (B) prohibits cruel and unusual punishment, including torture; the Fifteenth Amendment (C) prohibits state and federal governments from denying someone the right to vote based on race; the Twenty-sixth Amendment (E) lowered the national voting age to 18.

40. **A**   The Beat Generation was part of the broader countercultural movement that emerged in the 1950s and 1960s in America. Authors such as Jack Kerouac and William S. Burroughs wrote novels and poetry that emphasized a rejection of mainstream American values and expectations in favor of a rebellious youth culture.

41. **A**   The First Great awakening was a religious revival movement that took place both in Britain and in the American colonies in the 1730s and 1740s. One of its defining features was a move away from ritual and hierarchy toward a more personal and individualistic Christian faith.

42. **C**   During the pre-Revolutionary period, the triangular trade was foundational to the economy of New England. Ships loaded with rum would sail to Africa, where the rum would be traded for slaves. The slave ships would then sail to the Caribbean, where many of them were traded for sugar and molasses. The ships would finally sail back to New England, where the sugar and molasses would be used to produce more rum.

43. **A**   Rhode Island was founded by Roger Williams, who was an early advocate of freedom of religion. When he began to develop Providence in the 1630s, Williams envisioned the colony as a haven for religious minorities, a characteristic not emphasized in the other colonies at that time.

44. **E** The Quakers, Mennonites, and Amish are historically linked to the Christian Pacifism movement and do not participate in military activities.

45. **B** After the Progressive Era of the early 1900s, the Republicans gained control of the presidency in the years following World War I and promised a "return to normalcy." This period was marked by conservative attitudes and the environment was favorable to business interests. During this time period, Americans weary of war also sought to be less involved in international affairs.

46. **D** Roosevelt's first presidential inauguration took place in March 1933, only a few years after the stock market crash of 1929. The speech was widely broadcasted over the radio and millions of Americans looked to Roosevelt for leadership during the economically disastrous situation that they faced.

47. **A** President Dwight D. Eisenhower was mainly known for his foreign policy, but one domestic program he successfully implemented was the development of the interstate highway system (in part based on his observation of the efficiency of the German Autobahn network when he was stationed in Europe as Supreme Commander of the Allied Forces during World War II).

48. **C** Based on the idea of "Mutually Assured Destruction," American leaders in the 1950s and 1960s built up a huge arsenal of nuclear weapons because they believed that the effects of nuclear war would be so devastating that neither the United States nor the Soviet Union would dare to actually fire off their missiles.

49. **C** The domino theory held that if one state fell to communism, then other countries would follow suit (in a domino effect).

50. **D** Some Native Americans were captured or sold into slavery during the early years of European involvement in the New World, but such practices were never widespread or practiced on a large scale as was slavery of Africans.

51. **B** Most of the early colonial settlements were disproportionately populated by men, but the frontier regions had a more even distribution of the sexes.

52. **E** During the early years of the Massachusetts Bay Colony, only landholding men in good standing with the Puritan establishment were permitted to participate in the General Court.

53. **E** Henry David Thoreau was a prominent transcendentalist writer in the mid to late 1800s, well after the Constitution had already been written.

54. **A** The Harlem Renaissance was a cultural movement that took place mainly in the 1920s. James Baldwin, Langston Hughes, and Zora Neale Hurston were prominent African American writers associated with this movement.

55. **C** The cartoon depicts Abraham Lincoln and his Vice President, Andrew Johnson, attempting to repair the Union at the end of the Civil War. Andrew Jackson (A) was the seventh U.S. President, and therefore is a clear anti-era choice. Andrew Mellon (B) and Andrew Carnegie (D) were American industrialists, and therefore should not be paired with Lincoln. Andrew "Dice" Clay (E) is an American standup comedian who was popular in the 1980s and 1990s.

56. **D** In the election of 1824, Americans were able to vote directly for their presidential candidates for the first time. This experience brought out the factionalism and divisions within American society and returned the country to partisan politics after a period of several decades in which the Republicans faced very little real opposition.

57. **A** The sign indicating a separate room for "Colored" people is representative of the segregationist policies prevalent in the southern United States prior to the civil rights movement of the 1950s and 1960s.

58. **B** President Truman decided to use the atomic bomb in Japan because although the Germans had already surrendered, effectively ending World War II's European front, the Japanese refused to surrender. Truman thought (correctly) that the widespread devastation caused by atomic weapons would force the Japanese into an untenable position.

59. **A** President Truman desegregated the American military in 1948, an action that in many ways ushered in the modern civil rights movement. All of the events mentioned in the other answer choices occurred during the presidency of Dwight D. Eisenhower.

60. **E** Married women in colonial America had very few rights. They were legally able to work outside the home, but for the most part women were restricted to traditional roles revolving around motherhood and maintenance of the home or farm. Unmarried women and widows had a few more legal rights than those who were married.

61. **C** Thomas Paine's pamphlet *Common Sense*, published anonymously in 1776, explained in clear language the necessity for American independence. It was wildly popular and was read in many taverns and meeting houses, influencing the revolutionary movement.

62. **B** George Washington voluntarily left office after serving two terms as president, setting a precedent that was eventually codified in the middle of the twentieth century. The only president to serve more than two terms was Franklin Roosevelt.

63. **B** The 1803 Supreme Court case *Marbury v. Madison* was foundational in the development of judicial review and established that only the Supreme Court has the power to decide whether particular laws are constitutional.

64. **A** By means of the Indian Removal Act of 1830, President Jackson transplanted Native American tribes from their homelands to federally controlled areas west of the Mississippi River.

65. **C** After the Civil War, the United States experienced a huge influx of immigrants from southern (Mediterranean) European countries, Russia, the eastern European countries, and Asia. The term "New Immigrant" was coined in the 1880s and reflects the fact that these immigrants did not come from countries that had been the primary sources of immigration prior to the Civil War (Germany, England, etc.).

66. **D** The Whig Party started to decline in the 1850s after the slavery debates. Northern and Southern Whig Party members split over the issue of abolition, and the party never recovered after the Civil War.

67. **E** This quote comes from a speech given by Frederick Douglass in Rochester, New York. After escaping slavery himself, Douglass became a prominent author and activist in the antislavery movement. Choices (A), (B), and (D) are clear anti-era choices. Choice (C) could fit the time period in question, but the mention of "freedom" in the quote makes (E) the best answer.

68. **A** "Flappers" were free-thinking women associated with the cultural liberality of the 1920s and who were known for disdaining expectations of what was considered "proper" women's behavior at that time. Fairly or unfairly, these women were characterized as engaging in decadent behavior and participating in activities (such as smoking) that were traditionally thought to belong to men.

69. **D** The quote comes from Chief Justice Earl Warren's ruling in the 1954 case *Brown v. Board of Education*, in which the Supreme Court ruled that segregated schools could never be equal and that state laws enforcing such segregation were in violation of the Equal Protection Clause of the Fourteenth Amendment.

70. **D** One of the ways in which Jefferson's founding of the University of Virginia was unique is that he consciously established it as a secular institution of higher education, in contrast to the other universities of the eighteenth and early nineteenth centuries.

71. **C** Indentured servants were extremely poor or indebted individuals who were obligated to work in the colonies, often in exchange for passage across the Atlantic.

72. **B** Meriwether Lewis and William Clark left St. Louis in 1804 upon an exploratory expedition commissioned by Thomas Jefferson soon after the purchase of the Louisiana Territory. Their objectives were to explore and map parts of the new territory, find a practical route across the western region, and study the plants and animals they encountered (among other things).

73. **B** Anne Hutchinson was a charismatic woman whose opposition to the Puritan establishment led to her banishment from the Massachusetts Bay Colony in 1638. She is an important figure in the history of American religious freedom.

74. **A** In the eighteenth century, both the French and the British claimed to hold territory in the Ohio Valley, a fact that was one of the primary reasons behind the French and Indian War of 1754–1763.

75. **E** The Roosevelt Corollary states that the United States will intervene in European disputes with Latin American nations rather than allowing the European nations to interfere in the affairs of the western hemisphere. This policy is consistent with President Roosevelt's axiom, "Speak softly, and carry a big stick" (implying that the United States is justified in practicing an aggressive foreign policy that can be backed up with military might).

76. **C** It was Andrew Jackson, not Benjamin Franklin, who founded the Democratic Party.

77. **B** Unlike most religious sects of the eighteenth century, the Shakers embraced the idea of equality between the sexes and many women held prominent spiritual roles in Shaker communities.

78. **A** The references to race and nonviolence indicate that Martin Luther King, Jr. is the best match for this quote.

79. **E** The poster promotes better housing as a means to decrease infant mortality, and thus fits well within the Progressive Movement of the early twentieth century. As part of the New Deal, President Franklin Roosevelt promoted education, better housing, and a number of other reforms as part of his response to the crisis years of the Great Depression.

80. **D** The first documentation for Africans arriving in Jamestown comes from 1619, but it does not appear that there were many slaves in the colony until the second half of the century. In any event, there is no record of any slave insurrection until the late seventeenth century. The other answer choices correctly identify factors that made life in Jamestown exceedingly difficult.

81. **C** In the colonial period, the Iroquois (and some Algonquin) tribes who lived in the forested Mid-Atlantic and northeastern regions typically lived in huge longhouses that could sleep as many as 60 people. In fact, "Iroquois" means "people of the longhouse." Teepees (A) were typical of the tribes who lived in the Great Plains region. Semi-subterranean lodges (B) were typically used in the un-forested regions of the upper Midwest and West where there were few trees to use for materials. The Pueblo tribes of the Southwest typically lived in adobe houses (D). Native American tribes who lived in the southern plains regions typically lived in beehive-shaped grass houses (E).

82. **B** The colonists in New England had a difficult time producing wheat because the soil conditions were not favorable.

83. **E** After gold was first found in northern California in 1848, approximately 300,000 people rushed to the region in the span of just a few short years. San Francisco's population jumped from 200 to 36,000 in about four years.

84. **A** The Anti-Federalists were concerned that the Constitution did not grant sufficient provisions for individual liberties such as the right to free speech. The Federalists agreed to the first ten amendments, now known as the Bill of Rights, as a means to ensure that the Anti-Federalists were satisfied that the Constitution protected individuals from excessive governmental interference.

85. **C** This quote comes from Elizabeth Cady Stanton's keynote address at the Seneca Falls Convention, the first major women's rights convention in the United States. Among other topics, the convention addressed women's role in society, voting rights, and the abolition of slavery. Helen Keller's 1916 speech (A) argued against the United States entering World War I. Mother Jones's 1912 speech (B) was influential in the labor movement. Margaret Sanger's 1921 speech (D) was influential in the twentieth-century debate over reproductive rights. Sojourner Truth was a major women's rights advocate, but her quote "The Spirit Calls Me" (E) marked the beginning of her abolitionist activities.

86. **D** Prior to World War I, the Triple Entente was the alliance among Great Britain, France, and Russia. The United States did not enter World War I until 1917, when President Woodrow Wilson declared that the United States would join the Triple Entente nations.

87. **C**   After the Japanese bombed Pearl Harbor in December 1941, President Roosevelt signed legislation that uprooted Americans with Japanese heritage and placed them into internment camps.

88. **B**   In 1910, the majority of African Americans lived in rural areas, primarily in the South. In the early part of the twentieth century, a period sometimes called the "Great Migration," there was a mass exodus of African Americans to the northern cities. More than half of African Americans still live in the southern states, but nationwide more than 70 percent of African Americans now live in urban areas.

89. **E**   World War II was the last American war preceded by a formal declaration of war by Congress. Technically, the Korean War was a "police action."

90. **E**   Alexander Hamilton proposed a series of protectionist tariffs in 1791 with the intention of generating funds for the federal government, which he hoped would have the indirect effect of building up American industry. Jefferson and Madison opposed this plan because they feared that such protectionist measures would ultimately be detrimental to American industry and create too much reliance upon the federal government.

HOW TO SCORE PRACTICE TEST 3

When you take the real exam, the proctors will collect your test booklet and bubble sheet and send your answer sheet to the processing center where a computer looks at the pattern of filled-in ovals on your answer sheet and gives you a score. We couldn't include even a small computer with this book, so we are providing this more primitive way of scoring your exam.

Determining Your Score

STEP 1   Using the Answer Key at the beginning of this chapter, determine how many questions you got right and how many you got wrong on the test. Remember, questions that you do not answer don't count as either right answers or wrong answers.

STEP 2   List the number of right answers here.

(A) _____

STEP 3   List the number of wrong answers here. Now divide that number by 4. (Use a calculator if you're feeling particularly lazy.)

(B) _____ ÷ 4 = _____

STEP 4   Subtract the number of wrong answers divided by 4 from the number of correct answers. Round this score to the nearest whole number. This is your raw score.

(A) _____ – (B) _____ = (C) _____

STEP 5   To determine your real score, take the number from Step 4 above and look it up in the left column of the Score Conversion Table on the next page; the corresponding score on the right is your score on the exam.

PRACTICE TEST 3
SCORE CONVERSION TABLE

Raw Score	Scaled Score	Raw Score	Scaled Score	Raw Score	Scaled Score
95	800	55	680	15	440
94	800	54	670	14	430
93	800	53	670	13	430
92	800	52	660	12	420
91	800	51	660	11	420
90	800	50	650	10	410
89	800	49	640	9	400
88	800	48	640	8	400
87	800	47	630	7	390
86	800	46	630	6	390
85	800	45	620	5	380
84	800	44	610	4	370
83	800	43	610	3	370
82	800	42	600	2	360
81	800	41	600	1	360
80	800	40	590	0	350
79	800	39	580	−1	340
78	800	38	580	−2	340
77	800	37	570	−3	330
76	800	36	570	−4	330
75	800	35	560	−5	320
74	790	34	550	−6	320
73	790	33	550	−7	310
72	780	32	540	−8	300
71	770	31	540	−9	300
70	770	30	530	−10	290
69	760	29	520	−11	290
68	760	28	520	−12	280
67	750	27	510	−13	270
66	740	26	510	−14	270
65	740	25	500	−15	260
64	730	24	490	−16	260
63	730	23	490	−17	250
62	720	22	480	−18	240
61	720	21	480	−19	240
60	710	20	470	−20	230
59	700	19	460	−21	230
58	700	18	460	−22	220
57	690	17	450	−23	210
56	690	16	450	−24	210

Completely darken bubbles with a No. 2 pencil. If you make a mistake, be sure to erase mark completely. Erase all stray marks.

1.

YOUR NAME: _____
(Print)
Last   First   M.I.

SIGNATURE: _____ DATE: ___/___/___

HOME ADDRESS: _____
(Print)
Number and Street

_____
City   State   Zip Code

PHONE NO.: _____
(Print)

IMPORTANT: Please fill in these boxes exactly as shown on the back cover of your test book.

2. TEST FORM

_____

6. DATE OF BIRTH

Month		Day		Year	
○ JAN					
○ FEB	⓪	⓪	⓪	⓪	
○ MAR	①	①	①	①	
○ APR	②	②	②	②	
○ MAY	③	③	③	③	
○ JUN	④	④	④	④	
○ JUL	⑤	⑤	⑤	⑤	
○ AUG	⑥	⑥	⑥	⑥	
○ SEP	⑦	⑦	⑦	⑦	
○ OCT	⑧	⑧	⑧	⑧	
○ NOV	⑨	⑨	⑨	⑨	
○ DEC					

3. TEST CODE   **4. REGISTRATION NUMBER**

7. SEX
○ MALE
○ FEMALE

The **Princeton** Review®

© 1996 Princeton Review L.L.C.
FORM NO. 00001-PR

5. YOUR NAME

First 4 letters of last name   FIRST INIT   MID INIT

(Bubble columns A–Z)

Test 1

Start with number 1 for each new section.
If a section has fewer questions than answer spaces, leave the extra answer spaces blank.

1. Ⓐ Ⓑ Ⓒ Ⓓ Ⓔ
2. Ⓐ Ⓑ Ⓒ Ⓓ Ⓔ
3. Ⓐ Ⓑ Ⓒ Ⓓ Ⓔ
4. Ⓐ Ⓑ Ⓒ Ⓓ Ⓔ
5. Ⓐ Ⓑ Ⓒ Ⓓ Ⓔ
6. Ⓐ Ⓑ Ⓒ Ⓓ Ⓔ
7. Ⓐ Ⓑ Ⓒ Ⓓ Ⓔ
8. Ⓐ Ⓑ Ⓒ Ⓓ Ⓔ
9. Ⓐ Ⓑ Ⓒ Ⓓ Ⓔ
10. Ⓐ Ⓑ Ⓒ Ⓓ Ⓔ
11. Ⓐ Ⓑ Ⓒ Ⓓ Ⓔ
12. Ⓐ Ⓑ Ⓒ Ⓓ Ⓔ
13. Ⓐ Ⓑ Ⓒ Ⓓ Ⓔ
14. Ⓐ Ⓑ Ⓒ Ⓓ Ⓔ
15. Ⓐ Ⓑ Ⓒ Ⓓ Ⓔ
16. Ⓐ Ⓑ Ⓒ Ⓓ Ⓔ
17. Ⓐ Ⓑ Ⓒ Ⓓ Ⓔ
18. Ⓐ Ⓑ Ⓒ Ⓓ Ⓔ
19. Ⓐ Ⓑ Ⓒ Ⓓ Ⓔ
20. Ⓐ Ⓑ Ⓒ Ⓓ Ⓔ
21. Ⓐ Ⓑ Ⓒ Ⓓ Ⓔ
22. Ⓐ Ⓑ Ⓒ Ⓓ Ⓔ
23. Ⓐ Ⓑ Ⓒ Ⓓ Ⓔ
24. Ⓐ Ⓑ Ⓒ Ⓓ Ⓔ
25. Ⓐ Ⓑ Ⓒ Ⓓ Ⓔ
26. Ⓐ Ⓑ Ⓒ Ⓓ Ⓔ
27. Ⓐ Ⓑ Ⓒ Ⓓ Ⓔ
28. Ⓐ Ⓑ Ⓒ Ⓓ Ⓔ
29. Ⓐ Ⓑ Ⓒ Ⓓ Ⓔ
30. Ⓐ Ⓑ Ⓒ Ⓓ Ⓔ

31. Ⓐ Ⓑ Ⓒ Ⓓ Ⓔ
32. Ⓐ Ⓑ Ⓒ Ⓓ Ⓔ
33. Ⓐ Ⓑ Ⓒ Ⓓ Ⓔ
34. Ⓐ Ⓑ Ⓒ Ⓓ Ⓔ
35. Ⓐ Ⓑ Ⓒ Ⓓ Ⓔ
36. Ⓐ Ⓑ Ⓒ Ⓓ Ⓔ
37. Ⓐ Ⓑ Ⓒ Ⓓ Ⓔ
38. Ⓐ Ⓑ Ⓒ Ⓓ Ⓔ
39. Ⓐ Ⓑ Ⓒ Ⓓ Ⓔ
40. Ⓐ Ⓑ Ⓒ Ⓓ Ⓔ
41. Ⓐ Ⓑ Ⓒ Ⓓ Ⓔ
42. Ⓐ Ⓑ Ⓒ Ⓓ Ⓔ
43. Ⓐ Ⓑ Ⓒ Ⓓ Ⓔ
44. Ⓐ Ⓑ Ⓒ Ⓓ Ⓔ
45. Ⓐ Ⓑ Ⓒ Ⓓ Ⓔ
46. Ⓐ Ⓑ Ⓒ Ⓓ Ⓔ
47. Ⓐ Ⓑ Ⓒ Ⓓ Ⓔ
48. Ⓐ Ⓑ Ⓒ Ⓓ Ⓔ
49. Ⓐ Ⓑ Ⓒ Ⓓ Ⓔ
50. Ⓐ Ⓑ Ⓒ Ⓓ Ⓔ
51. Ⓐ Ⓑ Ⓒ Ⓓ Ⓔ
52. Ⓐ Ⓑ Ⓒ Ⓓ Ⓔ
53. Ⓐ Ⓑ Ⓒ Ⓓ Ⓔ
54. Ⓐ Ⓑ Ⓒ Ⓓ Ⓔ
55. Ⓐ Ⓑ Ⓒ Ⓓ Ⓔ
56. Ⓐ Ⓑ Ⓒ Ⓓ Ⓔ
57. Ⓐ Ⓑ Ⓒ Ⓓ Ⓔ
58. Ⓐ Ⓑ Ⓒ Ⓓ Ⓔ
59. Ⓐ Ⓑ Ⓒ Ⓓ Ⓔ
60. Ⓐ Ⓑ Ⓒ Ⓓ Ⓔ

61. Ⓐ Ⓑ Ⓒ Ⓓ Ⓔ
62. Ⓐ Ⓑ Ⓒ Ⓓ Ⓔ
63. Ⓐ Ⓑ Ⓒ Ⓓ Ⓔ
64. Ⓐ Ⓑ Ⓒ Ⓓ Ⓔ
65. Ⓐ Ⓑ Ⓒ Ⓓ Ⓔ
66. Ⓐ Ⓑ Ⓒ Ⓓ Ⓔ
67. Ⓐ Ⓑ Ⓒ Ⓓ Ⓔ
68. Ⓐ Ⓑ Ⓒ Ⓓ Ⓔ
69. Ⓐ Ⓑ Ⓒ Ⓓ Ⓔ
70. Ⓐ Ⓑ Ⓒ Ⓓ Ⓔ
71. Ⓐ Ⓑ Ⓒ Ⓓ Ⓔ
72. Ⓐ Ⓑ Ⓒ Ⓓ Ⓔ
73. Ⓐ Ⓑ Ⓒ Ⓓ Ⓔ
74. Ⓐ Ⓑ Ⓒ Ⓓ Ⓔ
75. Ⓐ Ⓑ Ⓒ Ⓓ Ⓔ
76. Ⓐ Ⓑ Ⓒ Ⓓ Ⓔ
77. Ⓐ Ⓑ Ⓒ Ⓓ Ⓔ
78. Ⓐ Ⓑ Ⓒ Ⓓ Ⓔ
79. Ⓐ Ⓑ Ⓒ Ⓓ Ⓔ
80. Ⓐ Ⓑ Ⓒ Ⓓ Ⓔ
81. Ⓐ Ⓑ Ⓒ Ⓓ Ⓔ
82. Ⓐ Ⓑ Ⓒ Ⓓ Ⓔ
83. Ⓐ Ⓑ Ⓒ Ⓓ Ⓔ
84. Ⓐ Ⓑ Ⓒ Ⓓ Ⓔ
85. Ⓐ Ⓑ Ⓒ Ⓓ Ⓔ
86. Ⓐ Ⓑ Ⓒ Ⓓ Ⓔ
87. Ⓐ Ⓑ Ⓒ Ⓓ Ⓔ
88. Ⓐ Ⓑ Ⓒ Ⓓ Ⓔ
89. Ⓐ Ⓑ Ⓒ Ⓓ Ⓔ
90. Ⓐ Ⓑ Ⓒ Ⓓ Ⓔ

Completely darken bubbles with a No. 2 pencil. If you make a mistake, be sure to erase mark completely. Erase all stray marks.

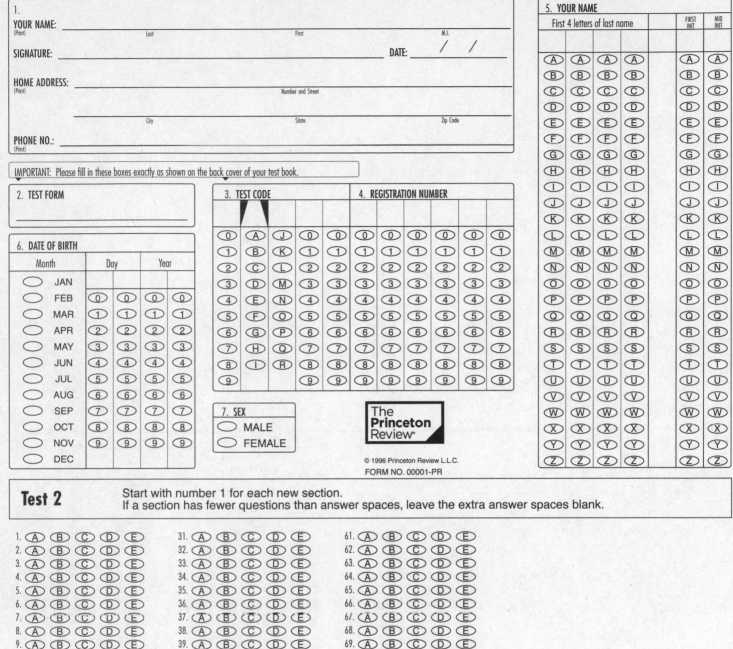

Test 2

Start with number 1 for each new section.
If a section has fewer questions than answer spaces, leave the extra answer spaces blank.

Completely darken bubbles with a No. 2 pencil. If you make a mistake, be sure to erase mark completely. Erase all stray marks.

IMPORTANT: Please fill in these boxes exactly as shown on the back cover of your test book.

2. TEST FORM
_____

6. DATE OF BIRTH

Month	Day		Year	
JAN				
FEB	0	0	0	0
MAR	1	1	1	1
APR	2	2	2	2
MAY	3	3	3	3
JUN	4	4	4	4
JUL	5	5	5	5
AUG	6	6	6	6
SEP	7	7	7	7
OCT	8	8	8	8
NOV	9	9	9	9
DEC				

3. TEST CODE

0	A	J	0	0
1	B	K	1	1
2	C	L	2	2
3	D	M	3	3
4	E	N	4	4
5	F	O	5	5
6	G	P	6	6
7	H	Q	7	7
8	I	R	8	8
9			9	9

4. REGISTRATION NUMBER

0	0	0	0	0	0	0
1	1	1	1	1	1	1
2	2	2	2	2	2	2
3	3	3	3	3	3	3
4	4	4	4	4	4	4
5	5	5	5	5	5	5
6	6	6	6	6	6	6
7	7	7	7	7	7	7
8	8	8	8	8	8	8
9	9	9	9	9	9	9

7. SEX
○ MALE
○ FEMALE

The Princeton Review®

© 1996 Princeton Review L.L.C.
FORM NO. 00001-PR

5. YOUR NAME

First 4 letters of last name				FIRST INIT	MID INIT
A	A	A	A	A	A
B	B	B	B	B	B
C	C	C	C	C	C
D	D	D	D	D	D
E	E	E	E	E	E
F	F	F	F	F	F
G	G	G	G	G	G
H	H	H	H	H	H
I	I	I	I	I	I
J	J	J	J	J	J
K	K	K	K	K	K
L	L	L	L	L	L
M	M	M	M	M	M
N	N	N	N	N	N
O	O	O	O	O	O
P	P	P	P	P	P
Q	Q	Q	Q	Q	Q
R	R	R	R	R	R
S	S	S	S	S	S
T	T	T	T	T	T
U	U	U	U	U	U
V	V	V	V	V	V
W	W	W	W	W	W
X	X	X	X	X	X
Y	Y	Y	Y	Y	Y
Z	Z	Z	Z	Z	Z

Test 3

Start with number 1 for each new section.
If a section has fewer questions than answer spaces, leave the extra answer spaces blank.

1. A B C D E
2. A B C D E
3. A B C D E
4. A B C D E
5. A B C D E
6. A B C D E
7. A B C D E
8. A B C D E
9. A B C D E
10. A B C D E
11. A B C D E
12. A B C D E
13. A B C D E
14. A B C D E
15. A B C D E
16. A B C D E
17. A B C D E
18. A B C D E
19. A B C D E
20. A B C D E
21. A B C D E
22. A B C D E
23. A B C D E
24. A B C D E
25. A B C D E
26. A B C D E
27. A B C D E
28. A B C D E
29. A B C D E
30. A B C D E

31. A B C D E
32. A B C D E
33. A B C D E
34. A B C D E
35. A B C D E
36. A B C D E
37. A B C D E
38. A B C D E
39. A B C D E
40. A B C D E
41. A B C D E
42. A B C D E
43. A B C D E
44. A B C D E
45. A B C D E
46. A B C D E
47. A B C D E
48. A B C D E
49. A B C D E
50. A B C D E
51. A B C D E
52. A B C D E
53. A B C D E
54. A B C D E
55. A B C D E
56. A B C D E
57. A B C D E
58. A B C D E
59. A B C D E
60. A B C D E

61. A B C D E
62. A B C D E
63. A B C D E
64. A B C D E
65. A B C D E
66. A B C D E
67. A B C D E
68. A B C D E
69. A B C D E
70. A B C D E
71. A B C D E
72. A B C D E
73. A B C D E
74. A B C D E
75. A B C D E
76. A B C D E
77. A B C D E
78. A B C D E
79. A B C D E
80. A B C D E
81. A B C D E
82. A B C D E
83. A B C D E
84. A B C D E
85. A B C D E
86. A B C D E
87. A B C D E
88. A B C D E
89. A B C D E
90. A B C D E

NOTES

NOTES

International Offices Listing

China (Beijing)
1501 Building A,
Disanji Creative Zone,
No.66 West Section of North 4th Ring Road Beijing
Tel: +86-10-62684481/2/3
Email: tprkor01@chol.com
Website: www.tprbeijing.com

China (Shanghai)
1010 Kaixuan Road
Building B, 5/F
Changning District, Shanghai, China 200052
Sara Beattie, Owner: Email: tprenquiry.sha@sarabeattie.com
Tel: +86-21-5108-2798
Fax: +86-21-6386-1039
Website: www.princetonreviewshanghai.com

Hong Kong
5th Floor, Yardley Commercial Building
1–6 Connaught Road West, Sheung Wan, Hong Kong
(MTR Exit C)
Sara Beattie, Owner: Email: tprenquiry.sha@sarabeattie.com
Tel: +852-2507-9380
Fax: +852-2827-4630
Website: www.princetonreviewhk.com

India (Mumbai)
Score Plus Academy
Office No.15, Fifth Floor
Manek Mahal 90
Veer Nariman Road
Next to Hotel Ambassador
Churchgate, Mumbai 400020
Maharashtra, India
Ritu Kalwani: Email: director@score-plus.com
Tel: + 91 22 22846801 / 39 / 41
Website: www.scoreplusindia.com

India (New Delhi)
South Extension
K–16, Upper Ground Floor
South Extension Part–1,
New Delhi-110049
Aradhana Mahna: aradhana@manyagroup.com
Monisha Banerjee: monisha@manyagroup.com
Ruchi Tomar: ruchi.tomar@manyagroup.com
Rishi Josan: Rishi.josan@manyagroup.com
Vishal Goswamy: vishal.goswamy@manyagroup.com
Tel: +91-11-64501603/ 4, +91-11-65028379
Website: www.manyagroup.com

Lebanon
463 Bliss Street
AlFarra Building–2nd floor
Ras Beirut
Beirut, Lebanon
Hassan Coudsi: Email: hassan.coudsi@review.com
Tel: +961-1-367-688
Website: www.princetonreviewlebanon.com

Korea
945-25 Young Shin Building
25 Daechi-Dong, Kangnam-gu
Seoul, Korea 135-280
Yong-Hoon Lee: Email: TPRKor01@chollian.net
In-Woo Kim: Email: iwkim@tpr.co.kr
Tel: + 82-2-554-7762
Fax: +82-2-453-9466
Website: www.tpr.co.kr

Kuwait
ScorePlus Learning Center
Salmiyah Block 3, Street 2 Building 14
Post Box: 559, Zip 1306, Safat, Kuwait
Email: infokuwait@score-plus.com
Tel: +965-25-75-48-02 / 8
Fax: +965-25-75-46-02
Website: www.scorepluseducation.com

Malaysia
Sara Beattie MDC Sdn Bhd
Suites 18E & 18F
18th Floor
Gurney Tower, Persiaran Gurney
Penang, Malaysia
Email: tprkl.my@sarabeattie.com
Sara Beattie, Owner: Email: tprenquiry.sha@sarabeattie.com
Tel: +604-2104 333
Fax: +604-2104 330
Website: www.princetonreviewKL.com

Mexico
TPR México
Guanajuato No. 242 Piso 1 Interior 1
Col. Roma Norte
México D.F., C.P.06700
registro@princetonreviewmexico.com
Tel: +52-55-5255-4495
+52-55-5255-4440
+52-55-5255-4442
Website: www.princetonreviewmexico.com

Qatar
Score Plus
Villa No. 49, Al Waab Street
Opp Al Waab Petrol Station
Post Box: 39068, Doha, Qatar
Email: infoqatar@score-plus.com
Tel: +974 44 36 8580, +974 526 5032
Fax: +974 44 13 1995
Website: www.scorepluseducation.com

Taiwan
The Princeton Review Taiwan
2F, 169 Zhong Xiao East Road, Section 4
Taipei, Taiwan 10690
Lisa Bartle (Owner): lbartle@princetonreview.com.tw
Tel: +886-2-2751-1293
Fax: +886-2-2776-3201
Website: www.PrincetonReview.com.tw

Thailand
The Princeton Review Thailand
Sathorn Nakorn Tower, 28th floor
100 North Sathorn Road
Bangkok, Thailand 10500
Thavida Bijayendrayodhin (Chairman)
Email: thavida@princetonreviewthailand.com
Mitsara Bijayendrayodhin (Managing Director)
Email: mitsara@princetonreviewthailand.com
Tel: +662-636-6770
Fax: +662-636-6776
Website: www.princetonreviewthailand.com

Turkey
Yeni Sülün Sokak No. 28
Levent, Istanbul, 34330, Turkey
Nuri Ozgur: nuri@tprturkey.com
Rona Ozgur: rona@tprturkey.com
Iren Ozgur: iren@tprturkey.com
Tel: +90-212-324-4747
Fax: +90-212-324-3347
Website: www.tprturkey.com

UAE
Emirates Score Plus
Office No: 506, Fifth Floor
Sultan Business Center
Near Lamcy Plaza, 21 Oud Metha Road
Post Box: 44098, Dubai
United Arab Emirates
Hukumat Kalwani: skoreplus@gmail.com
Ritu Kalwani: director@score-plus.com
Email: info@score-plus.com
Tel: +971-4-334-0004
Fax: +971-4-334-0222
Website: www.scorepluseducation.com

Our International Partners

The Princeton Review also runs courses with a variety of partners in Africa, Asia, Europe, and South America.

Georgia
LEAF American-Georgian Education Center
www.leaf.ge

Mongolia
English Academy of Mongolia
www.nyescm.org

Nigeria
The Know Place
www.knowplace.com.ng

Panama
Academia Interamericana de Panama
http://aip.edu.pa/

Switzerland
Institut Le Rosey
http://www.rosey.ch/

All other inquiries, please email us at
internationalsupport@review.com